Discount Rates for the Evaluation of Public Private Partnerships

Edited by
David F. Burgess and Glenn P. Jenkins

D1438422

JOHN DEUTSCH INSTITUTE FOR THE
STUDY OF ECONOMIC POLICY

Queen's
UNIVERSITY

McGill-Queen's University Press
Montreal & Kingston • London • Ithaca

ISBN: 978-1-55339-163-0 (pbk.), ISBN: 978-1-55339-164-7 (bound)
© John Deutsch Institute for the Study of Economic Policy
Queen's University, Kingston, Ontario K7L 3N6
Telephone: (613) 533-2294 FAX: (613) 533-6025
Printed and bound in Canada

Library and Archives Canada Cataloguing in Publication

Discount rates for the evaluation of public private partnerships /
edited by David F. Burgess and Glenn P. Jenkins.

Includes bibliographical references.
ISBN 978-1-55339-163-0 (pbk.).--ISBN 978-1-55339-164-7 (bound)

1. Public-private sector cooperation--Canada--Cost effectiveness.
2. Public investments--Canada--Cost effectiveness. 3. Capital costs--
Canada. I. Burgess, David F., 1942- II. Jenkins, Glenn P. III. John Deutsch
Institute for the Study of Economic Policy

HD3872.C3D57 2010   332.67'2520971   C2009-906620-3

Table of Contents

iii

iv

v

Preface

The papers and commentaries in this volume were all presented at the John Deutsch Institute conference on "Discount Rates for the Evaluation of Public Private Partnerships", held at Queen's University on October 2 and 3, 2008. The conference was organized by David Burgess of the Department of Economics, University of Western Ontario, and Glenn Jenkins of the Department of Economics at Queen's University, and Eastern Mediterranean University, Northern Cyprus. Funding for the conference was provided by the John Deutsch Institute and the John Deutsch International Executive Programs.

The objectives of this conference were twofold. First was to bring together academics from the field of Finance and Economics to work toward a synthesis of these two disciplines as they relate to the determination of this key parameter for public sector decision making. Second was to bring together practitioners and academics working internationally on the evaluation of public private partnerships to focus on what is viewed as best practice in arriving at the appropriate discount rate for the evaluation of benefits and cost over the life of such projects. This volume, while not producing a definitive consensus, brings together the current state of thinking in this field and lays out the advantages and disadvantages of alternative approaches.

The editors of this volume and conference organizers benefited from the assistance of a number of people in both the organization of the conference and the production of this volume. We especially wish to thank Sharon Sullivan of the John Deutsch Institute for her assistance throughout the project, her excellent job in the planning and managing of the conference, and her exceptional editorial and coordination activities in producing this volume. The conference benefited greatly from the assistance of Christopher Shugart and Arkins M. Kabungo in defining the themes in the research and professional practice of this field. We gratefully acknowledge the contribution of a number of others who provided advice and chaired sessions at the conference: Charles Beach, Arnold Harberger, Frank Milne, Finn Poschmann, and Rosalind Thomas.

It is also a pleasure to thank Stephanie Stone for her editing skills and the School of Policy Studies' Publications Unit for its valuable support in preparing the cover graphics and other publication aspects of the volume.

Finally, we wish to acknowledge the wonderful cooperation we received from the contributors to this volume.

David F. Burgess
University of Western Ontario

Glenn P. Jenkins
Queen's University and
Eastern Mediterranean University,
Northern Cyprus

Introduction

David F. Burgess and Glenn P. Jenkins

Introduction

This volume depicts the state of the debate about the appropriate discount rate for decision-making in the public sector, with particular emphasis on its role in evaluating public-private partnerships (P3s). How can public policy practitioners judge whether or not a P3 is a more efficient way to provide infrastructure and other services than a standard procurement contract? Any assessment will require a comparison of time streams of benefits and costs, so the choice of discount rate is often crucial. Should the discount rate reflect the economic opportunity cost of capital (EOCK), the rate at which society is willing to trade present for future consumption, the cost of capital of the preferred private provider, or the government's borrowing rate? Should the discount rate be adjusted for project risk, and if so, how should project risk be measured? The nine papers in this volume shed some light on these issues, and in the process, they make some progress toward the development of a more rigorous and defensible approach to the evaluation of P3s.

Some Background on How P3s Are Evaluated in Canada

A P3 is seen as an attractive alternative to purely public sector provision for a variety of reasons. Beyond the apparent fiscal advantage of shifting the burden of financing to the private sector, a P3 offers additional benefits, which include greater scope for innovation, stronger incentives to deliver desired results, the potential for cost saving through organizational/managerial efficiency, and a more efficient assignment of risk. However, in order to realize these benefits, contracts must be carefully designed, and performance must be monitored. Both of these are costly.

In Canada, different jurisdictions have different procedures for evaluating whether a P3 represents value for money, and one difference is the choice of discount rate. Infrastructure Ontario uses a discount rate that reflects the provincial government's cost of borrowing, whereas Partnerships British Columbia proposes to use a discount rate that reflects the weighted average cost of capital of the preferred private partner. Neither jurisdiction recommends a discount rate that reflects the EOCK.

Infrastructure Ontario regards a P3 as the preferred choice only if the value of the risk transferred to the P3, minus the premium that is paid to bear the risk, plus the estimated cost saving from improved incentives and more efficient management, is greater than the increase in transactions costs (e.g., costs of negotiating the contract and monitoring performance) plus the higher cost of financing. Is it appropriate to view the higher cost of financing as a social cost of the P3?

Partnerships BC proposes to compare the present discounted value of the stream of contractual payments made to the P3 with the present discounted value of the expected costs of purely public provision (including the value of the risks that would be transferred to the P3) by discounting at the private partner's weighted average cost of capital. The present discounted value of the stream of contractual payments will approximate the present discounted value of the P3's underlying costs if the bidding process is competitive, so the real resource cost of one option is being compared to the real resource cost of the other. Purely public provision enjoys no financing advantage in the comparison. However, the weighted average cost of capital of the P3 will not necessarily be equal to the economic opportunity cost of capital. Is this a problem, or should the discount rate for an investment decision differ from the

David F. Burgess and Glenn P. Jenkins

discount rate for an "asset portfolio" decision, i.e., whether to undertake the investment publicly or privately? Partnerships BC maintains that if a project is judged to be worth doing, whether under purely public provision or as a P3, the benefit of choosing a P3 is the present discounted value of the avoided costs of purely public provision discounted at the P3's weighted average cost of capital.

The view that different discount rates should be used for different types of decisions in the public sector is not unfamiliar. For example, Circular No. A-94 Revised: Guidelines and Discount Rates for Benefit-Cost Analysis of Federal Programs, issued by the US Office of Management and Budget in 1992, authorizes that a discount rate of 7% real (approximating the marginal pre-tax real rate of return in the private sector) be used to evaluate public investments with direct benefits to the public, but that the real treasury borrowing rate on marketable securities of comparable maturity be used for cost-effective analysis or for public investments whose benefits directly impact the federal budget. Is this dichotomy economically justifiable?

Infrastructure Ontario claims that it is counterintuitive to discount expected costs at a higher rate than the risk-free rate because projects with uncertain costs then become more attractive. However, if project costs are positively correlated with aggregate economic activity, there is nothing counterintuitive about their present value cost being lower. Moreover, if the market discounts costs at a higher rate to reflect their risk, why should governments do otherwise? Provided that the bidding process is competitive, the present discounted value of the underlying costs of the P3 will be a good approximation of the present discounted value of the stream of contractual payments when the discount rate is equal to the P3's weighted average cost of capital. If one can be reasonably confident that the cost stream of the P3 has the same systematic risk and inter-temporal structure as the cost stream under purely public provision, the choice of discount rate is not likely to affect the ranking of their present value costs.

Infrastructure Ontario maintains that once the relevant risks have been identified and their impacts quantified, the cost estimates will be virtually risk-free, so it is appropriate to discount at the risk-free rate. But does the risk analysis convert estimated costs into their "certainty equivalents", or does it simply remove bias, thus providing more realistic estimates of expected costs? If every risk was insurable, adding an insurance premium to the cost estimates would convert them into certainty equivalent costs that could be discounted at the risk-free rate. For each risk, the insurance premium would exceed the expected value of the risk, so the decision-maker's degree of risk aversion is taken into account. However, not all risks are insurable. Finally, even if the expected costs were converted into certainty equivalents, this would not justify using the provincial government's borrowing rate as the risk-free rate. The appropriate discount rate would be the risk-free economic opportunity cost of capital, which would be higher.

The difference between Infrastructure Ontario and Partnerships BC regarding the appropriate discount rate for evaluating P3s provides ample justification for this volume.

Summary of the Key Issues Discussed in the Papers

The papers in this volume are divided into three parts. Part I provides an overview of the theory and practice of discounting in the appraisal of P3s. Part II is devoted to theoretical approaches to the discounting of benefits and costs. Part III is focused on the empirical estimation of the social discount rate, with particular reference to Canada.

Part I: Discount Rates for PPP's: Overview of Theory and Practice

Chris Shugart opens the discussion of Part I by surveying the procedures used to evaluate P3s in various countries around the world, with particular attention to the choice of discount rate and the treatment of risk. His objective is to provide some guidance for assessing P3s in developing countries. A common feature of the procedures he surveys is the specification of a "public sector comparator" (PSC) to be used as a benchmark for judging whether a P3 represents value for money. The expected expenditures if the project was a capital works project within the public sector are then compared to the expected expenditures if the project was undertaken as a P3. The P3 represents value for money if the present value of the expected expenditures under the P3 minus the present value of the expected expenditures under the PSC is less than the value of the risk that is transferred to the P3.

Two things are striking about Shugart's survey. First, there are wide differences across jurisdictions with respect to the appropriate discount rate for comparing a P3 to a PSC. Second, many jurisdictions fail to

David F. Burgess and Glenn P. Jenkins

distinguish between the underlying real resource costs of the P3 and the stream of contractual payments that are made to the P3. This is important because, given that the contractual payments will be deferred relative to the underlying costs, the present discounted value of the stream of contractual payments will differ from the present discounted value of the underlying costs unless the discount rate reflects the P3's cost of capital and the bidding for the contract is competitive. Some jurisdictions, like the United Kingdom, recommend comparing the contractual payments to the P3 to the real resource costs of the PSC using a discount rate that reflects the social rate of time preference; others recommend comparing the financial costs using the government's long-term borrowing rate; others recommend using a discount rate that reflects the project's systematic risk; still others recommend using the government's long-term borrowing rate to evaluate the PSC but using a risk-adjusted discount rate to evaluate the P3. None of the jurisdictions surveyed use a discount rate that reflects the EOCK.

Shugart illustrates situations where comparing the real resource costs of the PSC to the contractual payments to the P3 (instead of the underlying real resource costs) by discounting at the EOCK can result in the P3 being rejected when, in fact, it may be the efficient choice. He also shows that comparing the direct capital and operating costs of each option without taking into account the real resource costs of financing the P3 can lead to purely public provision being rejected when it is the efficient choice.

However, it is not clear whether these problems would be rectified if competitive neutrality were applied. Thus, if the contractual payments to the private partner are treated as ordinary business income, it is the payments net of tax discounted at the private partner's cost of capital (market interest rate) that will equal the P3's underlying costs under competitive bidding. The underlying costs of the PSC option should then be compared to the contractual payments gross of tax discounted at the EOCK. On the other hand, if the contractual payments are tax-exempt, the analysis of the PSC option should take into account the business taxes that would be lost if the P3 were chosen instead.

Insofar as financing costs are concerned, one must ask why it is appropriate to include financial intermediation costs for the P3 but exclude them for the PSC. Unless the government can provide financial intermediation services at zero economic cost, it would seem inappropriate to ignore these costs when assessing the PSC. If the government is no better at financial intermediation than the private sector, competitive neutrality implies that the PSC should be subject to the same real financing costs as the P3.

With respect to risk, Shugart notes that in a well-functioning capital market, only a project's systematic risk requires compensation. A project's systematic risk, or its beta, refers to the covariance of its return with the rate of return in the market as a whole. The issue is to what extent the discount rate should be adjusted for differences in a project's systematic risk.

When comparing the stream of contractual payments to the P3 with the stream of costs for the PSC, the betas of these streams will differ. The beta of net revenue is the difference between the beta of revenue and the beta of cost. Shugart asks whether in comparing the P3 with the PSC one should apply a higher discount rate to the stream of payments to the P3 than to the stream of costs to the PSC when the payments stream is more highly correlated with the economy than the cost stream. This appears to be the approach taken by Partnerships Victoria. However, if the P3 and the PSC are interpreted as alternative ways to deliver the same stream of benefits, the benefit of pursuing the PSC can be treated as the stream of avoided payments to the P3. It is then appropriate to apply the same discount rate to the stream of costs for the PSC as to the stream of payments to the P3, and if the market can be trusted to price systematic risk, that discount rate should reflect the P3's weighted average cost of capital.

Given the lack of consensus among the experts about the appropriate discount rate and whether it should be adjusted for a project's systematic risk, Shugart proposes a sequential approach to isolate those situations where the choice of discount rate is crucial, namely, when higher initial costs of the P3 are counterbalanced by lower operating/maintenance costs. In these situations, he recommends that estimates of the stream of expected benefits be made, and benefits minus costs for each option be compared, using a discount rate that reflects the EOCK. If the PSC has higher net present value, the P3 can be rejected. If the P3 has higher net present value, the issue of systematic risk becomes crucial. If a project's systematic risk is virtually zero when undertaken in the public sector, the appropriate discount rate for the PSC should be the risk-free EOCK. If the net present value of the P3 discounted at the EOCK exceeds the net present value of the PSC discounted at the risk-free EOCK, then the case for the P3 option is strong. However, it should be noted that the results will depend upon the valuation of benefits, and benefits are difficult to

David F. Burgess and Glenn P. Jenkins

measure reliably. In addition, it remains contentious whether shifting a project into the public sector can eliminate its systematic risk.

The second paper in this section is by Michael Spackman. He first comments on three alternative views about the appropriate social discount rate: the efficient capital markets view that the required rate of return on a public investment should be the rate of return on a private investment of comparable risk; the view that the social discount rate should reflect the EOCK, which is the rate of return forgone in the private sector when the government borrows to finance the project; and the view that benefits and costs should be discounted at a rate that reflects the social rate of time preference, which is defined as the rate of impatience plus the product of the rate of growth of per capita consumption and the elasticity of the marginal utility of consumption.

Spackman dismisses the efficient capital markets view on the grounds that risk premiums observed in financial markets are not reliable measures of a project's systematic risk. He also rejects the view that the social discount rate should reflect the EOCK for three reasons: i) because there is no evidence of material crowding out of private investment by public investment in a world with highly elastic international capital flows; ii) because the pre-tax rate of return in the private sector contains a risk premium that should be treated as a cost rather than a forgone benefit; and iii) because if there is any private investment displaced by government financing, the appropriate way to take it into account is to apply a shadow price to convert displaced investment into its "consumption equivalent" and discount at the social rate of time preference.

These points will be addressed in later papers, so they will not be debated here. In Spackman's view, the social rate of time preference is the appropriate discount rate for all types of decision-making in the public sector, and that rate for the United Kingdom is currently 3.5% real. Countries with different rates of impatience, per capita consumption growth and the elasticity of marginal utility of consumption will have different social discount rates.

Insofar as the appropriate methodology for evaluating P3s is concerned, Spackman argues that the stream of contractual payments made to the P3 should be compared with the financing costs under purely public provision by discounting at the social time preference rate. He notes that if the social time preference rate is above the government's real long-term borrowing rate, the present value costs of each option will be understated, but the ranking will be unaffected. In his view, using a higher discount rate than the STP rate will bias the choice toward the P3, but of course, this depends upon whether the STP rate is the appropriate rate for making efficient choices.

Spackman describes a situation where the underlying costs of a project – whether as a P3 or under purely public provision – are the same, but purely public provision is deemed to be the efficient choice because the present value of the stream of contractual payments to the P3 exceeds the present value of the stream of payments under purely public provision when discounted at the social time preference rate. However, if the contract is awarded to the P3 under a competitive bidding process, purely public provision is being judged superior simply because it enjoys access to cheaper financing. Nonetheless, Spackman downplays the importance of the discount rate in determining whether to choose a P3 over a PSC. In his view, it is much more important to consider whether a P3 contract can be structured to elicit desired behaviour. He may well be right, but it is best to avoid errors when errors can be avoided.

Part II: Theoretical Approaches to the Discounting of Benefits and Costs

The first paper in this section is by David Burgess. He argues that at least some of the confusion about the appropriate social discount rate can be avoided once the different implicit assumptions behind the alternative positions are taken into account. Three views are identified: the view, espoused by Harberger and Sandmo-Dreze, that the social discount rate should reflect the economic (social) opportunity cost of capital (SOC) – a weighted average of the marginal productivity of capital, the consumption rate of interest, and the marginal cost of incremental foreign funding, where the weights reflect the proportions of funding drawn from each source; the view espoused by Marglin, Feldstein, Bradford, and Lind that the appropriate discount rate should reflect the social rate of time preference (which may or may not equal the after-tax rate of return), with all investment displaced or induced by financing, and executing the project being converted into its "consumption equivalent" by shadow pricing before discounting; and the view, recently put forth by Liu and co-authors, that benefits should be discounted at the after-tax rate of return, and costs minus any "indirect revenue effects" should be discounted at the pre-tax rate of return and multiplied by a parameter that reflects what Liu calls the marginal cost of funds (MCF).

Burgess shows that all three criteria can be reconciled once attention is paid to the different implicit assumptions that lie behind each viewpoint. Thus, the SOC criterion takes as its benchmark a project whose benefits are treated as income, whereas the MCF criterion takes as its benchmark a project whose benefits are fully consumed. Once these differences are taken into account, the two criteria yield equivalent results. The indirect revenue effects of a project under the MCF criterion refer to the *uncompensated* effect of the project on capital income tax revenue, whereas the indirect effects of a project under the SOC criterion refer to the *compensated* effect of the project on capital income tax revenue. Similarly, the shadow price algorithm implicitly assumes that the private sector is myopic. If the private sector has the same information as the planner, the shadow price algorithm will be equivalent to the SOC and MCF criteria, but it will be difficult to implement because the "consumption equivalent" value of a dollar of project expenditure will depend upon when that dollar is spent.

With respect to the evaluation of P3s, Burgess argues that if the P3 and the PSC are alternative ways to obtain the same stream of benefits, the appropriate discount rate to compare them should be the EOCK, not the government's borrowing rate or the social rate of time preference. The benefit of a P3 is the avoided costs of the PSC. The benefits, therefore, impact the government's budget rather than the private sector directly, but each dollar of government expenditure at given tax rates adds a dollar to the public debt, which has an economic cost that includes the government's borrowing rate plus the capital income tax revenue lost on any private investment displaced.

The second paper in this section is by Graham Glenday. He notes that the concept of the EOCK as a single national parameter to be used as the discount rate for all public sector investment decisions has come under increased criticism as governments have moved toward greater private sector participation in the risks and returns from public sector investment. The challenge is to incorporate into the discount rate a project's systematic risk, while at the same time taking into account that the funding for any project is drawn from a tax-distorted capital market. The EOCK for a project must not just compensate financiers for bearing systematic risk but also compensate the economy as a whole for the externality that is forgone in drawing funds from other projects. Thus, the EOCK for a project can be expressed as the sum of two components: the supply price of funding for the project, which is the minimum rate of return that financiers require to invest in the project, plus a term that represents the "economic externality per unit of capital". The beauty of

Glenday's approach is its empirical tractability. The minimum supply price of capital for a project (which includes its systematic risk) will be revealed in financial markets under competitive conditions, and the economic externality per unit of capital is a national parameter (i.e., common to all projects) that can be estimated using the same information required to estimate the standard weighted average social discount rate: information about the various tax distortions that drive wedges between the private and social rates of return on investment and on resident and foreign saving, and estimates of the responsiveness of demand for investment and supply of resident and foreign saving.

Glenday's approach also has the advantage of clarifying the distributional effects of a project. He shows that the difference between the economic value of a project and its value to the financiers consists of two components: the external benefit of the project minus the value of the externality forgone by investing in the project. If a project is worth doing from an economic perspective, but not from a financial perspective, it is important to choose instruments that induce the private sector to participate at the lowest efficiency cost. For example, a tax exemption for the project will increase private profitability, while increasing the value of the externality forgone by the same amount leaving the economic evaluation unchanged, whereas a subsidy that lowers the cost of debt financing will increase private profitability but at the cost of reducing the economic evaluation.

In the case of public sector projects that are not self-financing, Glenday recommends using the government's real long-term borrowing rate as the supply price of capital, which means that the EOCK is the risk-free EOCK. The implication is that taxpayers bear no systematic risk for such projects, either because risk is spread over all taxpayers or is uncorrelated with overall economic activity. The assumption that taxpayers bear no systematic risk for projects financed out of general government revenue seems strong. If the benefits of a project are pure public goods, spreading the risk over all taxpayers will not eliminate systematic risk. If the benefits are ordinary private goods, and are therefore appropriable through user fees, introducing such fees to make the project self-financing would raise its discount rate, according to Glenday's analysis (if project usage were positively correlated with economic activity) because private financiers would demand a risk premium to invest in the project. It is not obvious why a project with a given stream of expected benefits and costs should be evaluated using a different discount rate depending upon whether it is financed from general government revenue or from user fees. It is true that a project financed from general government revenue should be penalized for the excess burden of raising any revenue that is required to finance it, but this has a different effect on project assessment than increasing the discount rate. Infrastructure projects not financed with user fees will generate additional tax revenue indirectly to the extent that they facilitate ordinary commerce.

The final paper in this section is a brief cautionary note about risk by Antal Deutsch. He observes that risk is defined as the hazard of future loss. However, since the future is unpredictable, risk is immeasurable. The probability of a specific event happening is based upon an extrapolation from past experience, but the past is not a reliable predictor of the future. Insurance companies may appear to be scientific about risk and risk exposure, but since the future is unpredictable, their projections, in his words, are blind guesses. Insurance products may shift some risks around, but risk cannot be controlled or eliminated because it cannot be measured. Deutsch gives examples of events that were not covered by insurance because they were unforeseen.

Part III: Estimation of Discount Rates in Canada

The first paper in this section is by Arnold Harberger. He notes that for an economy in growth equilibrium, the rate of return to capital can be estimated from information on relatively few key parameters. The gross rate of return can be expressed as the ratio of capital's share of GDP divided by gross investment's share of GDP multiplied by the sum of the growth rate plus the depreciation rate. The net rate of return is then the gross rate of return minus the depreciation rate. Using plausible ranges for these parameters (e.g., capital's share equals 40%, investment's share equals 20%, the growth rate equals 3%, and the depreciation rate equals 4%), the implied net rate of return to capital is at least 10%. Harberger makes several refinements to the basic equation, such as allowing for out-of-equilibrium growth, introducing infrastructure capital that receives no direct compensation, taking into account the relatively low rate of return on residential housing, including R&D capital, etc. He concludes that it is hard to reject the view that the net rate of return to reproducible capital in a representative modern economy is at least 10%.

An inference that Harberger does not draw explicitly is that anyone who proposes to use a discount rate for public investment based upon a relatively low "social rate of time preference" like 3% or so (with no shadow pricing of private investment displaced) must explain how it is welfare-improving to shift resources from the rest of the economy, where they earn much higher rates of return. The two views can be reconciled if incremental funding does not displace private investment and displaces either consumption or net exports at an economic cost in the order of 3%. Without question, countries are increasingly well integrated into the global capital market, and a significant proportion of incremental funding for any project does come from abroad. But whether it is exchange rate risk, country risk, or home bias with respect to wealth holding, a country's investment rate is still much more sensitive to its own saving rate than to the saving rate in other countries. As long as the marginal source of funding for any project is the capital market, a significant proportion of the funding displaces private investment that appears to earn a real rate of return of 10% or more.

The second paper in this section is by Don Brean and David Burgess. They, too, are concerned about the potential errors involved in using a single measure of the EOCK to evaluate all projects when projects differ in terms of their systematic risk. A single economy-wide measure may be the best one can do in the absence of reliable estimates of a project's systematic risk, but this assumes that the project adds as much systematic risk to the economy as what is subtracted by the private investment and consumption it displaces. Following Bailey and Jensen, they express the EOCK for a project as the risk-free EOCK plus the project's systematic risk measured by its beta (defined as the covariance between a measure of project usage and overall economic activity, as reflected by GDP or GDP growth) multiplied by the difference between the economy-wide EOCK and the risk-free EOCK. Thus, unlike Glenday, a project's systematic risk is estimated rather than revealed in the market. The EOCK for a project with systematic risk β_j can be expressed as $EOCK_j = EOCK_f + \beta_j (EOCK - EOCK_f)$.

The risk-free EOCK is found by applying the tax distortions that are present in the single economy-wide EOCK to the risk-free market rate, interpreted as the average real rate of return on long-term government bonds. The risk-free EOCK is thus the EOCK in an economy with the same risk-free market rate and with the same tax distortions as those underlying the single economy-wide EOCK but with no risk premium embedded in rates of return. The social risk premium is the difference between the standard EOCK and the risk-free EOCK.

A project with no systematic risk should be discounted at the risk-free EOCK, whereas a project with a beta coefficient of one should be discounted at the standard economy-wide EOCK. If project usage is independent of GDP, the project has a beta coefficient of zero, whereas if project usage increases in tandem with GDP, it has a beta coefficient of one. They estimate beta coefficients for various investments in transportation infrastructure and find that for some (e.g., air transport, railway freight), the beta coefficient is statistically greater than one; for others (e.g., urban transit, water transport), it is not statistically different from one; and for others (e.g., passenger rail, passenger vehicles), the beta coefficient is not significantly different from zero. Their results suggest that if the standard economy-wide EOCK is estimated at 7.3%, it is appropriate to discount some investments at the risk-free EOCK (estimated at 4.7%), some at the standard economy-wide EOCK of 7.3%, and others at a risk-adjusted EOCK of 8.6%.

The next paper is by Glenn Jenkins and Chun-Yan Kuo. They use aggregate national accounts data for the period 1965-2005 to estimate the annual rate of return to reproducible capital in Canada. The return to capital is the sum of all the income attributable to capital divided by the replacement cost of the capital. The results indicate that the annual rate of return is in the order of 11%. They then deduct the various taxes plus financial intermediation costs to derive estimates of the annual net of tax rate of return accruing to Canadian savers in the order of 6.5%. The calculations incorporate the major changes in the tax treatment of income from capital that have occurred in Canada in recent years, including the replacement of the manufactures' sales tax with the GST, the harmonization of provincial and federal sales taxes in some provinces, and the lowering of the statutory corporate tax rate.

These updated estimates of pre- and post-tax rates of return are combined with estimates of the proportions of private and public investment that are financed by resident and foreign saving, the elasticities of supply of resident and foreign saving, and the elasticity of demand for investment with respect to the rate of return to arrive at an updated estimate of the EOCK.

There are two important innovations in their work. First, it is recognized that the net of tax return to capital includes financial intermediation costs incurred by savers to earn their returns, so this should be deducted to obtain the rate of return that is required to postpone consumption. Second, the rates of return contain a premium for systematic risk, which should be deducted in estimating the risk-free EOCK. The risk-free market rate is estimated as the after-tax rate of return on long-term government bonds minus the expected inflation rate. Jenkins and Kuo estimate this to be 1.9% and interpret it as an alternative to an investment in reproducible capital with an expected rate of return of 6.5%. If savers are uniformly distributed with respect to their degree of risk aversion, the most risk-averse savers will require the full premium between the two rates of return to forgo additional consumption, while a risk-neutral saver will require a zero premium. The average saver will require a premium of approximately 2%. This premium is then deducted from the pre- and post-tax rates of return to give a risk-free rate of return on displaced private investment of 9% and a risk-free rate of return on postponed consumption of 4.5%. Jenkins and Kuo assume that the net of tax rate of return paid to non-resident owners of capital in Canada is 6%. Combining these estimates of rates of return with estimates of the proportions of funding drawn from each source, they arrive at an updated estimate of the EOCK of 7%.

It should be emphasized that this is a risk-free discount rate, which is appropriate for evaluating projects with no systematic risk. For projects that add as much systematic risk to the national portfolio as what is forgone in financing, the appropriate EOCK will include the 2% risk premium. The baseline estimate for this rate of return is 8%.

The final paper in this section is by Peter Spiro. He argues that the appropriate discount rate for infrastructure investments in Ontario should reflect the rate of return that Ontarians are able to earn on a balanced portfolio that is passively invested in Canadian corporations and real return bonds issued by the provincial treasury. He estimates this rate of return to be 5% under current conditions. In Spiro's view, it would not be appropriate to use the government's borrowing rate as the discount rate because market conditions could change – in particular, real interest rates could increase – during the life of the project. A discount rate that reflects the pre-tax rate of return in the private sector would not be appropriate either because there is no evidence of material crowding-out of private investment in Ontario when the provincial government increases its borrowing by significant amounts. His compromise is to base the discount rate on the rate of return on a balanced portfolio but to reassess its value annually. With respect to risk, Spiro believes that the systematic risk borne by individual projects is negligible because the government can spread it over all Ontario taxpayers. With respect to crowding out, Ontario is closer to a small open economy than Canada as a whole, but if all jurisdictions in Canada ignored the crowding-out effects of their investment decisions on other jurisdictions, Canadians as a whole, meaning Canadians in all provinces, would suffer because projects just passing muster at the provincial borrowing rate would be undertaken at the expense of other investments in Canada that earn higher rates of return.

References

Making Projects Happen, Assessing Value For Money: A Guide to Infra-structure Ontario's Methodology. 2007. Queen's Printer for Ontario. At www.infrastrucureontario.ca.

Methodology For Quantitative Procurement Options Analysis. 2009. Discussion Draft for Partnerships BC. At www.partnershipsbc.ca.

Part I

Discount Rates for PPPs: Overview of Theory and Practice

1

PPPs, the Public Sector Comparator, and Discount Rates: Key Issues for Developing Countries

Chris Shugart

Introduction

During the past 10-15 years, many countries around the world have turned to long-term contractual arrangements with private sector companies to provide public infrastructure and services. These arrangements are often referred to as "public-private partnerships" (PPPs).[1]

This paper draws on a longer and broader-scope study prepared by the author for the NEPAD Secretariat and funded by PPIAF: *Quantitative Methods for the Preparation, Appraisal, and Management of PPI Projects in Sub-Saharan Africa* (August 2006). Some of the original ideas have been modified – and perhaps improved – in writing the present paper.

[1]Although the term "public private partnership" may have objectionable connotations of *partnering, joint venture, and informal relations* rather than a rigorous and objective arm's-length contractual relationship (which is the concept that should be at the core of the arrangement – even though a trusting relationship is required to make the arrangement work well), the term "PPP" has become a popular slogan and is difficult to avoid. Note that in the UK, "PPP" has a slightly different meaning; arrangements of the type discussed in this paper are usually referred to as "PFI" (Private Finance Initiative) projects.

PPP projects are complex. They require careful design, preparation, appraisal, procurement, contracting, and vigilant oversight if they are to succeed in yielding net benefits to society. Deficiencies in any of these aspects can lead to failure – sometimes disastrous failure.

The preparation of the *public sector comparator* for a PPP project has been a hallmark of most institutionalized PPP programs around the world. The basic idea is that it is important to demonstrate quantitatively that the PPP project is superior to an alternative public sector project that would deliver the same (or very similar) services. This hypothetical public sector project is often referred to as the "public sector comparator" (PSC).[2]

What might be the sources of the differences between the PPP project and the PSC? It is unlikely that one would estimate, *ex ante*, that the PPP project will have higher investment or operating costs than the PSC – for the same level of services. (If this is true in mature economies, it is even truer in most developing countries.) So the question is not usually whether the PPP project is likely to be more efficient in a technical sense. The main issue is whether there are other factors tending in the opposite direction – factors that might favour the PSC. The two main candidates are *financing costs* (possible additional costs due to private sector financing) and *transaction and contract oversight costs* (additional bidding, contracting, and monitoring costs in a PPP setting).

Either of these factors might bring additional costs that would outweigh the efficiency gains expected from private sector participation. One way to assess this would be to carefully examine and compare all the costs of both alternatives. If the costs of the PPP alternative were significantly higher than those of the PSC, then one could argue that it would be more beneficial to implement the project on a public sector basis.

In many countries, the PSC has played an important role in justifying PPP projects. If the PSC costs are higher, this can help counter the arguments of critics who may be resistant to the idea of private sector involvement, who are not convinced by theoretical arguments in favour of private sector participation, and who regard the PPP project as a way of benefiting private business interests at the expense of taxpayers, consumers, or workers.

---

[2]Morallos and Amekudzi (2008) give a useful summary of "value for money" analysis and the PSC exercise, as practised in a number of different PPP programs around the world.

The PSC may be used at different stages of the project preparation process. The main distinction is between using the PSC before the private sector bids are received and after the bids are received. An additional issue that arises when the PSC is used before the bids are received is that, in that case, a *hypothetical* PPP project ("reference PPP project") has to be modelled in addition to a hypothetical public sector alternative. Ideally, this should be based on good data from a sufficient number of actual PPP projects undertaken in the specific country. More often in developing countries, the reference PPP project is based on a few public sector projects in the country, adjusted to take into account the efficiency gains one might expect based roughly on experience with PPPs in developed countries – with a great deal of subjective judgment used. When the PSC is used after bids are received, the PSC is compared against the bid price of the preferred bidder.

The PSC exercise has come under increasing criticism in recent years. Some of the identified weaknesses are the following:

- Great inaccuracy: an enormous amount of uncertainty in the results, made even greater when a hypothetical PPP project is used as opposed to an actual bid price.
- Omitted risks: some important risks are very difficult to estimate and are often ignored.
- Manipulation: strong bureaucratic incentives to adjust the inputs to achieve the desired results.
- High cost: a full PSC study can be time-consuming and costly. Critics argue that requiring a PSC exercise for every PPP project is a boondoggle for consulting firms.
- In many developing countries, it cannot be assumed that a feasible public sector project will deliver roughly identical services. In that case, the comparison becomes more complicated and speculative.
- In many cases, there is no realistic public sector alternative at all. If in fact no public sector funding will be made available, the PSC is not feasible and is therefore irrelevant.

Regardless of these criticisms, there remains the need to assess, in some way, whether the PPP project would be expected to bring net benefits compared with the realistically best public sector project (presuming that it is realistic even to consider a public sector project). If this appears unlikely, then the PPP project – at least, one with the envisaged design – should not be undertaken.

One possible approach would be not to require a PSC analysis for every PPP project but only for representative *types* of projects. Simpler rules of thumb – both qualitative and quantitative – could then be developed for routine use by those deciding whether to embark on a PPP project in a particular case.

This paper does not examine the PSC exercise in all its aspects; it looks only at one issue that must be addressed in carrying out a PSC exercise. The comparison between the public sector comparator and the PPP project must be made in terms of *present values*. The discount rate used can therefore have an important impact. Since the costs of the PPP, as seen by the public sector through the contractual payments it will make, are spread out over time to a greater extent than the PSC costs, using a lower discount rate will often increase their present value and hence disfavour the PPP project,[3] and in that case, the comparative gains in PPP efficiency would have to be greater to make the PPP project worthwhile.

There is considerable controversy over how to determine the correct discount rate for this purpose. No consensus exists among respected economists, policy makers, and practitioners about the fundamentals of what the rate should be and whether it should be the same for the PSC and the PPP project.

This paper does not attempt to give a definitive solution. Instead, the more modest goal is to lay out some of the main issues as a way to help clarify the debate. The approach taken is to avoid taking sides where no strong consensus exists. In that sense, the paper takes the perspective of informed but non-specialist policy-makers in developing countries who are grappling with these questions. To keep it from becoming too long, however, the paper does assume basic familiarity with discounted cash flow techniques and with the Capital Asset Pricing Model (CAPM).

The *ultimate* goal, of course, is to give appropriate guidance to governments in developing countries. How *should* they deal with this complex issue, given that eminently qualified experts around the world differ about which methodology to use and what inputs to use in the calculations?

---

[3]For PPP projects that involve mainly recurrent operating and maintenance costs, the discount rate may not make much difference.

Overview of Practice in Several Countries

This section gives a summary of how several different countries approach the issue of the discount rate to be used in the PSC exercise. The assumptions and approaches differ widely. It is understandable that PPP units in developing countries that are looking to PPP programs in more advanced economies for guidance are likely to come away confused. The common solution will then be to hire a reputable consulting firm to recommend a methodology. This may protect the PPP unit against criticism, but it usually does not help get any closer to a sound understanding of the underlying issues.

United Kingdom (UK)

The 2003 UK "Green Book" (the Treasury's guidance for appraisal and evaluation of government projects – applicable to PPP-PSC comparisons) (HM Treasury, 2003a) uses a "social time preference" (STP) rate, deriving from classic concepts in welfare economics fleshed out in the 1950s and 1960s. The Green Book STP rate is the sum of three components:[4]

- a "pure time preference" rate;
- a "catastrophe risk" rate;[5] and
- a third component that takes into account the idea (roughly) that as per capita income increases, people will care less about additional income, and this increases their preference for money today relative to money in the future.

The Green Book estimates the pure time preference rate plus the catastrophe risk rate at 1.5% (with the pure time preference rate probably around 0.5%) and the third component at 2.0%. So the STP rate comes

---

[4]The first and third bullet points are the classic Ramsey formula.

[5]This is based on the idea that the typical risk adjustments to future cash flows do not take into account low-probability catastrophic events – climate-change catastrophe, nuclear devastation, massive asteroid impact, etc. – and so it is legitimate to include such risks in the discount rate.

out to *3.5%*, which is the real discount rate that must be used in (among other things) comparing the PSC with the PPP project.

Ireland

Central guidance in Ireland states that the discount rate to be used for comparing a PPP project with an equivalent public sector project "should reflect the relative value of the cash flows from the State Authority's perspective" (Central PPP Policy Unit, 2006). This is not "an economic discount rate ... which may be applied at an earlier stage of the evaluation of capital investment projects (including PPP projects) for conducting a cost-benefit analysis ..." Instead: "The discount rate is based on the risk free cost of debt to the public sector – the yield on the appropriate long term Government Bond" (the maturity of the bond presumably being the main characteristic of interest). This same rate should be used in discounting all cash flows.

If any adjustment for risk is called for, it should be made to the cash flows, not to the discount rate.

The PSC exercise is therefore clearly considered to be a type of *financial* appraisal – from the perspective of the government department.

Victoria, Australia

Partnerships Victoria takes a different approach from both the UK and Ireland. It builds up the discount rate by beginning with a risk-free rate and then adjusting for risk using classic methods based on the CAPM.[6]

Related to this, Partnerships Victoria says that only financial costs and benefits should be considered in the PPP-PSC comparison. Economic analysis is needed as part of the rationale for the project in general, but this appraisal should already have been carried out by the line department before the PSC exercise takes place.

The risk-free rate is taken to be the yield to maturity of a ten-year Commonwealth Bond. In 2003, this was 3% in real terms. In January 2005, the figure had risen to 3.5%.

---

[6]This section is based mainly on Partnerships Victoria (2003b). The values given may not reflect the values currently used.

The market risk premium is taken to be 6%. The risk adjustment is based on three "risk bands" according to type of project, with asset betas of 0.3, 0.5, and 0.9 yielding risk premiums of 1.8%, 3.0%, and 5.4%.[7] Water, transport, and energy projects are considered to be in the middle band. For these, the real discount rate to be used should be *6.5%* (= 3.5 + [0.5 × 6]), which is three percentage points above (almost double) the rate used in the UK.

But this is not the end of the story for Partnerships Victoria. The rate given above is the rate that would be used for net cash flows of the underlying project (before financing). Partnerships Victoria sees two further considerations in determining the rates to be used for the PPP-PSC comparison:

- It is *costs* that are being considered – negative cash flows. It makes no sense to say that a future cost is necessarily less onerous the riskier it is; this is the effect that normal discounting would have.
- Risks should be seen from the perspective of the public sector. For the PPP project, these are not the underlying risks of the project but the risks that are intentionally or unintentionally borne by the public sector – principally through the payments that the public sector makes to the private company.

It then proposes a pragmatic (rule of thumb type) way to deal with these two issues. According to Partnerships Victoria, the PSC cost flows should always be discounted using the risk-free rate; the PPP outflows (seen from the public sector perspective) should be discounted using the risk-free rate *plus* a risk premium that is proportional to the systematic risk that has been transferred to the private company (with 100% risk transfer meaning that the full, conventional risk-adjusted rate would be used). It should be stressed that these discount rates are meaningful *only* for purposes of comparing (ranking) the PSC present value against that of the PPP project. The guidance material makes it clear that using the risk-free rate for the PSC will not necessarily give the present value of the true costs to the government of that option. It is not the right rate to use in a stand-alone analysis of the PSC project.

---

[7]The term "asset beta" and several other terms and abbreviations are defined at the end of this paper.

The Partnerships Victoria approach may seem confusing and, at first glance, counterintuitive. The correct intuition is to think only about the ranking: the *less* systematic risk borne by the public sector with respect to a PPP project, the *higher* the discount rate that should be applied to the cost stream because the costs are less onerous to the public sector the less risky they are.

Partnerships Victoria guidance material states that this method will give the correct ranking of the PSC and the PPP project. It should be noted, also, that for routine projects, in practice the same discount rate – the full risk-adjusted rate – will often be used for both alternatives because of the complexity of trying to determine the risk allocation, and hence a more appropriate rate, with any accuracy.

It should be noted that Partnerships Victoria is the only PPP program of those discussed here to identify these issues as important.

Netherlands

The Netherlands Ministry of Finance has taken the position that the discount rate should be very close to the private sector weighted average cost of capital for both the PPP and the PSC.[8]

The risk premium should be based on non-diversifiable risk, as in the CAPM. This risk premium will be in the range of 1.5% to 4.5% for PPP projects, depending on what they call "market spread risks" – essentially the project beta (but in principle based on a wider portfolio of assets – not just financial assets). They consider the market risk premium to be 3%, so this implies an asset beta of 0.5 to 1.5.

The Ministry assumes a real risk-free rate of 4%; so the real discount rate to use will be in the range of *5.5% to 8.5%.*

The Ministry of Finance changed its position to this market-based one following the recommendations of a special commission in 2003 (see Ewijk and Tang, 2003). The key change was that it decided to use the observed price of risk in the equity market (market risk premium), along with the underlying idea that risks are something that depend on the project; so there is no good reason why risks should change just because of the source of funding.

---

[8]The following is based on PPP Knowledge Centre (2002a and 2002b) and discussions with the Centre in The Hague in February 2006. It is not known whether the policy has changed since then.

Chris Shugart

An unusual feature of the Netherlands method is that, when doing the PPP-PSC comparison before receiving the bids, the Ministry of Finance looks at the underlying cash flows of the PPP project, not the envisaged *payments* that the public sector will make to the project company, as is more common. But the result is the same, since the discount rate the Ministry uses is the same as, or close to, its best estimate of the appropriate project weighted average cost of capital from the private company's perspective.

South Africa

The PPP Manual (National Treasury 2004, p. 22) states: "For practical purposes, the discount rate is assumed to be the same as the risk-adjusted cost of capital to government." Although acknowledging that the government bond yield is not really the correct value for the risk-free rate – because of, e.g., "tax implications of diverting funds from private to public consumption" – it ignores these factors as being too difficult to quantify.

The Treasury does not prescribe a rate to use for the discount rate. But it states that one should begin by using the yield of a government bond with a remaining maturity similar to the duration of the project. Then, in principle, risks should be accounted for as cash flow items and not in the discount rate. But for some projects, on a project-by-project basis, a risk premium could be added but only in cases "where it is not possible to accurately reflect the effect of all risks in the cash flow of the project". It says that transaction advisors should advise on this. No mention is made of any possible difference in the treatment of systematic and non-systematic risks.

The rate selected for the project must then be used for both the PSC and the PPP models.

The Discount Rate before Adjusting for Risk

Financial Flows or Economic Flows?

As we have seen in the second section, all the countries cited, except for the UK, build up the discount rate by beginning with the financial risk-free interest rate; the UK begins (and ends) with an independently derived social time preference rate. A separate but related question is whether the PSC exercise should be considered a type of *financial* or *economic* appraisal. Partnerships Victoria guidance states explicitly (2003a, p. 7): "The PSC is intended as a quantitative financial benchmark against which to assess bids. Therefore only financial costs and benefits should be included in the PSC. Economic and cost-benefit analysis form part of the investment rationale for the project and will have already been considered at the investment decision stage." Ireland is equally explicit. This approach implies the use of a financial, as opposed to economic, discount rate.

This paper takes the position that the discount rate used for the PPP-PSC comparison should be one appropriate for economic flows (costs and benefits), not financial cash flows only. It may be that the managers of a particular government department are concerned only with the government borrowing rate, as if the department were an individual person or company borrowing money. It is difficult to see the rationale for adopting that view as government policy, however. Surely the government should be concerned with costs and benefits in the economy as a whole and therefore should use an *economic* discount rate.

One justification for treating the PSC exercise as a form of financial appraisal might be to assume that the time-pattern of costs is likely to be roughly the same (e.g., as between capex and opex) in both the PPP project and the PSC and that the economic discount rate will not be much different from the government borrowing rate. These assumptions, however, may not hold up in many developing countries.

Economic Discount Rate

Let us assume, then, that the PSC exercise is a form of economic appraisal and that we must therefore begin with the economic discount rate: the cost (or opportunity cost) of public expenditures to society as a whole.[9] This paper will not describe in any detail how to estimate the rate. This is a topic exhaustively treated elsewhere. A summary will suffice for present purposes.

---

[9]This rate is referred to variously as the economic discount rate, social discount rate, economic (or social) opportunity cost of public expenditures, etc. This paper uses the qualifier "economic" to avoid any confusion that "social" might entail (e.g., social policy, concerned especially with distributional issues, pro-poor focus, etc.). Cf. Harberger (1997, p. 79, endnote 1).

The classic approaches to the economic discount rate (before any specific risk adjustment) all involve looking at the sources of the funds that the government uses and what their cost or opportunity cost is. The assumption is often made that in the short run, the funds come from the capital market.

There are three possible sources for these funds at the margin: increased lending (or, more generally, financial investment) by members of society, displaced private investment, and foreign lending. In a textbook-case perfectly efficient economy, the three marginal rates would be equal. But since there are distortions in the economy, especially taxes, subsidies, and transaction costs, the rates will tend to be different – and, some would argue, different for different people and different situations.

According to the weighted average approach (the "sourcing" approach), widely used by practitioners, all three sources may be used to some extent when the public sector draws more funds from the capital market, which is assumed to be the immediate or marginal source of funds, and so a weighted average of the three rates should be used as the economic discount rate. It is also necessary to determine the weights, and this presents another source of divergence among final values. Some people argue that the weights may vary from time to time and according to how a project is funded.

Another method should be mentioned briefly: the shadow-price-of-capital approach, which looks differently at a project's effect on consumption and investment and converts the effect on investment into an equivalent effect on consumption. This method increases the effective cost to society of capital expenditures by looking at consumption equivalents rather than discounting all net cash flows by a higher (weighted average) discount rate. Depending on assumptions, the result may not be exactly the same as when using the weighted average approach.

Proponents of the method say that it enables them to distinguish between public expenditures that displace private investment from those that do not; the latter would not have an associated shadow price if they displaced only consumption. The issues become complex, depending on, among other things, assumptions about hypothetical future patterns of consumption and reinvestment.[10]

---

[10]For an in-depth examination of the shadow-price-of-capital method, see the classic article by Sjaastad and Wisecarver (1977). See also Burgess (2009).

The shadow-price-of-capital method is not widely used by *practitioners* because of the somewhat arbitrary (or at least highly discretionary) assumptions that need to be made. There is no general agreement about these assumptions.

The main reason for mentioning this method in the present context is that there is an argument associated with it that in cost-effectiveness analysis – where only expenditures are considered and the benefit stream is assumed to be the same in both project alternatives, as in the typical (or at least ideal) PPP-PSC comparison – the shadow price of capital is irrelevant since it applies across the board, and so the cost flows, expressed in "consumption equivalents", should simply be discounted at the social time preference rate.[11]

Two critical assumptions in reaching this conclusion, however, are (i) that all types of expenditure considered in the analysis have the same shadow price of capital (note that one might be comparing trade-offs of capex and opex), and (ii) that the shadow price of capital is constant in all time periods. If these assumptions do not hold, the opportunity cost of displaced private investment may matter in a cost-effectiveness analysis, even within the shadow-price-of-capital framework.[12]

The last issue to be mentioned is the question of whether the marginal rate of return on private investment (e.g., in the weighted average approach) should include the average market risk premium, which it usually does, implicitly, if determined in a typical way. If instead one started with the financial *risk-free* rate – i.e., government borrowing rate – and grossed this up to a pre-tax level for the relevant component of the weighted average, then this might give a rough economic discount rate that does not include a premium for systematic risk.[13]

---

[11]See Feldstein (1970) and Spackman (2004, 2006). To put the basic argument in the simplest of terms, suppose one multiplies every cost in both alternatives by the same factor. The ranking of present values would not change, regardless of the value of the factor.

[12]With respect to (i), if in one project alternative recurrent operating and maintenance expenditures are wholly or partially covered by user charges, then (within the framework of the shadow-price-of-capital method) there is no shadow price of capital associated with that part of the expenditures since the cost to the economy is determined simply by consumers' willingness to pay. With respect to (ii), in Burgess's (2008, 2009) analysis, the shadow price of capital decreases over time.

[13]The question of how to derive a risk-free economic discount rate is discussed in Brean *et al.* (2005, 75ff.). The method suggested in the text above is

In any event, the idea to retain for the purposes of this paper is that if one contemplates making a specific risk adjustment to the economic discount rate for systematic risk (as in CAPM), it is important to know the extent to which the rate one begins with already includes an *average* risk premium for the economy.

As noted at the start of this section, most PPP programs begin the calculation of the discount rate to use in the PSC exercise with the government borrowing rate. In a healthy open economy with low taxes, a risk-free rate based on the weighted average method will often not be far from the government borrowing rate. But we cannot depend on that result in many developing countries. There could be major distortions. If private investment with a high marginal return is displaced, or if the country's stock of foreign debt is becoming uncomfortably high, the correct rate might be significantly higher than the government borrowing rate – even before considering risk. This could easily add several percentage points to the resulting figure. PPP programs in developing countries that use the government borrowing rate as the risk-free discount rate may therefore be distorting the results, as will be discussed further in the next section.

Apart from the issue of how to deal with systematic risk, the various controversies over how to determine the correct economic discount rate will not be discussed any further in this paper.

Should the PPP-PSC Comparison Be Done through the Veil of Financing?

Cash flows viewed after financing

One important but neglected feature of the way the discount rate is used in the PPP-PSC comparison is that in the case of the PPP project, it is

---

roughly the approach they use. The method proposed by Glenday (2009), however, would seem to be more conceptually correct: the economic externalities should be calculated based on appropriate *market* rates, not the risk-free rate. For example, corporate income tax is based on actual profit, even if that profit contains a component remunerating companies' shareholders for bearing systematic risk. The externalities, related to average systematic risk in the market, would be considered to be a national parameter and would apply even if the specific project being appraised involved no systematic risk.

typically project cash flows *after financing* that are discounted since cash outflows from the public-sector perspective are mainly the payments made to the private company under the PPP contract – i.e., the revenue required by the private company after it has financed its capital expenditures. This is in contrast to general practice in economic appraisal, in which the economic discount rate is applied to a project's underlying cash flows *before* financing.[14] Does this make a difference? The possible complications involved in using the economic discount rate for the *post-financing* cash flows of the PPP project have been ignored in most of the literature on the subject.[15] Most PPP programs ignore the problem because they assume that they should be using a *financial* discount rate, but, as maintained in this paper, this cannot be right.

Throughout this section, we assume that there is no systematic risk (or no economic cost associated with systematic risk). The question of systematic risk will be introduced in the next section.

We also need to make an assumption about the impact of financing from foreign sources since the economic treatment of foreign and domestic financing can be different. The assumption made in this paper keeps to the assumption on which the method of the weighted average economic opportunity cost of capital is based: given the marginal rates of substitution among different sources of funds, it will be assumed that, regardless of the project-specific source, it is *as if* every marginal project is financed by all the sources according to their respective weights in the weighted average. Therefore, since the foreign financing component of the economic discount rate takes the government borrowing rate as the starting point, if the PPP project were financed by foreign sources at the government borrowing rate, the underlying project costs should simply be discounted using the economic discount rate, and we would not need to make any other adjustments for the cost of foreign financing.[16]

---

[14]One exception is Jenkins (2001), who looks at the economic costs and benefits arising from the foreign financing of PPP projects.

[15]Grout (2003) is an exception.

[16]Jenkins (2001) discusses how the economic appraisal would have to be modified in the two extreme cases (i) where new foreign financing is entirely additional to the pool of capital in the country, and (ii) where new foreign financing simply substitutes for other foreign capital inflows. Trying to add these considerations to the paper would introduce too many complications for present purposes.

One way to motivate the discussion is to consider two projects with identical capital and operating costs, as illustrated in Table 1 (lines 1 and 4). For present purposes, we assume that there are no transaction costs and that borrowing and lending rates are the same – i.e., a unique market interest rate.

In the PSC, it is the underlying costs (line 1) that are considered in the comparison. In the PPP project, capital costs are financed at the market interest rate, here assumed to be 5%; the resulting capital charge is given in line 5. After adding the recurrent costs of 50 in each year starting in year 1, the final costs, as paid by the public sector, are 205 in each year (line 6). The PSC exercise would typically compare line 1 and line 6.

Suppose we determine the present value of the costs using a weighted average economic discount rate that is higher than the market interest rate because of various price distortions in the economy – in the illustration, assumed to be 10%. Carrying out the analysis *after financing* appears to increase the economic value of the PPP project (i.e., the present value of costs is lower) – compare lines 2 and 7. If we assume that both the PSC and the PPP project are sourced in the same way from the capital market, something must be wrong.[17] What is it? The answer surely is that it is not correct to apply the economic discount rate to the cash flows obtained after financing the project (more precisely, not correct unless various compensating adjustments are included). The underlying costs to the economy remain the same, regardless of how the financial impact is spread over time by the financing per se (ignoring for the moment any true economic costs *associated with* the financing).

Table 1: Comparing the PPP Project with an Identical PSC

	Rate	PV	0	1	2	3	4	5	6	7	8
PSC											
1 Underlying costs			-1000	-50	-50	-50	-50	-50	-50	-50	-50
2 Present value	10%	-1267									
3 Present value	5%	-1323									
PPP project											
4 Underlying costs	10%	-1267	-1000	-50	-50	-50	-50	-50	-50	-50	-50
5 Financing of capex	5%			-155	-155	-155	-155	-155	-155	-155	-155
6 Costs as seen by public sector				-205	-205	-205	-205	-205	-205	-205	-205
7 Present value	10%	-1092									
8 Present value	5%	-1323									

[17]The discussion in this section might not hold if we assumed different sources of funds in the economy for the PPP project and the PSC.

If instead we use the market interest rate, we get the same present value for both projects (see lines 3 and 8). The reason is simple: discounting at the market interest rate eliminates the effect of financing from the cash flows for the purposes of comparing the two projects. Note, however, that it does not yield the *correct* present value, given in line 2.

One upshot is that if the PPP project and the PSC have identical underlying cash flows and the only difference is financing, and we assume a unique market interest rate and no financial transaction costs, then, looking at cash flows after financing, we can simply use the market interest rate for the purposes of comparing the two projects (but not for more general purposes); this gives the same comparative result that would be obtained using the *economic* discount rate before financing. But this conclusion may not seem to be of much use if it applies only when the projects have the same underlying cash flows.

The conclusion is still helpful as an insight, however, for the following reason. Most PPP programs use the government borrowing rate as the discount rate (before adjusting for risk – which we are not considering in this section). *To the extent* that differences between the costs (as seen by the public sector) of the PPP project and the PSC are solely the result of a change in the timing of expenditures through financing in a way that does not give rise to any costs to the economy, then using the financing rate as the discount rate gives the correct comparative result. But this is not because the appropriate analysis is a financial, rather than economic, appraisal. It is because the analysis is carried out looking at cash flows after financing. In other words, PPP programs that consider after-financing cash flows and use the government borrowing rate as the risk-free component of the discount rate (for comparative purposes only) may, in some circumstances, be doing roughly the right thing after all – but for the wrong reason.[18]

But that is not the end of the story. Even if using the government borrowing rate were roughly the right way to address the issue of financing the PPP, it would not necessarily be correct, especially in many developing countries, as a way to deal with the net result of different underlying (economic) costs in different time periods – e.g., the *benefit*

---

[18]One correct reason for using just the government borrowing rate as the economic discount rate would be if all incremental financing (from the perspective of the economy) came from government borrowing and if the marginal cost of foreign financing were constant. These assumptions are questionable for many developing countries.

of greater capex efficiency in the initial years of a PPP project, but with additional oversight *costs* on a recurring basis throughout the life of the arrangement. The approach used for PPP programs in developing countries must address this issue, and for this, the economic discount rate is the appropriate rate to use.

This is illustrated in Table 2. The duration of the projects has been limited to eight years to fit conveniently on the page. The comparative effects would be greater if a more realistic duration for the projects was used – say, 25 years.

The PPP project now has different underlying costs in two respects (compare line 4 with line 1): initial costs are higher because (let's suppose) despite greater capex efficiency, the PPP transaction costs are very high relative to the size of the project; but recurrent costs are one-half the PSC costs because of more efficient O&M (e.g., reduced costs for personnel). Applying the economic discount rate of 10% to the underlying costs shows that the PPP project is more costly (lines 4 and 2). But what happens if we use the *financial* discount rate applied to the after-financing cash flows, as would be done in most PPP programs? The PPP project now erroneously appears *less* costly (lines 3 and 8). The problem is that we are trying to do two things with one rate: correct for the effect of financing the PPP *and* compare the differing underlying costs. This cannot necessarily be done; it will not give the right result in all cases. In this respect, the approach used for the public sector comparator analysis in most PPP programs rests on shaky grounds.

The tendency to use the government borrowing rate instead of the economic discount rate is an example of how PPP programs in developing countries have often blindly copied PPP programs in advanced economies without going back to fundamentals. In developing

Table 2: Comparing the PPP and PSC When Costs Differ

	Rate	PV	0	1	2	3	4	5	6	7	8
PSC											
1 Underlying costs			-1000	-50	-50	-50	-50	-50	-50	-50	-50
2 Present value	10%	-1267									
3 Present value	5%	-1323									
PPP project											
4 Underlying costs	10%	-1283	-1150	-25	-25	-25	-25	-25	-25	-25	-25
5 Financing of capex	5%			-178	-178	-178	-178	-178	-178	-178	-178
6 Costs as seen by public sector				-203	-203	-203	-203	-203	-203	-203	-203
7 Present value	10%	-1083									
8 Present value	5%	-1312									

countries, there can be a large difference between the economic discount rate and the government borrowing rate. The PPP-PSC comparison of underlying project costs must be made using the economic discount rate.

Why might this make a difference, in practical terms? One can think of a number of examples. Here are three.

- PPP projects involve high up-front transaction costs, and because of their partially fixed nature, these costs make up a greater proportion of initial costs the smaller the size of the project. Suppose that for a certain kind of project, these higher initial costs for a PPP project may be offset by lower recurring costs because of the expected greater O&M efficiency of a private operator.[19] The higher the discount rate, the greater will be the impact of the higher costs in initial years relative to the lower recurrent costs. So one might expect that for a certain type of project, the threshold in size below which a PPP simply does not make sense – because transaction costs are too high – will be *higher* in countries that have a higher economic discount rate. This sort of effect may not be discovered by using the government borrowing rate as the discount rate for the PPP-PSC comparison.

- In countries with a high economic discount rate, achieving operating efficiencies through a PPP will not be as important as reducing design and construction costs occurring during the first few years. So the focus should be more on these aspects. Once again, we may not see how this plays out in a particular project unless we carry out the comparison using the right discount rate and the right set of cash flows.

- If demand is growing, it might be optimal to increase capacity in stages rather than build the full capacity needed at the start of the PPP. But it is easier and less risky from a transaction point of view not to include major construction stages later in the contract. The economic cost of *not* choosing a staged approach, where this is optimal, will be greater the higher the economic discount rate.[20]

---

[19]They may also be offset by lower capex, but we are ignoring that here. Since both the main capex and the transaction costs occur in the initial period, the discount rate used will be of less importance in this comparison.

[20]As an approximation, the optimal design period is inversely proportional to the discount rate (for a given economies-of-scale exponent and assuming that demand is a linear function of time). So, for example, if in using a discount rate of 5% the optimal design period is 25 years (i.e., the full term of the PPP), it

Chris Shugart

Financial intermediation costs

So far, we have been considering only the effect of financing that involves no economic costs. But financial intermediation involves true costs to the economy, and the PPP-PSC comparison should take these costs into account. One way to do this would be to carry out the comparative analysis using the economic discount rate applied to: (i) the underlying costs (i.e., before any financing), *plus* (ii) the economic costs associated with financial intermediation. Financial intermediation costs will almost certainly be greater for the PPP project than for a public sector project financed by government loans.

In general, the costs that might be considered for domestic sources of credit – costs that make up the spread between a bank's borrowing rate and lending rate – are the following:[21]

- *Bank operating and administrative costs.* These are true costs to the economy and should be included.
- *Markup for required cash reserves.* If the reserve requirement is R (expressed as a proportion of funds borrowed), then the bank has to borrow $1+R$ pesos for every peso it lends.[22] The economic discount rate takes into account the cost to the economy of one peso for every peso of funds provided to the project. So the markup for R should be accounted for as a separate cost item in the calculation.
- *Provision for loan losses.* The cash flows used in the economic analysis should be *expected values*.[23] (See the next section.) So on

---

would be optimal to build a stage with half the capacity at the start and then another similar stage after about 12.5 years if the correct discount rate were instead 10%.

[21]Note that the purpose here is not to carry out a full economic appraisal with respect to these costs. It should be considered sufficient for purposes of the PPP-PSC comparison (given the considerable uncertainties involved) just to make sure that one takes into account the major cost *items* that would otherwise have been neglected.

[22]This component of the spread is determined by multiplying the bank's borrowing rate (e.g., the interest rate on deposits) by $R/(1-R)$. For example, if the reserve requirement is 20% and the interest rate on deposits is 3%, this component of the spread will be 0.75 percentage points.

[23]In this paper, the term "expected value" is used in its technical sense. See the definition on page 76.

average, this item does not represent a cost to the economy: some borrowers will pay the full interest rate; some will pay less because they default. (The costs incurred by the bank in dealing with a defaulting borrower – workout costs – should be considered true economic costs, however.)

- *Bank profit.* Normal profit should be included as an economic cost since it is a return to capital invested in the financial institution. Strictly speaking, supra-normal profits of domestic banks should not be included. But it is probably a good rule of thumb simply to include the entire amount of this item as a cost unless there are convincing reasons not to do so.[24]

As an example, Table 3 shows the interest rate spread for banks in three East African countries.

So as a rough rule of thumb, the entire spread should be considered to be an economic cost except for the loan-loss component, which would typically be in the range of 10–30% of the total spread in most developing countries. In addition, one should add the various fees that banks would charge – e.g., up-front fee, commitment fee.

Table 3: Interest Rate Spreads for Banks in Three East African Countries

	Kenya	Tanzania	Uganda
Interest rate spread (% points)	**14.9**	**11.4**	**14.4**
Operating (and misc.) costs	5.9	7.5	8.7
Cash reserves	0.3	0.1	0.2
Loan losses	2.5	2.1	3.5
Residual (pre-tax profit)	6.2	1.7	2.1

Source: Čihák and Podpiera (2005). For Kenya and Tanzania, based on 2002 data; for Tanzania, data for June 2001–June 2002.

---

[24]For example, Čihák and Podpiera (2005) attribute the high profit component in the interest rate spread in Kenya shown in Table 3 to a lack of effective competition in the sector. It might then be a policy question for a PPP program (or the Ministry of Finance) whether one should deem these supra-normal profits to be a cost or not for purposes of the PPP-PSC comparison.

Chris Shugart

A further question is what time-profile to give to the economic costs associated with the interest rate, for the purpose of adding them to the costs of the project before discounting. The simplest way would be to treat them as a fixed proportion of the interest payments (which are not included in full since the simple financing effect is not considered in the analysis).[25] They would then be discounted, along with all other costs, at the economic discount rate.

Table 4 illustrates one way that the PPP-PSC comparison could take into account the financial intermediation costs associated with the financing, using this approach.

In this case, looking only at the underlying costs, the PPP project is less costly in present value terms (compare lines 1 and 2): up-front costs are greater (1100 compared with 1000), but more than offset by lower recurrent costs. We do not consider the after-financing costs as seen by the public sector contracting party (line 3), but as an intermediate step, we do need to calculate the interest costs paid by the PPP company (line 4). Suppose that this is a loan of 1100 from a local bank, to be repaid in constant, annuity-style debt service payments over eight years, and of the 7% interest charged, the spread between this rate and the bank's borrow-

Table 4: Taking Financial Intermediation Costs into Account

	Rate	PV	0	1	2	3	4	5	6	7	8
PSC											
1 Underlying costs	10%	-1267	-1000	-50	-50	-50	-50	-50	-50	-50	-50
PPP project											
2 Underlying costs	10%	-1233	-1100	-25	-25	-25	-25	-25	-25	-25	-25
3 Debt service	7%			-184	-184	-184	-184	-184	-184	-184	-184
4 Interest paid	7%			-77	-69	-61	-53	-44	-34	-23	-12
5 Economic costs re financing				-22	-20	-18	-15	-12	-10	-7	-3
6 Total costs for comparison			-1100	-47	-45	-43	-40	-37	-35	-32	-28
7 Present value	10%	-1312									

---

[25]This may not always be the best way to handle these costs. For example, some of the preparation costs for a project finance loan may be included in the interest rate margin instead of charging all of them in a specific up-front fee. If there is reason to believe that the time-profile of actual costs diverges substantially from the time-profile of interest payments, the actual profile should be used.

ing rate – but excluding the project-specific *default* component[26] – is two percentage points. That means that the intermediation costs we need to consider equal two-sevenths of the interest payments (line 5). Given the *total* costs of the PPP project, including the economic costs associated with the financing (line 6), the PPP project is now seen to be more costly than the PSC in present value terms (line 7). In this illustrative case (designed to give this result), financing has made a material difference.

The Treatment of Risk

Non-Systematic Risk

This section and the next section deal with the question of risk adjustments to the discount rate. Most of the controversy over the right rate to use involves systematic risk, but it is good to start by briefly reviewing other kinds of risk, too.

Asymmetric risk

"Asymmetric risk" is risk whose expected value is not equal to zero – i.e., upside or downside risk. The upside or downside impact cannot, of course, be eliminated by simple diversification or spreading.

There is a general consensus that asymmetric risks should ideally be handled by adjustments to cash flows rather than to the discount rate. "Optimism bias" is one kind. If project cash flows are built up as expected values, as they should be, then an adjustment for optimism bias should not be included in the discount rate.[27] The net present value (NPV) of the project will be lower because of the downward adjustment to net cash flows, not because a "risk premium" has been added to the

---

[26]We assume here that the default component is correctly priced and does not include transaction costs (e.g., legal fees, which can be considerable) related to a default or potential default. In other words, the *expected value* of what the bank will receive (according to best judgment) is equal to the interest rate excluding this default premium.

[27]Following the British example, in the method used by most PPP programs, it is assumed that the base cost estimates for the PSC are optimistically low and so a separate "optimism bias" adjustment must be made.

discount rate. A typical mistake is to ignore optimism bias in estimating the costs of the public sector project, whereas the costs of the PPP project, as estimated by the project developers, are closer to expected values. This makes the PPP project look worse.

Another example is the default premium in the cost of debt. Corporate and project finance lending rates include a default premium because there is some probability that borrowers will default on their debt service payments. The interest rate including the default premium is the *stated* cost of borrowing, i.e., the rate the borrower promises to pay. What the lender *expects* to receive is lower. The economic discount rate should not include a borrower- or project-specific default premium so long as the cash flows have been estimated on an expected-value basis. (Nevertheless, there are likely to be transaction costs associated with a default or impending default, and these should be included, ideally in the cash flows.)

This issue comes up frequently in comparing the cost of government debt with the cost of PPP company debt. Critics of PPPs have often pointed to the higher cost of debt to the PPP company as an argument in favour of public sector financing. But if the default premium is based on a good estimate of the probability of default, the premium does not result in an added cost, on average.[28] (The expected value of the transaction costs associated with a debt workout, however, would be an added cost of a PPP project and should not be ignored.)

Another way of conceptualizing this issue is to assume that project costs have been *underestimated* in the cash flows, and it is appropriate to consider the default premium in the loan to the PPP company loan as a true cost. But in that case, to be able to compare like with like, something equivalent is needed for the PSC: if there is no possibility of a default on the government loan, then contingent costs have to be funded somehow – e.g., an implicit guarantee from taxpayers to be called on if project cash flows are not sufficient to repay the debt.[29]

---

[28]But if you have good reason to believe that because of, e.g., lack of good information, wary *foreign* lenders are charging a default premium that is higher than a premium based on the best estimate of the probability of default, then the high cost of PPP financing would constitute an economic cost to the host country.

[29]Klein (1996) takes this approach in demystifying problems encountered in comparing the costs of PPP financing and government debt.

An analogous issue may arise with respect to the equity returns that investors say they expect. When investors say they need to be assured of very high rates of return in certain emerging markets (sometimes 20% or higher, in real terms), in some cases they are implicitly assuming that the purported "expected" cash flows are overly optimistic, sometimes because they ignore low-probability financial-disaster scenarios.[30] The rates may build in a cushion against downside risk – analogous to a lender's default premium. Once again, the question to ask is whether this premium appears to be based on a correct assessment of future risks.[31]

Non-systematic variability risk

It is generally accepted that both the public sector, through taxes, and the private sector, through dispersed shareholding, can in most cases diversify away or sufficiently spread symmetric non-systematic variability risk – i.e., the volatility around the expected value that is not correlated with the economy (national income).

According to some, this may not be quite true for the private sector because of agency considerations: managers might not have the same viewpoint as shareholders with regard to non-systematic risk. There are two ways to respond. First, from a financial point of view, in a competitive market, one would have to explain how this could be sustained for very long; strategic investors should try to increase the competitive advantage of their companies by finding clever ways around this agency problem so as to reduce the cost of capital. Second, from the economic point of view, any added premium would not be an economic cost (provided we are considering only domestic shareholders) – just

---

[30]One would have to look at all the components – especially the sovereign risk premium for the country and the leverage of the capital structure of the company – to have a good idea of whether a rate like this seems excessive if interpreted as an expected value.

[31]This can be problematic, however. Suppose that one of the largest risks for equity investors is that the public entity will renege on the PPP contract or resort to creeping expropriation of some kind – and that investors must therefore add a substantial risk premium in expectation of that contingency. It is hard to imagine the PPP unit admitting this officially and therefore being willing to exclude this premium in estimating true cost of equity. The irony is that the PPP project may then appear prohibitively expensive, even though it is the propensity of the *public entity* to act in an opportunistic way (as perceived by investors) that makes it seem so.

Chris Shugart

supra-normal returns to shareholders. Irrespective of whether these responses are adequate, it is generally accepted that symmetric non-systematic variability risk should not be considered to affect the cost of capital for either the private or the public sector.

Most discussion of the impact of non-systematic risk in the public sector context relates to taxpayers. The issue might be different with regard to customers of the PPP service who pay user charges. There could be a big difference between risks borne by all taxpayers in a country and risks borne by a much smaller group of service users. What is most important to understand is that if people face *significant* non-systematic risk (i.e., it is not spread very thinly) and they cannot remove it by diversification or insurance, then *even non-systematic risk can have an economic cost.*[32]

The following thought experiment highlights the issue.[33] Let's assume that some groups in society cannot completely diversify away or hedge non-systematic risk. Now consider the case of non-systematic risky costs and benefits that are fully, and negatively, correlated with each other so that *net* cash flow does not vary at all. If one group in society receives both streams, there is no risk-related economic cost. But if the costs and benefits are split and different groups (who cannot contract with each other) receive the two different streams, there will be a risk-related economic cost *for each group*.

Some monetary impacts of PPP projects that involve customers who pay for services might well remain concentrated among these service users and not fall on the entire population of taxpayers; so even non-systematic risk might require a premium if the effects are large enough.

In conclusion, non-systematic risk could increase the cost of either the PPP project or the PSC because of the impact of idiosyncratic risk on a relatively small group of customers; the group may be small enough so that people cannot achieve the full benefits of risk spreading and may not be able to diversify or hedge the risks sufficiently. It is probably more likely that risky customer payments figure more prominently in the PPP project than in the PSC; there is likely to be more emphasis on cost recovery from customers in the PPP project instead of filling deficits by government subsidies or by decreases or deferrals of maintenance expenditure. On the other hand, it is more likely that there will be greater

---

[32]The possible importance of this in public sector projects is discussed in Arrow and Lind (1970, p. 377).

[33]This illustration is based on Arrow and Lind (1970, p. 377).

risks in service quality – and hence risky coping costs – in the PSC. All in all, owing to the lack of good information, non-systematic variability risk should therefore probably be ignored in the analysis.

Systematic Risk

"Systematic risk" is risk that co-varies with the entire market or, depending on the type of analysis one is doing, with national income (loosely speaking, with the "economy" – the way it will often be expressed in this report). This means that it will not disappear through diversification or spreading.

Might a premium for systematic risk matter in the PPP-PSC comparison? Suppose for the moment (just to start the discussion) that the appropriate premium to use is the same as that used for a single-purpose PPP company.[34] The cost of capital for private sector companies engaged in PPP-type activities does include a risk premium. Empirical results show a range of values for the asset beta (i.e., what the beta would be for an *unlevered* company – a company with only equity and no debt in the capital structure).[35] As one would expect, given these companies' reduced exposure to market forces (being regulated by contract or by agency), the asset beta values tend to be below the average asset beta for the market as a whole (which is around 0.65–0.75 in Western economies). Let's say the asset beta for a typical PPP project company (assuming a PPP contract with a good-practice allocation of risk) is between 0.3 and 0.5.[36] Given a market risk premium of 6% (an oft-cited figure – perhaps somewhat on the high side), this translates into a project risk premium of between 1.8 and 3.0 percentage points to be added to (or subtracted from – see the next section) the discount rate.[37] That is not

---

[34]In fact, this may not be the right benchmark to use, as will be discussed in the fifth and seventh sections. But this sets the scene.

[35]See definitions of beta and leverage on pages 75-76.

[36]See, e.g., the figures given in PricewaterhouseCoopers (2002).

[37]The discussion in this paper assumes that the project-specific risk premium, using CAPM, is calculated using a market risk premium and a beta similar to those found in advanced economies. Some would argue that in many emerging markets, adjustments must be made that might greatly increase the risk premium. See, e.g., Estrada (2007) for a concise review of different models.

insignificant. But how often would it switch the ranking of the PPP project and the PSC – especially in developing countries where the economic discount rate is relatively high? (If very infrequently, perhaps the whole issue should be ignored.)

Systematic risk might not disappear just because the government borrowing rate does not include a premium for systematic risk and the government does not raise its funds in the equity market. Variability risk is not reflected in the stated cost of government financing; to the extent that it exists, it falls on taxpayers instead.[38]

The standard argument to support the idea that systematic risk adds a cost to government financing goes something like this. Suppose, for example, that consumers pay a fixed price per unit consumed of some service, that demand for the service decreases when the economy is in a slump, and that the production process involves a certain proportion of fixed costs. Then in the case of a private sector company providing the service, shareholders' returns will decrease during an economic downturn. If we keep the same pricing policy, but this is a *public sector* project instead and the net cash flows go to and from the government's coffers, then in an economic slump, taxpayers will have to pay more taxes than they otherwise would and so will have less money to use for consumption purposes.[39] So the impact of a project on taxpayers' consumption would be positively correlated with the state of the economy.

In this story, it does not matter if the government practises tax smoothing by increasing its borrowing when there is a deficit so long as we subscribe to some form of *permanent income hypothesis* according to which present consumption is determined by long-term income expectations – in which case there is a close analogy between an investor's *asset* in the capital market and a taxpayer's perceived long-term *wealth*. This analogy may seem strained to some people – especially since investors in the capital market, as opposed to taxpayers, engage in a continual process of explicitly quantifying asset values and of trading –

---

[38]Klein (1996) makes a related point: if the cost of risk associated with public finance is truly low, we need to ask "what it is about the tax system that allows it to tap lots of 'investors' with low costs of risk-bearing". Are "all the financial advantages of sovereign finance ... due to [the] coercive powers" of the government?

[39]It may well be that pricing policy would tend to be different in a public sector project, but for the purposes of comparing private sector and public sector projects, it is simpler to hold this aspect constant.

but many economists will view the two cases as virtually the same, despite empirical studies that show departures of consumers' behaviour from the permanent income hypothesis.

Nevertheless, the question of whether a premium for systematic risk should be included in the *economic* discount rate is generally ignored in the economic appraisal of public expenditures – even by those economists who basically accept the story outlined above,[40] leading to the view that the risk premium should not be the same for the PPP project and the PSC. This view is based on the belief that there is something different about public sector and private sector financing in terms of risk and hence cost to the economy. In particular, there might be something peculiar to the equity markets that makes the financing of the PPP project especially risky and costly.

In the following discussion, we are concerned only with the financing of the projects and monetary costs – and not with benefits and non-monetary costs – on the assumption that these will be the same for both the PSC and the PPP projects. In fact, this assumption is unrealistic in some developing countries since we would expect service quality to be lower and riskier with the PSC, and perhaps riskier in a way correlated with the economy. But trying to take this into account would only add to the complications of the analysis.[41]

What is the basis for the view that risk (or the cost of risk) is different for private and public sector financing? The landmark Arrow-Lind article (1970) is often brought out to dismiss the idea that there is a risk premium related to public sector projects. It is sometimes stated categorically that according to Arrow and Lind, one should use a risk-

---

[40]In the weighted average sourcing approach, one component of the economic discount rate does include a premium for *average* market systematic risk. The question here is whether the overall premium should be adjusted to reflect the systematic risk of the particular project being appraised.

[41]It is not clear how to deal with the riskiness of non-monetary impacts (e.g., risky non-monetary benefits to users of the service). One view is that risk aversion is not relevant here (see, e.g., Spackman, 2001). But risky benefits from an infrastructure project could affect disposable income by way of coping behaviour: e.g., if a water system breaks down, people might have to spend more money or time getting water from standpipes, carriers, or tankers – and these extra expenditures (or reduced income) might be correlated with the economy if the service breakdowns are.

Chris Shugart

free discount rate for public sector investment projects.[42] In fact, Arrow and Lind focus their attention on cases involving non-systematic risk; they state explicitly that their main contention does not apply to *systematic* risk. It is true that they do not believe that systematic risk is relevant or significant for public sector projects, but this is not a conclusion they reach through a detailed examination; they express it almost as a passing thought.

One preliminary point is that according to the general view, if systematic risk has a cost to the economy, it must be because of how it impinges on *individuals* somewhere along the line. Statements, therefore, that government departments should perhaps add risk premiums for systematic risk (using the CAPM methodology) "in the case of large investment projects where the risk is borne by an individual [government] agency" are puzzling or at least incomplete.[43] An organization, per se, does not experience the kind of risk aversion referred to in conventional theory.[44]

A major stumbling block is that economists do not yet fully understand the causes of the observed high equity risk premium in the capital market – referred to as the "equity premium puzzle". The puzzle, first noted in the mid-1980s, results from the conclusion from theory that the equity premium should be no more than about one-half a percent, rather than the 4-7% based on empirical data on actual market returns. Many explanations have been proposed, but there is not yet a consensus among economists.

This leads to a serious problem for deciding whether something similar to the equity premium should apply to public sector projects. In discussing the question of a risk premium for the economic discount rate, it is common for economists to refer to theory, and to empirical studies of the variability of national income and its correlation with project costs and benefits, and to conclude that even if a premium for systematic risk should be included for public sector projects, it is surely very small.

---

[42]For example, Klein (1996, p. 6): "Arrow and Lind argued that government finance was indeed cheaper than private finance. They claimed that the government discount rate should be a risk-free rate reflecting risk-neutrality on the government's part."

[43]Taken from Department of Treasury and Finance, Western Australia (2002, p. 142).

[44]If an organization per se is posited as experiencing risk aversion, we have left behind the usual assumptions of methodological individualism.

But since we do not really know why the observed premium in the equity markets is so high relative to theory – and it is the same basic theory that applies – it is difficult to say with confidence whether the same discrepancy should or should not also apply to public sector financing. Authors steeped in the welfare economics tradition tend to believe that this cost is negligible; those schooled in financial economics generally see no reason to apply different assumptions from those applicable to private sector financing.[45]

This is not the place to review all of the possible explanations advanced for the equity premium puzzle, of which there are many.[46] There is an important distinction, however, for the purposes of this paper: some explanations would apply only to financing from the equity markets, and some might apply across the board.

- *Peculiarities of equity markets.* Explanations of this type would probably not apply to public sector financing. This is the kind of explanation usually cited by those who believe that there is no reason to think that systematic risk involves a significant cost in the public sector. If reasoning along these lines is correct, this would tend to support the idea that there is indeed a significant extra cost associated with PPP projects. (But note that the efficiency gains and quality improvements brought about by the PPP project could still outweigh these extra costs; so this would not be the end of the story.) Some examples of this category of explanation (or description) are the following:
  - The pattern of returns in the equity market exhibits extreme values ("fat tails") – for example, because of traders' irrational behaviour (e.g., noise trading, speculation, contagion, bubbles, information cascades). This might cause concern to investors but might not be captured adequately by the statistical variance of the returns.
  - Emergent characteristics of market behaviour – e.g., fractals – with unspecified causes but having broadly the same effect as in the first point.[47]

---

[45]Spackman (2006), among others, makes this comparison among different academic traditions.

[46]See, e.g., Grant and Quiggin (2004) and Spackman (2006) for summaries.

[47]For "fractal finance", see Mandelbrot and Hudson (2004).

Chris Shugart

- Systematic risk in the capital markets might be concentrated on a relatively small group of people because the markets are not complete and frictionless – for a number of possible reasons.

- *More general features of beliefs, preferences and psychology.* Explanations in this category might possibly affect the cost of risk in the public sector as well as in the equity market, but much would depend on the details. Examples:
  - People's risk aversion may be greater than is generally believed.[48]
  - Anticipated impact of low-probability economic disasters.[49]
  - "Myopic loss aversion": people may be more concerned about losses than about gains, and they may focus too much on short-term volatility.
  - Other unconventional specifications of people's utility functions (e.g., habit persistence).
  - People may believe there is more uncertainty about future economic growth than one might predict based on past data (e.g., there may be uncertainty about model type and parameters) – a problem of "unknown unknowns".[50]

Another possibly important distinction affecting some of the explanations in both categories – but probably more so in the capital-market explanations – is whether a *mistake* may be involved.[51] Explanations along these lines would not involve any economic cost since the error would simply result in someone in the economy getting a windfall –

---

[48]But see Layard, Mayraz, and Nickell (2008). Using data from six surveys of reported well-being and happiness, they estimate the coefficient of risk aversion (assuming a CRRA utility function) to be around 1.2–1.3, well within the usual range as estimated by other methods (e.g., choice under uncertainty and intertemporal choice).

[49]See, e.g., Barro (2006).

[50]Economists tend to use point estimates based on past sample averages for their model parameters; this may be an inadequate way to model future uncertainty. For example, see Weitzman (2007). Weitzman is concerned with capital market phenomena, but the idea of subjective structural (parameter) uncertainty could be applied more broadly.

[51]For example, a mistake about what will happen in the future or perhaps about one's own true preferences.

someone ends up earning more or less than they bargained for.[52] We might not object to this in developing countries if it benefited *domestic* shareholders: strengthening local business groups is likely to help develop the economy. This would, however, involve an economic cost if the error resulted in a *foreign* investor receiving the windfall – e.g., a foreign investor believing that the project is more risky than it really is.

In short, most specialists addressing the issue come down strongly on one side or the other: either the systematic risk premium appropriate for public sector financing is negligible, or it should be the same as for private sector financing. Since competent, highly regarded economists are ranged on both sides of the issue, the best policy advice to governments is perhaps to say simply that the question is undecided at present. The implications of this noncommittal position will be developed more in the seventh section.

Taking Systematic Risk into Account in the PPP-PSC Comparison

In this section, we assume, *solely for purposes of argument*, that it is appropriate to make a CAPM-type adjustment for systematic risk in the discount rates used for the PPP-PSC comparison. In that case, how should one go about it?

As noted in the second section, Partnerships Victoria has identified two problems with the way discounting is often done in the PPP-PSC comparison.

- In the case of costs, we are looking at negative cash flows. It makes no sense to say that a future cost is less onerous the riskier it is[53] – which is the effect that normal discounting would have. (The greater the riskiness, the higher the discount rate and so the lower the present value of the cost.) So we have to approach the discounting issue in a different way.

---

[52]This is like the notion of the *happy pessimist*: the person who habitually prepares for the worst and is continually pleased by outcomes more favourable than he or she expected.

[53]Assuming here that the risky cost (expressed as a negative value) co-varies positively with the state of the economy.

- Riskiness should be seen from the perspective of the public sector. So, in discounting the payments to be made to the private company under a PPP contract, it is not the underlying risks of the project that matter but the risks that are intentionally or unintentionally borne by the public sector – principally through the payments that the public sector pays to the private company. Supposing (hypothetically) that *all* systematic risks were borne by the private company, then the rate to use in discounting the PPP project cash flows, from the public sector's perspective, should be the risk-free rate.

Most PPP programs discuss the question of risk adjustment as if they were using the discount rate in the canonical way – i.e., to discount the *net* cash flows of a project. But we are not looking at net cash flows; we are looking just at costs.

Within the CAPM framework, there is nothing wrong with disaggregating various inflows and outflows so long as one applies the appropriate risk premium to each flow. The sum of the present values of each line must equal the NPV of bottom-line net cash flow, discounted at the appropriate project rate. The risk premium that should be used for each flow is based on the covariance of that particular cash flow with the market or economy. The rules to be used for the sign of the risk premium (i.e., the sign of conventional CAPM beta) are shown in Figure 1.

The reason that the sign of the risk premium (i.e., of beta) is different for outflows and inflows is that the conventional CAPM beta (project beta) is based on correlations of *returns*, not cash flows, and with respect to outflows, this introduces a negative value in the denominator.[54] The relevant algebra is summarized in Annex 1.

---

[54]The sign of the *cash-flow* beta is the same as the sign of the correlation (see Annex 1), but it is the conventional CAPM beta (the project beta, based on returns, not cash flows) that must be used to determine the sign of the risk premium; for outflows, the signs of the two different types of beta are different. There has been an ongoing debate about how to apply the CAPM-type risk premium to negative cash flows. See the discussion in Ehrhardt and Daves (2000), which includes an appendix setting out the basic algebra. One concern in the literature has been whether flipping between positive and negative risk premiums could present arbitrage opportunities, which would not make sense (see Brealey, Cooper, and Habib, 1997). The rules given in Figure 1 would not lead to this problem.

Figure 1: Determining the Sign of the Risk Premium to Be Added to the Discount Rate

Correlation of cash flow with the
market or economy

	Positive ("bad risk")	Negative ("good risk")
Inflow	Positive risk premium	Negative risk premium
Outflow	Negative risk premium	Positive risk premium

For convenience, let's refer to cash flows that are positively correlated with the economy as "bad-risky" cash flows (risk reduces value) and cash flows that are negatively correlated with the economy as "good-risky" cash flows (risk increases value).

In the projects we often consider where the *net cash flow* is bad-risky, we have to include a positive risk premium above the risk-free rate. That can come about either because both inflows and outflows are bad-risky, which amplifies the effect in the net cash flow, or because inflows and outflows are different in this respect but the effect of the bad-risky cash flows outweighs that of the good-risky cash flows. For example, take the case of a project in which demand, and hence revenue, is positively correlated with the economy. One would expect variable costs to be good-risky since they will also be lower when demand is less (they are negatively correlated with the economy). But the bad-risky revenue outweighs this, and so the net result is bad-risky.

What happens when we do a PPP-PSC comparison? The ideal case is one in which benefits are the same for both alternatives; so we will ignore the benefit side and look only at the comparison of costs. When we look at the costs, what kind of cash flows are we looking at? They are outflows. If they are bad-risky, by the rules above we would use a *negative* risk premium in the discount rate.

But it is not at all clear why all the costs should be bad-risky. As noted in the example above, *variable costs* might well be good-risky in an overall bad-risky project, and this is a type of cost that will extend throughout the life of the PPP project. We should use a *positive* risk premium for good-risky costs. Moreover, one can imagine bad-risky projects in which almost all the systematic risk comes from the revenue (or benefit) stream. In that case, one should use the risk-free rate to discount the costs.

In fact, even though the PPP-PSC comparison typically involves analyzing only costs, any adjustment made for systematic risk has to be the adjustment appropriate for *net* cash flow since part of the risk – and often the major part – arises on the revenue side. This does little to make the adjustment easily comprehensible.

Partnerships Victoria is certainly on to something important in recognizing that within the CAPM framework, the discount rate to be used for components of disaggregated cash flows is not necessarily the discount rate that would be used for the overall net cash flow – i.e., the normal project discount rate. But it is not immediately obvious that there is an easy solution: it would seem that a careful case-by-case, line-by-line examination is needed. (It may be that with further study, some useful rules of thumb would emerge.)

The second novel aspect of the Partnerships Victoria approach is that it looks at the riskiness of the PPP cash flows *as faced by the public sector*. The overall systematic risk of the PPP project is not what matters to the public sector in discounting the payments it will make to the company if the company's shareholders bear most of that risk. In the extreme case, where shareholders bear all systematic risk, the payment stream made to the private company would have zero systematic risk from the public-sector perspective. (The internalized risk may affect the cost of financing for the private company, but that would affect the size of the contractual payments to be made, not their riskiness.)

In contrast, the public sector would face the full risk in the PSC because no one else is taking any of it. Since we are looking at outflows in each case from the public sector's perspective, if we assume that we are dealing with outflows with zero or positive correlation with the economy (i.e., neutral or bad-risky outflows), if there is any risk premium to use in the discount rate, it will be negative. So in the extreme case, where all systematic risk has been transferred to the private company, the discount rate to use for the PPP outflows will be the risk-free rate, and the rate to use for the risky PSC outflows will be lower than the risk-free rate.

The Partnerships Victoria method may seem confusing at first because it uses the risk-free rate for the PSC costs and possibly a higher rate for the PPP outflows. It may have the right ranking of rates and the right difference in percentage points between them, but the rates are at the wrong levels.[55]

Does this matter? In fact, it may indeed matter because of the non-linear relation between discount rates and present values. Suppose the real risk-free rate is 3% and the appropriate risk premium is 4% (the figure is exaggerated to show that the discount rate could actually be negative). For the typical cash flow profiles, and assuming that all types of costs require the same risk premium, there would be a significant difference between (i) comparing the PSC using a discount rate of 3% with the PPP at a discount rate of 7%, and (ii) comparing the PSC at a discount rate of -1% with the PPP at a discount rate of 3%. It can easily be shown that method (i), the method used by Partnerships Victoria, distorts the results in favour of the PPP project. How often that might matter with actual cases is another question.

Apart from this question, there are difficult issues in knowing what the risk premiums should be for the PSC and for the PPP project from the public sector perspective. (Here we ignore the added problems of understanding just what the cost of systematic risk is outside the context of the capital market. We assume here that the public sector costs the risk in the same way that the equity market does.)

For the PSC, it is typical to suggest looking at publicly traded private sector companies that are engaged in similar types of activities (i.e., PPP projects in the same sector) and determining their betas based on equity prices over a past period. But this would reflect the systematic risk faced by the company's *shareholders*.[56] Some of the systematic risk may well have been passed on to customers or a public entity. What we are really interested in knowing is what the beta of a PPP company would be, hypothetically, if *no* systematic risk were passed on to customers or the public sector through the PPP contract – i.e., if all of it were borne by shareholders. But there may be no market benchmark for that.

For the PPP project, from the perspective of the public sector, we would need to understand the systematic risk inherent in the payment

---

[55]According to Gómez-Ibáñez (2005, p. 7): "Victoria's Treasury did not recognize that the betas for the Partnerships projects were likely to be negative, …" (It is true that Partnerships Victoria [2003b] does not mention the idea of negative betas.) If this is correct, this would explain why Partnerships Victoria used the risk-free rate and a *higher* rate.

[56]A similar point is made in Gómez-Ibáñez (2005).

Chris Shugart

formula,[57] including all adjustment provisions (indexation, specified events, price resets, etc.), as well as in any guarantees that might be given by the government outside the PPP contract. This is no easy matter. Suppose the contract passes demand risk through to government or customers but only under certain conditions. First, one has to understand the extent to which demand risk in this sector and for this project is systematic. Second, one has to figure out how the specific contractual allocation mechanism allocates that systematic risk. This is likely to be highly speculative.

In conclusion, even if we assume that the cost of systematic risk is the same in the public sector as in private sector financing (and it is not clear that this is so), deciding how to take this into account in comparing the PPP project with the PSC is hardly straightforward.

Questions and Puzzles

One way to sum up the discussion in this paper – before turning to a possible practical way forward – is to highlight a number of key questions and puzzles that arise when looking at how PPP programs in different countries conceptualize the discount rate issue and also in other writings on the subject oriented for the practitioner or the public. The following gives some of the key questions that often arise. Short and informal responses follow each question. Not all specialists will agree with all the responses given below. What is most important to note for the purposes of this paper is that these are the kinds of issues that PPP programs must wrestle with to determine the appropriate discount rate to use. PPP units should attempt to understand what these issues involve and not unthinkingly take on board the conclusions in a consultants' report.

(1)   **Q.** Should the PSC exercise and the discount rate be based only on financial costs to the government (or to the particular government department), or should they be based on costs to society as a whole? That is, is the PSC exercise

---

[57]See Grout (2003) for a careful examination of what the result might be if the private company is paid a fixed unit cost while the sales quantity varies with demand.

fundamentally a form of *financial* appraisal or *economic* appraisal?

A. PPP programs have not taken a consistent position on this. But it is difficult to see why the government should not look at costs and benefits in the economy as a whole.

(2)   *Q.* Is the correct discount rate, before possibly accounting for systematic risk, the government borrowing rate?

A. This would make sense from the purely financial perspective. If the economic perspective is taken, however, in principle, externalities (if any) should be taken into account. See (1). In some countries, the economic discount rate will be (or will be close to) the government borrowing rate.

(3)   *Q.* Why is the UK, which has led the way in the PPP movement in so many respects, the only country (of those noted in the second section) that seems largely to ignore market rates and the opportunity cost of displaced private investment in its determination of the appropriate discount rate (or at least, not use them in a straightforward way)?

A. UK Treasury guidance does not give a direct answer to this question. In most of the usual approaches to the economic discount rate, the opportunity cost of capital plays some role, and it had a prominent place in the thinking of the UK Treasury before 2003. Some cynics suspect there was pressure to lower the rate to make it more favourable to the public sector solution for infrastructure projects (as well as responding to pressure from interest groups in other sectors), and using just the social time preference rate was a convenient way to accomplish this. Others note that the rate arrived at (3.5% real) is fairly close to the government borrowing rate plus a corporate profit-tax gross-up; so the result may not be far from what the risk-free economic discount rate would be, derived that way, even if there appears to be a gap in the conceptual story. It is important to note, however, that the economic opportunity cost of displaced private investment could have a much greater effect on the rate in developing countries.

(4)   **Q.** Should the cost of risk be accounted for as a cash flow adjustment or as an adjustment to the discount rate?

A. This depends on the type of risk. Symmetric variability risk can be accounted for in the discount rate in certain circumstances. Asymmetric risk – e.g., the expectation of a future downside shock of some kind – should ideally be accounted for in cash flows. Default risk would fall into the latter category. Optimism bias is another example.

(5)   **Q.** Do risks and the cost of risk depend only on the underlying project and not at all on the way the project is financed?

A. This statement is often made, taking cue from modern finance theory. But this theory looks at risk in capital markets, so it begs the question. There is no reason, a priori, to think that the cost of risk must be the same in funding projects from the capital market, from user charges, and from taxes.

(6)   **Q.** Does risk disappear in the public sector financing of infrastructure projects because it is diversified or spread over all taxpayers?

A. There is a consensus that the cost of non-systematic variability risk will tend to go to zero when spread over a large number of people – the oft-cited Arrow-Lind (1970) result. But this can occur by way of taxation *or* through the capital market. Moreover, it does not happen with systematic risk.

(7)   **Q.** Suppose we grant that the discount rate should take into account "systematic risk". How do we know what the economic cost of systematic risk is in a public sector project?

A. This is not a simple matter; there is no consensus among experts or practitioners.

(8)   **Q.** Supposing that it is correct to adjust the discount rate for systematic risk, should one use as the discount rate the market-derived weighted average cost of capital (WACC) that would be appropriate for the same kind of project implemented by a company in the private sector?

A. Even if we ended up with a rate close to that, it would be after we carefully thought through all the issues and made calculations, not because it simply seemed natural to use this rate.

(9) **Q. Isn't it true that public sector funding cannot be less costly because if it were, it would mean that the government should finance all investment projects, and that would be absurd. As Partnerships Victoria (2003b, p. 27) puts it: If the government's borrowing rate were used as the discount rate, "the logical consequence would be that government would finance everything, and replace commercial sources of finance".**

A. This is not a good argument because there are other reasons why we would want certain organizations rather than others to bear the risk of financing projects. Often the way to ensure that an organization puts adequate effort into reducing costs or improving service is to make it bear the associated risks. It is often too complicated to unbundle financing from the rest of the business without disturbing the incentive structure – too complicated to find ways to transfer risks to the private sector in a different way.

(10) **Q. Shouldn't the same discount rate (including risk premium, if any) apply to both the PSC and the PPP project since the underlying project is the same?**

A. The answer depends on the approach used. Most PPP programs use the same discount rate even when they discount project cash flows on an after-financing basis, as they generally do. But if the discount rate is applied to the stream of payments that the public sector will make under the PPP contract (along with some other adjustments), then the risk characteristics of the cash flows may have changed since risks have been allocated between the private company and the public sector. In one extreme case, where all variability risk is borne by the company, clearly a *risk-free* discount rate should be used to discount the PPP contract payments if the discount rate is applied after financing. (The contract payments might be expected to be greater, however, because investors would require a higher return to compensate them for bearing all the systematic risk.)

If the view is taken that systematic risk does not have a significant cost to the public sector, then it is correct to use the same (risk-free) discount rate for both the PPP project and the PSC when the discounting is done after financing: in both cases, one is looking at cash flows from the perspective of the public sector.

It is argued in the present paper, however, that discounting the PPP project and the PSC on an after-financing basis is unsound: it is the true resource cost of the projects that is relevant, and so one should ignore the financing per se. But one still has to account for the costs to the economy of systematic risk (certainly for the PPP project, perhaps for the PSC too). The most conceptually appealing way to deal with this would be to use certainty equivalents. A rougher screening test is proposed in this paper that adjusts the discount rate for systematic risk. Using that test, if it assumed (as one possibility) that systematic risk has a significant cost for the PPP project but not for the PSC, then one should indeed use different discount rates.

(11)   **Q.** Is the risk premium (more fundamentally, the appropriate CAPM beta) *negative* for negative cash flows?

A. This depends on whether the negative cash flows are positively or negatively correlated with the market or economy (as the case may be). In the case of negative cash flows that are positively correlated with the economy (i.e., where systematic risk reduces value), one should indeed use a negative beta and a negative risk premium so that the appropriate discount rate will be *below* the risk-free rate – thus making the present value of outflows *greater*.[58] This is something that appears to have been ignored by all PPP programs, although Victoria has got it partly right.

---

[58]The beta referred to here is the project beta (i.e., based on returns). Since we are looking at cash flows, we may think more naturally in terms of cash flow betas. But for outflows, the corresponding project (or "return") beta is opposite in sign to the cash flow beta. See footnote 54, Annex 1, and Ehrhardt and Daves (2000).

A Practical Approach to Carrying Out the PSC Exercise

Regardless of the complexities, in some circumstances PPP units may want to use a method of some kind to compare a PPP project with the public sector comparator. What follows is a sketch of a possible approach. The purpose is to provoke thought and encourage people to test and then develop these ideas further in a more operational way. The approach is developed in more detail in Annex 2.

▶ *Carry out a PSC comparison for different* **types** *of projects, not for each specific project.*

There is no need to carry out the PSC exercise for each project. It is sufficient to determine that a type of project with certain key features is likely to yield greater benefits if implemented as a PPP. So long as a specific project conforms well enough to the general type, there is no need to repeat the exercise. The country's PPP unit can develop routine-level instructions and guidance (as appropriate) for the appraisal of individual projects of a specified type.

The fact that the initial assessment would be made for *types* of projects offers some new ways to decide whether to embark on a PPP project instead of a public sector one. For example, suppose that the PPP unit's assessment does not yield a clear conclusion that the PPP project will offer greater benefits than a well-designed public sector alternative. Instead of treating the issue as having been decided by the evidence one way or the other, one solution would be to embrace the ex ante uncertainty and recommend that the line department undertake, on a random basis, some of the projects on a PPP basis and some on a public sector basis, while setting up a system to carefully monitor the comparative results. A solution like this would not emerge naturally from a project-by-project PSC analysis.

Most important, the PPP unit's attention would shift to modelling the envisaged PPP project not for purposes of comparison with a PSC but to better understand and hence improve the PPP arrangement and transaction itself.

▶ *Consider the cash flow streams* **before** *the financing of the project (for both the PPP and the PSC), but include costs* **associated with** *the financing.*

This eliminates the problem discussed in the third section (cash flows viewed after financing). The costs to be included – those associated with the financing – are (i) financial intermediation costs and, if applicable, (ii) the cost of systematic risk (see below).

▶ *Carry out the analysis looking at both costs and benefits – i.e., net cash flow – especially whenever a premium for systematic risk is included in the discount rate.*

The PSC exercise is normally carried out as a comparison of costs only. If the exercise is restricted to apply to project *types* rather than individual projects, fewer PSC exercises will be conducted, and there is no reason not to spend more time and conduct a full cost-benefit analysis. There are several advantages. First, it is likely that a sound economic cost-benefit analysis has not yet been carried out (contrary to the common assumption in more advanced economies); so the exercise will bring out problems on the benefit side. Second, a complete analysis will permit a comparative distributional analysis (who gains and who loses and by how much), which is a very useful tool in PPP appraisal and comparison with the PSC. Third, discounting net benefits instead of cost streams, makes it possible to retain the conventional, and more intuitively appealing, practice of *adding* the risk premium to the discount rate.

▶ *See if the issue of systematic risk can be sidestepped by examining critical test cases for the PPP project and the PSC.*

Given that there is no consensus among experts about whether and how systematic risk might constitute a significant cost in the context of a publicly financed project, it would be best to try to avoid the issue completely. If the analysis is carried out by adding a risk premium to the discount rate for both the PPP project and the PSC, and the PSC wins (i.e., has the highest NPV), then one can accept this result as decisive since this is the toughest test for the PSC to meet. If, on the other hand, the analysis is carried out by including the cost of systematic risk only for the PPP project and the PPP wins, then one can accept this result as decisive since this is the toughest test for the PPP. It is expected that most projects would meet one or the other of these conditions, and hence the issue of systematic risk could be avoided.

If neither of these conditions holds – i.e., if the PPP project wins when a risk premium is applied to both projects but ranks below the PSC when a risk premium is applied only to the PPP – then one should conclude that systematic risk might make a difference. It would then be best to look more closely at the details of the projects and consider a wider range of factors. One should pay particular attention to the underlying characteristics of the PPP project that, based on theory and experience, argue in favour of or against using the PPP approach (e.g., is a fairly *complete* long-term contract feasible, or is it likely that the public sector will want considerable flexibility as the project advances?).

Conclusions

The issue of what discount rate to use in comparing a PPP project and an equivalent public sector project is complex and in some ways confusing. This paper has tried to show that the way the issue is being addressed at present in many countries is too simplistic and for some aspects clearly incorrect. The main conclusions of the paper can be summarized as follows:

- The appropriate rate to use is some variant of, or is based on, an *economic* discount rate.
- There are differences of professional opinion about how to determine the discount rate – even before any adjustment for systematic risk. An important consideration is whether the rate should include a component reflecting the marginal economic rate of return on private investment. Doing that could make a significant difference, especially in developing economies.
- There are peculiarities that arise from applying the economic discount rate to PPP project cash flows viewed *after* financing (the typical practice in the PSC exercise) – especially in countries in which the government borrowing rate is not a good approximation of the economic discount rate. Not enough attention has been given to this issue in the developing country context.
- Whether or not, and the extent to which, systematic risk adds significant cost to public sector projects is a matter of debate and speculation.

o   Even if one accepts in principle that the cost of systematic risk is significant for public sector financing, the analytical issues remain complicated: we cannot easily rely on market benchmarks to determine the beta of the PSC since we want to know the impact of the *entire* underlying systematic risk, not just the part typically borne by PPP company shareholders (the part that would show up in market benchmarks).

o   Adding to the complications, risk to the public sector from the PPP project should be viewed after being filtered through the PPP contract. So in addition, we have to understand how the PPP contract allocates systematic risk – not always an easy matter.

- In any event, for many developing countries, it would probably be better to focus on analyzing financial intermediation costs in comparing public sector and private sector financing rather than possible differences in a premium for systematic risk.

- One solution to the question of systematic risk would be simply to ignore it in the PPP-PSC comparison. The previous section and Annex 2 suggest an alternative, pragmatic approach (which needs to be tested, refined, and developed further in a more operational way) that might be used by PPP units. It might be used as a preliminary exercise that would lead to a more general conclusion by the PPP unit that systematic risk should henceforth be ignored in the PPP-PSC comparison. The analysis would separate the question of underlying project costs from the effect, if any, of private sector financing. The analysis also would be carried out in a number of different ways, with a view to determining whether the PPP project should definitely be eliminated or definitely be selected. For a range in the middle, given the uncertainties of the discount rate issue, the PPP-PSC comparison would not yield definitive results. One would then have to give more attention to other factors tending to favour or disfavour the PPP project.

Annex 1

Determining the Sign of the CAPM Beta

This annex summarizes the algebra underlying Figure 1 (see page 52).
The conventional CAPM *project* beta can be expressed as follows:

$$\beta = \frac{\text{cov}(r, r_m)}{\sigma_m^2},$$

where r is the rate of return for the asset in question, r_m is the market rate of return, and σ_m^2 is the variance of the market returns.

This is equivalent to:

$$\beta = \frac{\text{cov}\left(\left(\frac{CF_1}{V_0} - 1\right), r_m\right)}{\sigma_m^2} = \frac{\text{cov}(CF_1, r_m)}{V_0 \times \sigma_m^2},$$

where V_0 is the value of the asset, or stream of future cash flows, at the end of period 0 (i.e., the starting value or present value) and CF_1 is the risky cash flow occurring at the end of period 1 (assuming a one-period model, with CF_1 being the total return received).

So long as CF_1 and r_m tend to move together in the same direction along the real number line, the covariance will be positive, regardless of whether CF_1 is positive or negative. This is systematic risk that *reduces* value ("bad risk" in the shorthand used in the fifth section). Likewise, the value often referred to as the "cash flow beta" will be positive:

$$\text{Cash flow beta} = \frac{\text{cov}(CF_1, r_m)}{\sigma_m^2}$$

But the conventional CAPM beta ("β" above), the project beta (sometimes referred to as the "return" beta), will depend also on the sign of the cash flows: in the case of negative cash flows (e.g., costs), V_0 in the denominator will be negative, and therefore so will β. So in the case of a stream of *costs*, value-reducing systematic risk will lead to a *negative* risk premium to be applied to the discount rate.

Chris Shugart

Annex 2

One Possible Practical Approach

This annex develops in more detail the approach sketched out in the seventh section.

PPP programs need a pragmatic way to deal with the discount rate issue – a way that makes sense given all the uncertainties involved. This annex sketches a possible way forward. First, a few caveats and other considerations.

- Although this scheme involves a method for carrying out the PPP-PSC comparison, the more limited focus here is on the discount rate and how it should be used and on how the additional costs of private sector *financing* are to be taken into account.
- What follows should not be taken to be a recommendation. It is simply one possible solution, put forward to stimulate thought and discussion. What is most important is the approach being suggested, not the details; some details may be misguided or impractical. More work needs to be done using real PPP projects to test approaches like the one sketched out below (and others also) and then to modify and refine them before including them in any guidance material for PPP units.
- Given all the uncertainties, the quantitative findings of the PPP-PSC comparison should not necessarily be decisive in themselves. They will be one factor to examine, along with others. This consideration is even more pertinent if the PPP-PSC comparison is carried out not for each individual project but instead for representative *types* of projects.
- To simplify matters, and in keeping with common PSC practice, it is assumed in steps 1 and 2, below, that the gross benefits of the alternative projects will be the same, and so we will look only at costs. As noted above in the first section, this may well be an unrealistic assumption, especially in developing countries. In that case, adjustments would have to be made to the details outlined below.
- The PPP-PSC comparison referred to in this section is assumed to be carried out *before* the bids are received and is therefore based on a hypothetical PPP project. There is a danger that a PPP-PSC comparison done after the bids are received turns into more of a

bureaucratic exercise in ex post justification than a serious decision tool. In any case, the approach given · below is not suitable, without further modification, for that purpose. Note, however, that the PSC model is to be distinguished from a sensible financial model of the expected PPP project (reference PPP project), which is indeed an essential tool to be used throughout the process of project preparation.

The tentatively suggested approach would consist of three steps. Step 1 begins by making some comparisons of costs without doing any discounting. It may be possible to reject the PPP project without going any further. Step 2 involves discounting and includes financial intermediation costs but not the costs of any systematic risk. Step 3, in which the possible cost of systematic risk is introduced, is separated from Step 2 because the issue of systematic risk is problematic, and there is no consensus about its relevance for the public sector comparator. So Step 3 gives a rough cut and simply looks at the two extremes with respect to the issue of systematic risk.

The three steps are as follows.

Step 1

The first step would involve examining the cash flows of the PPP project and the PSC *before any discounting*. An important purpose is to try to understand what is likely to be driving any cost advantages and disadvantages of the PPP project relative to the PSC.

Two broad kinds of comparison are the most important. For each of the two categories, (1) and (2) below, (a) is compared with (b), and if (a) > (b), then the PPP project is considered more advantageous with respect to that aspect.

(1) Costs during the early years of the project – the development and construction phases:
    (a) Capex for the PSC *minus* capex for the PPP project.
    (b) Transaction (and early contract oversight) costs due for the PPP project *minus* costs of a similar type for the PSC.
(2) Recurrent costs during the operating phase (for a typical year or years after completion of construction):
    (a) Opex for the PSC *minus* opex for the PPP project.

(b)   Costs of ongoing contract monitoring and management for the PPP project *minus* costs of a similar type for the PSC. (This is worded as if we expect these costs to be higher for the PPP project. We might expect them to be lower in a specific case, in which case the value of (b) would be negative.)

The following decision rules would be used:

- If *clearly* (1)(a) < (1)(b) and (2)(a) < (2)(b), then we can see that the PPP project is a bad choice without needing to go any further. We can assume that the added effect of private sector financing would be negative, or at best neutral, for the PPP project.
- If *clearly* (1)(a) > (1)(b) and (2)(a) > (2)(b), we can see that the PPP project is the better solution before taking private sector financing into consideration, but that step might switch the ranking. So we need to go to Step 2.
- In the two other cases, namely:
  (1)(a) < (1)(b) & (2)(a) > (2)(b), and
  (1)(a) > (1)(b) & (2)(a) < (2)(b),
  we need to proceed to Step 2 because the comparison must be done across time using present values.

Step 1 is important for several reasons. First, it is done on the basis of underlying costs without need to estimate any economic costs associated with private sector financing. Second, no discount rate is needed. Third and perhaps most important, it brings out the main underlying reasons why the PPP project might be more or less costly than the PSC. It is better to try to understand these reasons rather than to crank out a PPP-PSC comparison as a black-box exercise, ending up simply with a present value – which can easily lead to a specious sense of precision.

Step 2

In Step 2, a discounted PPP-PSC comparison is made using the underlying project costs of the PPP project (not the net cash flows, just the costs), considered before financing, *plus* the economic costs associated with the financing (e.g., certain financial intermediation costs – see the third section), except for costs that might arise from systematic risk. The discount rate used for both alternatives would be the usual economic discount rate.

This analysis gets at the comparison between cost advantages and disadvantages occurring in different time periods. For example, suppose that the project is relatively small and so the PPP transaction costs are proportionally large and outweigh any expected capex efficiency of the PPP project, but it is expected that there will be considerable opex efficiency gains with the PPP project, offset to some extent by financial intermediation costs. Do these gains tip the balance in favour of the PPP project? Discounting is needed to make the comparison. The higher the discount rate (and the economic discount rate could be fairly high in a developing country), the greater are the opex efficiency gains that will be needed to outweigh a cost disadvantage in the early years.

If the PPP project comes out ahead in this step (i.e., present value of costs lower than for the PSC), we must proceed to Step 3. If the PPP project does worse than the PSC in this step – i.e., if the PPP looks worse even before we take into consideration the question of systematic risk – then it is likely that the PPP route is not the way to go. This does not mean that the PPP project should automatically be rejected; a deeper analysis should be carried out to see what is giving rise to this result and whether it makes sense.

Step 3

In the final step, we would do a discounted comparison of economic *net cash flows* (economic benefits minus economic costs), taking into account a premium for possible systematic risk.

We would do the analysis in two ways:

(A)   *Best case for PPP and private sector financing.* Here we assume that systematic risk requires a premium for both projects. This is the most favourable assumption for the PPP project. The appropriate risk premium (see below) is added to the risk-free economic discount rate for both the PPP project and the PSC. Doing this in a *carte blanche* manner, applying the risk-adjusted discount rate to all economic flows, is surely too coarse − e.g., should a risk premium really apply to *non-monetized* consumer benefits? But trying to disaggregate the flows and applying the risk-adjusted rate (or determining certainty equivalents) for some but not all flows would be complicated and would once again run into the controversies set out in section five. A crude adjustment is perhaps the best we can do here.

Given that we are making the same adjustment to the discount rate for both the PPP project and the PSC, it is unlikely that this will change the ranking determined in Step 2 (where the same rate, but with no risk premium, was used), but it might do so in some circumstances. If the ranking changes relative to Step 2, the cash flows should be examined in detail to understand what the factors are that switch the ranking and whether there is a reasonable explanation.

(B) *Best case for PSC.* For this case, we make an adjustment for systematic risk only for the PPP project. This is the most favourable assumption for the PSC. This reflects the view of some authors that the premium for systematic risk associated with the PSC is insignificant (see the fourth section).

Rather than add a risk premium to the discount rate used for the PPP project, it might be better to look at just the PPP financing flows (debt and equity), estimate the cost of systematic risk, add that cost to the overall project costs, and then use the usual economic discount rate in the cost-benefit analysis.

Ideally, the cost of systematic risk should be estimated using certainty equivalents.[59] This would be consistent with separating the issue of the cost of systematic risk from the discount rate. But the assumptions needed for the required calculations – e.g., the covariance between each risky cash flow in each year and the market return – are likely to be unknown.[60] An easier, if rougher, alternative method would be to estimate the present value (PV) of systematic-risk costs by taking the difference between the NPV of the financing flows, discounted at the risk-free financial rate, and the NPV of the same financing flows, discounted at the risk-adjusted financial rate.

---

[59]See page 75 for the definition of "certainty equivalent".

[60]For a detailed discussion of how to use certainty equivalents instead of a risk-adjusted discount rate in a CAPM framework, see Sick (1986).

If the PPP project has the higher NPV even in case (B), where the PPP project has a handicap, then this is a favourable result for the PPP project. In this case, we can feel fairly confident about going ahead with the PPP project.

If the PSC has the higher NPV in case (A), then things do not look good for the PPP project. This does not mean that the PPP solution should be rejected out of hand. A deeper look should first be taken to understand what produced this result and whether it seems plausible.

If the PPP project wins (i.e., has the higher NPV) in the case of (A) but not (B), then we can see that the thorny issue of systematic risk is critical – systematic risk might make a difference. After looking more deeply to see what led to the overall results (apart from the possible systematic risk premium), we should probably give somewhat more weight to other positive or negative factors (e.g., a qualitative assessment of why this *type* of project might or might not be conducive to being implemented as a PPP project) in reaching our decision about whether to go ahead with the project on a PPP basis.

The risk premium to be used in the analysis would be determined in the following way: For simplicity, the risk premium could be based on the standard CAPM paradigm. In case (A), we would want to include the *total* systematic risk of the project, not just the systematic risk faced by a typical PPP company. The total systematic risk would be captured in the increased cost of financing for the PPP company, in markups charged by subcontractors to the extent that they bear part of the systematic risk, and possibly in the contractual payments made to the company by the public sector (i.e., unless the public sector takes no systematic risk). For present purposes, we do not need to distinguish between these components since we are interested only in the total effect – an advantage of the method outlined here, which begins with the underlying costs before financing.

What value should we use for the asset beta in case (A)? As noted in the fourth section, the market average (*unlevered* beta) in developed economies is around 0.65-0.75.[61] Demand risk is an important driver of

---

[61]In this discussion, since the purpose is just to outline an approach and methodology, we will look at values for beta and the market risk premium applicable to mature equity markets – e.g., the US and the UK. Estimating these values for an emerging market is much more problematic, especially if we assume that the market is not fully integrated with the global equity market. Another problem is that even though we want to exclude downside country risk from this particular calculation (since it is picked up elsewhere), in some models the beta coefficient itself is assumed to be related to the country risk premium. See Sabal (2004) for a good summary of the different views.

Chris Shugart

asset betas. Many infrastructure and utility-type projects produce necessities (as opposed to luxuries) – they are not cyclical businesses – and so they face a lower income elasticity of demand than the average market-based project. We might therefore think that the appropriate asset beta would be lower than the market average. On the other hand, the scope of activities of PPP companies is tightly regulated: they are often locked in to their technologies and market, and so they have much less flexibility to adjust to changing market conditions. That characteristic might tend to increase the asset beta.

Given that we are not aiming for precision in Step 3 but intend simply to compare the two extreme possibilities, for want of better information, perhaps using a rough market average would be best in case (A) – say, 0.7. Alternatively, one could take the approach of Partnerships Victoria and use three different values depending on the type of project. Partnerships Victoria uses 0.3, 0.5, and 0.9 (see section two).

The calculation used in case (B), however, must be different. Since the assumption in case (B) is that systematic risk has a negligible cost to the public sector, any systematic risk transmitted to the public sector through risky contractual payments to the PPP company should be ignored. But we would still want to include the systematic risk passed on to subcontractors of the PPP company, unless the cost estimates used for this purpose implicitly incorporate this already. As noted in the fourth section, one might expect the asset beta of a PPP company (with a good contract) to be in the range of 0.3–0.5. So perhaps we should take 0.5 as the figure to use for the rate applicable to the PPP project in case (B). The difference between the asset beta for the PPP project in cases (A) and (B) – namely, 0.2 in the assumptions we are using here – reflects the assumption in case (B) that systematic risk passed on to the public sector by way of risky contractual payments has no societal cost.

If we assume an asset beta 0.5 in case (B) and a market risk premium of 6% (a figure sometimes used these days for many advanced economies, although some would say it is on the high side), we should add three percentage points to the risk-free economic discount rate to account for systematic risk when applied to the financing flows for the PPP project. We can see that the maximum impact of systematic risk in the PPP-PSC comparison is likely to be less than the impact of the financial intermediation costs that are typically found in many developing countries (see the examples from East Africa, Table 3, section three). It might be advisable, then, to focus more in the PPP-PSC comparison on assessing economic financial intermediation costs than to spend time trying to refine the CAPM calculations.

In fact, it may well be that after testing this approach with a range of typical PPP projects in developing countries, one will be able to conclude that it is a waste of effort to try to take the possible cost of systematic risk into account in the PPP-PSC comparison: perhaps the three percentage points would hardly ever switch the ranking of the PPP project and the PSC, and even if they did, this itself might not be considered decisive in deciding to reject the PPP project. Other aspects of the analysis might be much more important.

In any case, by separating the effects of financial intermediation costs (Step 2) from the possible effects of systematic risk (Step 3), the disaggregated three-step approach outlined in this section can help reveal the underlying drivers better than does the typical PPP-PSC exercise.

References

Arrow, K.J. and R.C. Lind. 1970. "Uncertainty and the Evaluation of Public Investment Decisions", *American Economic Review* 60(3), 364-378.

Barro, R.J. 2006. "Rare Disasters and Asset Markets in the Twentieth Century", *Quarterly Journal of Economics* 121(3), 823-866.

Brealey, R.A., I.A. Cooper, and M.A. Habib. 1997. "Investment Appraisal in the Public Sector", *Oxford Review of Economic Policy* 13(4), 12-28.

Brean, D., *et al.* 2005. *Treatment of Private and Public Charges for Capital in a "Full-Cost Accounting" of Transportation.* Prepared for Transport Canada. Final Report, 31 March.

Burgess, D.F. 2008. "A Critique of Feldstein's Shadow Price Algorithm". Unpublished paper. Department of Economics, University of Western Ontario, London, Canada, 25 November.

_____. 2009. "Toward a Reconciliation of Alternative Views on the Social Discount Rate", in this volume.

Central PPP Policy Unit (Ireland). 2006. "Discount Rate Principles for Public Private Partnership Capital Investment Projects", Central Guidance Note No. 7. February.

Čihák, M. and R. Podpiera. 2005. "Bank Behavior in Developing Countries: Evidence from East Africa". IMF Working Paper WP/05/129. June.

Department of Treasury and Finance (Government of Western Australia). 2002. *Project Evaluation Guidelines.* January.

Ehrhardt, M.C. and P.R. Daves. 2000. "Capital Budgeting: The Valuation of Unusual, Irregular, or Extraordinary Cash Flows", *Financial Practice and Education* 10(2), 106-114.

Estrada, J. 2007. "Discount Rates in Emerging Markets: Four Models and an Application", *Journal of Applied Corporate Finance* 19(2).

Ewijk, C. and P.J.G. Tang. 2003. "How to Price the Risk of Public Investment?", *DE Economist* 151(3).

Feldstein, M.S. 1970. "Choice of Technique in the Public Sector: A Simplification", *The Economic Journal* 80(320), 985-990.

Glenday, G. 2009. "The New (but Old) Approach to the Economic Opportunity Cost of Capital", in this volume.

Gómez-Ibáñez, J.A. 2005. "Partnerships Victoria: The Public Sector Comparator". Case. Kennedy School of Government, Infrastructure in a Market Economy Executive Program. Revised 11 August.

Grant, S. and J. Quiggin. 2004. *The Risk Premium for Equity: Implications for Resource Allocation, Welfare and Policy.* Risk & Uncertainty Program Working Paper 8/R04. Risk & Sustainable Management Group, Schools of Economics and Political Science, University of Queensland. August.

Grout, P.A. 2003. "Public and Private Sector Discount Rates in Public-Private Partnerships", *The Economic Journal* 113(March), C62-C68.

Harberger, A.C. 1997. "New Frontiers in Project Evaluation? A Comment on Devarajan, Squire, and Suthiwart-Narueput", *World Bank Research Observer* 12(1), 73-79.

HM Treasury (UK). 2003. *The Green Book: Appraisal and Evaluation in Central Government.* London.

Jenkins, G.P. 2001. "Economic Aspects of Foreign Financing". Unpublished paper, 23 February.

Klein, M. 1996. "Risk, Taxpayers, and the Role of Government in Project Finance". Policy Research Working Paper No. 1688. Private Participation in Infrastructure Group. Washington, DC: World Bank. December.

Layard, R., G. Mayraz, and S.J. Nickell. 2008. "The Marginal Utility of Income". SOEP Papers on Multidisciplinary Panel Data Research. Berlin, April.

Mandelbrot, B. and R.L Hudson. 2004. *The Misbehavior of Markets.* Basic Books.

Morallos, D. and A. Amekudzi. 2008. "The State of the Practice of Value for Money Analysis in Comparing Public Private Partnerships to Traditional Procurements", *Public Works Management & Policy* 13(2), 114-125.

National Treasury (South Africa). 2004. "Module 3: PPP Feasibility Study", *Public Private Partnership Manual.* Issued as National Treasury PPP Practice Note No. 4 of 2004.

Partnerships Victoria. 2003a. *Public Sector Comparator.* Supplementary Technical Note. Department of Treasury and Finance. July.

_____. 2003b. *Use of Discount Rates in the Partnerships Victoria Process.* Technical Note. Department of Treasury and Finance. July.

PPP Knowledge Centre (Netherlands). 2002a. *Public Private Comparator.* Ministry of Finance. August. The Hague.

_____. 2002b. *Public Sector Comparator.* Ministry of Finance. August. The Hague.

PricewaterhouseCoopers. 2002. *Study into the Rates of Return Bid on PFI Projects.* Academic advisor: Prof. Julian Franks. Commissioned by the UK Office of Government Commerce (OGC). London. October.

Sabal, J. 2004. "The Discount Rate in Emerging Markets: A Guide", *Journal of Applied Corporate Finance* 16 (Spring/Summer), 155-166.

Sick, G.A. 1986. "A Certainty-Equivalent Approach to Capital Budgeting", *Financial Management* 15(4), 23-32.

Sjaastad, L.A. and D.L. Wisecarver. 1977. "The Social Cost of Public Finance", *Journal of Political Economy* 85(3), 513-548.

Spackman, M. 2001. "Risk and the Cost of Risk in the Comparison of Public and Private Financing of Public Services". NERA, London. March.

_____. 2004. "Time Discounting and of the Cost of Capital in Government", *Fiscal Studies* 24(4), 467-518.

_____. 2006. "Social Discount Rates for the European Union: An Overview". Working Paper 2006-33, October. Fifth Milan European Economy Workshop.

Weitzman, M.L. 2007. "Subjective Expectations and Asset-Return Puzzles", *American Economic Review* 97(4), 1102-1130.

Abbreviations, Acronyms, and Definitions

asset beta

Refers to the beta (see below) of an asset (e.g., company or project) after removing the effect of financial leverage – i.e., what the beta would be if the financing consisted entirely of equity capital. Sometimes called "unlevered beta". The asset beta indicates the systematic risk intrinsic to the project or company and permits comparison among projects or companies, regardless of their leverage.

Roughly: $\beta_{asset} = \beta_{equity} \times \dfrac{E}{D+E}$,

where β_{equity} is the beta of the equity shares of the company, E is the value of equity in the capital structure, and D is the value of debt. (This simplified formulation assumes that there is no debt beta.)

beta

A coefficient used in the CAPM that measures the degree to which the return on a specific asset co-varies with the return on the entire portfolio of assets (in financial analysis, usually defined to be the stock market). So beta indicates the proportion of the asset's riskiness – i.e., referred to as *systematic* risk – that cannot be removed by a diversified portfolio.

capex

capital expenditures

CAPM

Capital Asset Pricing Model

certainty equivalent

The certainty equivalent of a risky cash flow is the amount that the recipient (respectively, payer) would need to receive (pay) *with certainty* to leave the recipient (payer) indifferent between receiving (paying) the risky cash flow and the certainty equivalent. If the recipient (payer) is risk averse, the certainty equivalent will be less (more) than the expected value of the risky cash flow.

expected value	The sum of the values obtained by multiplying the probability of each possible outcome by the value of that outcome. Strictly speaking, this definition applies only to *discrete* random variables.
leverage	Used in this paper to mean, roughly, the ratio, in the capital structure of a company, of (i) debt to (ii) the sum of debt and equity. The common British term for this concept is "gearing".
NPV	net present value
opex	operating expenditures (including maintenance)
PFI	Private Finance Initiative (a British program)
PPP	public-private partnership
PPI unit	Used in this report to mean either: (i) a central unit in the country that has the main responsibility for structuring and appraising PPP projects or for issuing guidance for these activities, or (ii) a unit in a line department with similar functions, relating to sectoral projects.
PSC	public sector comparator
PSP	private sector participation
PV	present value (i.e., the NPV when all the cash flows are either positive or negative, so no netting is required)
systematic risk	See the fourth section.
WACC	weighted average cost of capital

Summary of Discussion

Finn Poschmann: I learned some interesting things from Chris's paper. Such as what's going on with P3 policy in some other places and how people talk about the various risks they consider when they analyze cash flows, or cost flows. And Chris does focus on costs, I should point out, because that is where the choice of discount rate and the public sector comparator is arguably most important.

But for a market-oriented person like me, this might be a little unsatisfying because it allows Chris to say things like, "it is unlikely *ex-ante* that a P3 has a higher investment or operating cost than the PSC". Which is no doubt true. But not to discuss the benefits in the public-private cases, and the risks associated with those, as I said, that feels a little unsatisfying. I want to know a little more about all those flows. And I want to be careful about what risk assumptions are around those.

As I was saying, this is problematic if you think that in comparing public and private delivery you need to disaggregate those flows and make estimates about the incentives and the risks attached to each of those costs and net flows.

There's another sense in which I feel slightly detached from reality, and this is just framing the question, because it's possible to contract out public-service delivery without knowing much at all about pricing or discounting. And that's by having a contracting agency run an auction in which the public sector is allowed to bid. We do this frequently in transit or in waste collection. If the auctioneer can certify that the bids are essentially comparable, he ought to feel comfortable accepting the low bid. Bidders will worry about what discount rates they should be carrying around in their mind.

The main problem for me here is that Chris doesn't really discuss the details of contracting and the allocation of risks. We always need to keep in mind that risk is a probability times a magnitude, and that where it lies is affected by the contract. Of course, the discount rate is critical in calculating and comparing present-value costs and benefits over time, but in comparing public and private delivery, we need to know what risks are travelling with which costs and benefit flows.

For example, Chris states that "… accounting for the risks that come with the particular benefits, or the service delivery, would overly complicate the analysis". But I think this is absolutely central to the contracting process, which is what P3s are all about. In comparing public and private delivery, we need also to remember that we are writing incomplete contracts in the presence of not just risk but uncertainty, and imperfect information. And the contract specifies where certain risks lie. I think that makes it difficult to speak generically about which discount rate is best. Chris sought to ward off this line of argument by saying we've got reasonably complete contracting and reasonably complete information sets. But, of course, we don't actually.

Chris spends a little time with the question of whether the relevant discount rate is the government financing rate or something economic, which recognizes the true cost of public financing and some of the other things that go along with the process. What I find is amazing is that we still have this discussion because the so-called risk-free rate is clearly wrong in the context where the purpose of the contracting is to move risks around. I find myself again referring to contract structure, which Chris doesn't really do. And I do so because it can be helpful in clarifying a suitable P3 contract that would parsimoniously allocate risks and rewards, and if the contract permits the government effectively to lay off risk, it has to that extent acquired a put option on the risk of default. Once that concept is ingested, and it does come up in Chris's paper, we can stop talking about the government's borrowing rate as an important comparator.

There's a caveat to what I've just said. And that's the discontinuity associated with the possibility of bankruptcy in the context of limited liability. So risks that a government thought it had laid off might actually come back to bite everyone. But that doesn't change the underlying point about the purpose of the contract being to manage risks.

Another issue for a domestic-policy guy like me is the developing-country approach that often comes up. This allows Chris to say that financial intermediation raises the cost of financing for private contractors, more so than government. Whereas everything I know about financial intermediation says that it should lower the cost for both, and I don't care to speculate what institutional constraints would lower it more for one than the other. In the development literature that *I* know, we actually use the depth and breadth of financial intermediation as a proxy for development because we know that it better facilitates the distribution of risk within an economy. So I don't know why we'd be talking about it as a cost.

And I also don't know why foreign versus domestic sources of capital would affect the analysis. Because each of the public or private sectors may or may not use foreign-source capital, and I think this should stand way outside a framework for analyzing contract choices.

I mentioned that Chris has a small catalogue of risks and other influences on cash flow estimates. Some were new to me, like one he mentions, the optimism bias. Now I don't understand these things because if an agent consistently overestimates benefit flows, then that agent is going to meet Poschmann's pink-slip corrective factor. And that's going to damp down future occurrences of excessive optimism.

Chris also discusses systematic risk, and he takes on the equity premium. I really don't know why. I mean, if you track the equity-premium literature, all those high estimates are way, way too high. And if you think it's reasonable to expect or to book a long-run rate of return on capital that exceeds the real growth rate of the economy, you're planning on taking over the planets and solar systems and you're thinking way bigger than I am.

At the end of his paper, Chris offers some practical decision trees for choosing project delivery modes. I don't have a lot to say about that because it seems to me, the hard part is all in the contracting for risks.

To lead to Chris's defence, at numerous points, he says that the risks I'm talking about probably ought to be handled upstream in the contract process – which is what I'm saying – and that these should be accounted for in the cash flow analysis. What he's talking about is what happens next, and I think that would be a fair response.

Christopher Shugart: The issue of contracting really is in there; it couldn't be presented given the time constraint, but if you look on the sheet with the table, I carefully underline all the costs needed to produce a service's expected values on both sides. So, in doing the exercise one should look at all the different scenarios, and one should look at how the different contract clauses pay out. And if a certain risk has been transferred to the PPP operator that will show up in a higher expected value of cost.

So the contracting is surely in there, and that's the way costs will be allocated. What then the final risk issue, of systematic risk, is those zero-mean risks that are justifiable. But all the other kinds of risk are definitely in the way you construct these cash flows; you cannot do it without sitting there, looking at the contract, and seeing how various risks have been allocated. Perhaps I should emphasize that more.

Graham Glenday: My experience in dealing with PPPs in countries like India is such that I find the whole concept of a public sector comparator very difficult to absorb. The reason why they might not have done as well is simply because the public sector can't do what is being asked. Also, the PPP has run the whole gamut from self-financing projects to projects where users are charged for benefits. As soon as you start charging for benefits, the risk allocation changes. Now you run into some governments, say India, where the government regards itself as providing free public services because it's politically impossible to do otherwise. The only way to move to user charges is to get the PPP to do the charging for you. So the move from public to private is also a move from free access to user pay. Comparing a PPP to a PSC without taking this into account is misleading.

Christopher Shugart: I think that what's missing here is absolutely right. The concern of this paper may seem strange to those of you who are actually doing real work in real countries. The problem is, the concern emerges more out of this growing administrative PPP culture. There are PPP units, there are advisors running around all the development agencies. And within this PPP culture, the public sector comparator is "You must do one!" And this paper was mainly in response to that. I think for a lot of you who aren't part of that culture, you'll say: Is this tempest in a teapot? What are you worrying about it for? And I tend to agree.

Rosalind Thomas: On this discussion on the public sector comparator, I think the point that has been made is correct. Chris, we've worked together a lot on these issues, but it seems to me that the public sector comparator is not feasible in Africa, except for South Africa. And I think it comes out in your paper, the absence of data. There actually isn't any public sector project you can compare with to get that kind of information, to see whether you benefit from a PPP or from a public sector-financed project. I think to have that kind of approach for countries in Africa that are trying to set up their PPPs just doesn't make sense.

Christopher Shugart: I agree entirely with you, and I guess this was more, as I say, directed towards a lot of the agencies that were pushing it. Maybe if they'd come around to your view, we can throw my paper out; it's no longer relevant.

2

Time Preference, the Cost of Capital, and PPPs

Michael Spackman

Introduction

Discounting in the public sector was a source of vigorous controversy when it first emerged in earnest in the 1960s. Over the decades, some issues have faded and new ones have arisen, and some limited international consensus has been achieved within academic welfare economics. Some consensus trends are also emerging, even across governments. However, controversy persists on some aspects, in academia and across (and quite often within) government administrations.

This paper first, in the next section, reviews this story, excluding issues raised by private financing. The three main positions on government discounting still promoted by different schools are summarized, together with their main strengths and weaknesses. Some international conventions are compared, and a consistent analytical and practical framework is presented that has been fairly widely established within welfare economics for a decade or two and is becoming fairly widely accepted in government within Europe.

The third section which begins on p. 99, reviews the appraisal from a government perspective of proposals that include private financing, as is

I am grateful for helpful comments from David Burgess of the University of Western Ontario. All errors or omissions are, however, my responsibility.

often the case in proposed public private partnerships (PPPs). This is an area that has attracted very little academic interest, except from some financial economists.

The last section summarizes the main observations and conclusions.

The Main Approaches to Government Discounting and the Opportunity Cost of Public Expenditure

It is standard practice in private and public project or policy analysis to discount costs and benefits over time, usually at a constant percentage rate per year.[1]

In the private sector, the discount rate is based on the financial cost of capital for the activity in question – namely, the weighted average cost of the relevant debt and equity financing. For government, the financial cost of capital is the market cost of government borrowing. However, this cost of capital does not in welfare economics define the social discount rate.[2]

This section reviews the three main conceptual approaches that have evolved to discounting in government.[3] Each has advocates in some government administrations.

Until the 1970s, debate about public sector discounting focused on two concepts often described, then as now, as "social opportunity cost" (SOC) and "social time preference" (STP). In the 1970s, these approaches were joined by the capital asset pricing model (CAPM), which was in turn derived

---

[1] In recent years, increasing concern with the very long term has made prominent the issue of discount rates that decline over time, often described as "hyperbolic discounting". This is outside the scope of this paper.

[2] A few countries, notably the US Office of Management and Budget (OMB) (http://www.whitehouse.gov/omb/circulars/a094/a94_appx-c.html), use the government borrowing cost at least for cost-effectiveness analysis and for lease versus buy comparisons, but in these countries the reason for this approach, as discussed below, appears to be administrative simplicity and political acceptability rather than technical rigour.

[3] This paper is not concerned with the concept described in European Commission guidance as the "financial discount rate" for publicly supported commercial projects (European Commission, 2008). A required *financial* return on public commercial assets is distinct from the financial cost of capital or a social discount rate.

Michael Spackman

from the efficient markets hypothesis, underlying the then blossoming developments in financial economics. The CAPM approach has been given a modest new lease on life by the development of PPPs.

The CAPM approach to government discounting is discussed below; it proposes case-specific discount rates, with risk premiums equal to those of a similar privately financed investment. Another approach examined is the social opportunity cost of public expenditure (whether classified as capital or current), following a literature that was developed in the 1990s. Next is a discussion of the traditional SOC approach to government discounting, which proposes a government discount rate equal to the financial return to be expected if investment were to be made, instead, in the private sector. Hybrid approaches are then described that combine the traditional SOC approach with the concept of STP, followed by a discussion of the conceptual basis and application of STP; the latter is elaborated upon in Appendix A.

CAPM as a Basis for Government Discounting

It is uncontentious that in a competitive market, equity risk premiums measure a cost of "systematic risk" – that is, the risk of volatility that is correlated with the equity market average volatility and so cannot be diversified away.[4] Many financial economists believe that financial markets are so efficient that this premium must be measuring an *inherent social cost* of the volatility of the costs and benefits of the activity being financed. Thus, if the activity is financed by public debt, this makes little or no difference: the cost of systematic risk that would be revealed by the equity premium if it were privately financed is still there (Brealey, Cooper, and Habib, 1997; Grout, 2003).[5]

This implies that the social cost of capital for a publicly financed activity, and the discount rate appropriate for comparing its costs or benefits over

---

[4]This is quite distinct from the risk of, for example, optimistic bias in estimates of capital costs or of benefits.

[5]In practice, financial economists appear generally to accept that the systematic risk associated with public expenditure *costs* is usually very low. These therefore should be discounted at the risk free government borrowing rate (which is normally lower than estimates of the rate of STP). However, for discounting benefits there should generally, within the EMH framework, be a significant risk premium, as revealed by the private equity financing cost of similar activities.

time, should be derived, as in the private sector, by the familiar capital asset pricing model (CAPM). In the CAPM, the cost of capital for an activity is the sum of the risk-free rate (generally a government borrowing rate) and a risk premium equal to the equity market average risk premium multiplied by a factor (beta) reflecting the correlation between the expected return to the investment and the market average.[6] The efficient markets hypothesis (EMH) school proposes that for a publicly financed activity, this risk premium should be derived from that expected for a similar privately financed activity.

The mechanics of how such a social cost would arise from a publicly financed activity are, however, never explained.[7]

Welfare economists generally regard the average equity risk premium as a function mainly of equity markets themselves. Crucial though equity markets are to market economies and to prosperity, they are in this view subject to, for example, fads or fashions among investors and to largely mean-reverting impacts from factors such as oil crises, wars, business cycles, or, indeed, financial crises.

In the 1960s and early 1970s, these opposing views were argued among the heavyweights. An early skirmish over the implications of the EMH for publicly financed activities was a critique, by Bailey and Jensen (1972), of arguments made by Arrow (1965, 1966) that the cost of risk may be lower for government than for the private sector. The still widely quoted paper by Arrow and Lind (1970) developed these arguments, commenting, for example, in contrast in particular to Hirshleifer (1966), that "many insurance markets do not exist" and on "clear evidence that the existing capital markets are not perfect". They conclude that the cost of *GDP-covariant* variability with public financing is negligible, the variance of GDP fluctuations being far less than that of equity markets. The two sides were never reconciled, and it is no longer an issue of high-level debate. However,

---

[6]CAPM is often applied to company stock, in which case beta (the covariance of the stock's return and the market average return divided by the variance of the market average) measures the stock's volatility in relation to the market. In the context of investment appraisal, beta is derived from the expected *project* returns, either as an equity beta or as a (generally lower) project beta when gearing is taken into account.

[7]Many benefits and costs of public service activities are correlated with fluctuations in GDP, but as noted below, the covariances are too small to impose any material social cost or benefit.

Arrow and Lind (1970) continues to be attacked by EMH proponents in some UK literature (e.g., Klein, 1997; Currie, 2000).[8]

Several subsequent developments support the welfare economist's scepticism about equity markets being so efficient that they reveal a hidden cost of debt or tax financing. In the 1990s, distinguished commentators such as Wadhwani (1999) set out, before the general market downturn, reasons why the market appeared at that time to be overvalued, which in the EMH view of the world cannot happen except perhaps very briefly.[9] A parallel finance literature (Mandelbrot and Hudson, 2004) develops models of financial markets based on fractal analysis, showing that equity market fluctuations are very different from the Gaussian distribution generally assumed in financial economics. Research evidence is also accumulating on the impact of investor behaviour on such markets.[10]

The insights into financial markets revealed during 2007 and 2008 may further cause some observers to doubt the hypothesis that financial markets are driven by well-informed participants, generally valuing assets correctly on the basis of all the information available.[11]

---

[8]The arguments deployed, such as the fact that per capita benefits of non-rival goods (such as national defence) do not diminish as they are more widely spread, are concisely presented by Currie (2000), with a response to each in Spackman (2001).

[9]For example, successive editions of the leading textbook by Brealey and Myers (e.g., 2003, pp. 563-564, and six previous editions from 1981 to 2000) say that "managers generally favour equity rather than debt after an abnormal price rise. The idea is to catch the market while it is high. … But *we know that* the market has no memory and the cycles that financial managers seem to rely on do not exist." (Emphasis added.)

[10]For example, Kirman (1995, p. 290) presents the results of a simple model of interactive investor behaviour, demonstrating that the statistical tests often quoted in support of the EMH random walk (as opposed to mean reverting) model of equity markets are not robust.

[11]Indeed, Wadhwani (2008) suggests that leading up to the financial crisis, "a common thread running through many of the policy mistakes is a belief in the Efficient Markets Hypothesis".

The Social Opportunity Cost of Public Expenditure

An extra $1 of taxation is not merely a transfer between taxpayers and the government. It also imposes a social cost because of its distortionary impacts on consumer, employee, and corporate behaviour.

Feldstein (1997) notes that the common textbook assumption that a tax increase will reduce aggregate demand, with some consequent fall in tax revenue, does not apply in practice because other instruments are used to maintain demand, but that many supply impacts, and distortions in the distribution of demand, are usually overlooked or underplayed. He estimates, mainly from analysis of the large reduction in US marginal income tax rates between 1985 and 1988, that spending from marginal taxation should be given a shadow price of two or more, relative to a loss of consumption. Other authors, looking at other countries, suggest much lower values of around 1.2 to 1.3 (Ruggeri, 1999; Warlters and Auriol, 2005).

UK public sector guidance on cost-benefit analysis (CBA) in transport records that "this principle might imply a 30% uplift to expenditure costs" (Department for Transport, 2004–6, paragraph 13). Australian Guidance (Department of Finance and Administration, 2006, p. 37) suggests a 25% uplift (although this is subsumed in a SOC discount rate, as discussed below).

It would be technically sound in CBA to apply a shadow price to public spending relative to consumption, but few (if any) public administrations generally do so. However, when a public infrastructure cost is being compared with consumption benefits, all discounted at an STP rate, as discussed below, it is often accepted that to merit consideration for approval, the ratio of benefits to public expenditure costs has to be very much more than 1. This ratio can readily accommodate the opportunity cost of public spending (as well as possibly reflecting other concerns, such as optimism bias in cost or benefit projections).

SOC as a Basis for Government Discounting

Suppose that a government has decided that the "social time preference" (STP) rate (i.e., society's preference for marginal consumption sooner rather than later) is 4% per annum and that the rate of return from marginal investment by the private sector is 7%. Then suppose, as a stylized numerical example, that an investment proposal is made in the public sector in which $100 would be spent in year 0 to give a single benefit of $175 in year 10.

Discounting this benefit over 10 years at the STP rate of 4% gives a benefit to cost ratio of 1.18, implying that this investment is worth considering.

However if, instead, $100 were invested in the private sector, it would be expected after 10 years to yield a benefit of $100 x $(1.07)^{10}$ = $197, implying that the proposed public investment is not worth considering because more would be gained by investing in the private sector. This test can be applied more simply by discounting the costs and benefits of the government project at the 7% "social opportunity cost" (SOC) rate of return.[12] Discounting the benefit of $175 over 10 years at this SOC rate of 7% gives a benefit to cost ratio of 0.89.

This approach to government discounting is sometimes perceived as being obviously correct. However, it does not stand up to closer examination for several reasons. Some of these are discussed below under "the nature of the opportunity cost of public spending" and "the nature of the social value of private sector returns to equity".

The nature of the opportunity cost of public spending

Capital versus current public spending. Capital and current spending, public or private, are in many respects very different. They have overlapping but different implications for planning, management, budgeting, and accounting. However, a dollar of marginal public capital spending imposes no more nor less social cost than a marginal dollar of public current spending.

Many countries may explicitly or implicitly aim to apply a convention such as confining changes in government borrowing over the economic cycle to the level of net government investment (sometimes described as a "golden rule"), and this may at the level of macroeconomic planning affect the balance between aggregate borrowing and taxation. However, public fiscal and debt management in practice, at the aggregate level or in spending units, does not generally consider any explicit financing of specific capital expenditure proposals. They are funded from the capital budget of the

---

[12]Sometimes the CAPM approach is also presented as measuring an "opportunity cost". However, the CAPM approach claims to measure the direct social cost of public investment, not the opportunity cost of activities that the public investment might displace.

relevant spending body, which in turn is funded from the same central fund as current expenditure.[13]

It is doubtful that even if marginal public capital spending were financed by marginal debt, this would nowadays have any significant impact on private investment. Even nearly 20 ago, Lind (1990) concluded (p. S16) that because of international capital mobility, "the crowding out [of private investment by public investment] that has been the focus of most of the closed economy models does not appear to be very important to the analysis of the social discount rate".

It is sometimes suggested that capital spending may nonetheless physically displace private capital and in this way have a higher social opportunity cost than current spending. However, it looks unlikely that this could today be a material effect. Construction is a competitive international industry. Tenders for major projects routinely cross national boundaries. Major activities such as tunnelling are carried out by international teams moving around the world with their equipment. Both intermediate products such as cement and steel, and final products such as pumps, turbines, pipes, locomotives, signalling systems, rails, or IT hardware or software, are international commodities. The most that can plausibly be said is that a major construction project may combine with a peak in other local projects to inflate local wages for construction skills, despite the considerable mobility of such labour. However, this is an issue that needs to be considered in the costing and planned time scheduling of the specific project.

The SOC of public expenditure applies equally to capital and to current dollars.

Public "spend to save" versus public spending for consumption benefits. The opportunity cost of public spending is the present value of the stream of consumption displaced by the tax (or borrowing) used to fund it.[14]

---

[13]The immediate marginal impact of all government spending, or revenue, or expenditure savings is of course on borrowing, as neither aggregate spending nor aggregate revenue can be precisely determined in advance.

[14]This opportunity cost is finite so long as the STP rate exceeds the long-run rate of growth of this stream of lost consumption. This is normally the case, as indefinite compounding of the consequences of $1 of public spending cannot exceed the long-term growth rate of the whole economy, which for any developed economy is less than any defensible rate of STP. This might possibly not be the case for an economy with a prospect of low per capita income growth and high population growth. In this

In cost-effectiveness analysis – that is, comparing alternative cost streams to achieve given non-monetized benefits – even this opportunity cost is irrelevant because it applies equally to all costs and benefits (Feldstein, 1970). In developed economies, cost-effectiveness analysis is more common than the "cost-benefit analysis" of projects such as transport or flood protection investment, or overseas aid projects, where the benefits are often consumption benefits such as time savings, lower risks of flood damage, or higher incomes for poor communities.[15]

Thus, returning to the stylized numerical example on pages 88-89, the answer to the question of whether the $100 investment would be worthwhile depends in part on whether the projected benefit is a saving in public spending or a consumption benefit. If the $175 of benefit in year 10 were a public expenditure saving, and there were no other factors to consider, such as risk or non-monetized impacts, then the investment looks worthwhile. If, on the other hand, the benefit were a consumption benefit, then, even with no other factors to consider, a benefit to cost ratio of only 1.18 looks too small to justify the SOC of the $100 of public spending.

This illustrates the need, as was noted by Feldstein (1973, p. 313), for two different "prices" – one for the value of future consumption relative to current consumption (i.e., a discount rate) and one for the value of public spending relative to contemporary consumption (i.e., an SOC for public expenditure). The handling of two different objectives requires two instruments.

The nature of the social value of private sector returns to equity

The risk premium in private sector returns, as was set out by Arrow and Lind (1970, p. 376), is a cost, not a net social benefit. Forgoing it, therefore, does not incur an opportunity cost.[16] However, the assumption in the SOC literature is nearly always that it is an opportunity cost.

---

case, the long-run economic growth rate provides a floor for the public sector discount rate.

[15] Examples of cost-effectiveness analysis might include administrative relocation decisions, the comparative costing of medical treatments, administrative IT innovations, or military equipment design.

[16] Although it is sometimes argued that the premium is "irrationally" high and that the irrational excess is not a social cost. However, even if the premium revealed by the market is irrational, it is still a social cost, as is, for example, the fear of a person who is terrified of a Martian invasion.

A possible rationale for such an assumption is that the government could invest in a "private sector" opportunity, to earn the same return, but without incurring the equity risk premium. However, the transition from public to private financing has other consequences, not least for incentives, which, as commented by Arrow (1995b), make this an unreal option.

The SOC approach to discounting in practice

Whatever its technical merits, an SOC discount rate has a strong intuitive appeal.

A Harvard professor of international economics, in an otherwise authoritative article on climate change, presented a two-page argument for the use of a 10% SOC discount rate (Cooper, 2000, pp. 152-155), bringing a firm response from Arrow that "… the observed rate of return in the private sector is not the correct one for assessing public investment projects" (Arrow, 2000).

It appeals also to senior administrators or ministers, and is easy for a minister to explain plausibly in public. Perhaps for such reasons, it remains influential in many countries and international bodies, at least for presentational purposes. The US OMB rate for comparing public investment with subsequent benefits in kind of 7% (OMB, 2003) is presented as an SOC rate.[17] The UN (Economic Commission for Europe, 2003) and the World Bank (Birdsall and Steer, 1993) also, for comparing public investment with subsequent benefits in kind, adopt SOC or weighted rates.

The EC (European Commission, 2008) recommends an SOC rate for financial (as opposed to economic) analysis, but this is a required financial rate of return to public sector commercial activities, not a social discount rate.

SOC / STP − Hybrid Approaches to Discounting

It is sometimes proposed that STP should be used for discounting, as on pages 94-95, but a shadow price of more than unity should be applied to public investment. This shadow price is derived as the present value (discounted at the STP rate) of the flow of consumption that investment of a dollar in the private sector would have yielded. Early proponents of this

---

[17]http://www.whitehouse.gov/omb/circulars/a094/a094.html#8, section 8.b.1.

Michael Spackman

approach included Eckstein (1957, 1958, 1961),[18] Marglin (1963b), and Feldstein (1964). It remains popular in some American literature (e.g., Boardman *et al.*, 1996).

It has since the 1950s generated much algebra, reflecting assumptions about, for example, how the financing of the public investment is distributed between borrowing and taxation, the consequent impact on private investment, and the subsequent social return.

This approach is fairly similar in practical terms to the use of an STP rate for discounting combined with a shadow price for *all* public spending or receipts to reflect their impact on taxation, as discussed on page 88. However, in confining the SOC estimation to capital spending, and assuming that private returns measure a social benefit, it is subject to most of the problems of the SOC approach to discounting discussed earlier – namely, the implausible assumption of strong displacement of private investment by public investment (but not by other public spending) and the implicit assumption that the cost of risk in returns to private equity financing measures a net social benefit rather than a social cost.

Another hybrid approach, rarely advocated in recent years, is to apply an averaged discount rate, on the basis that STP and SOC both matter but cannot be reconciled in a single rate, so that an average is a second-best solution. However, this retains the assumption, rejected earlier as unsustainable, that private sector financial returns are relevant to public sector discounting over time.[19]

---

[18]Eckstein (1958) noted that he had advocated different conventions on different occasions but suggested that they were equivalent.

[19]Averaging of discount rates is anyway unsatisfactory because, as the time duration increases, the effective average rate falls toward the lower number. Thus, the average of the present values of $100 discounted over five years at 4% and at 7% is $76.74, implying an "average discount rate" of 5.4%. But if the same procedure is applied over 50 years, the "average discount rate" is 5.0%. This is one of the arguments for using lower discount rates for the very long term if discounting is considered suitable for such analysis.

STP as a Basis for Government Discounting

STP, as normally defined, is the time preference of the population as a whole for marginal income or consumption.[20]

Leading early exponents of an STP discount rate for public sector analysis were Eckstein (1958) and Feldstein (1964) and, later, an influential paper by Bradford (1975). Others, taking a growth theory perspective, were Marglin (1963a, 1963b) and Arrow (1965, 1966), the latter work being developed into a powerful book by Arrow and Kurz (1970). All of these authors adopted the principle that the social value of a public investment is the present value of all of its impacts on consumption, discounted at the STP rate for consumption. As the basis for deriving the rate of STP, they mostly[21] applied equation (1).

$$STP = \delta + \eta g \tag{1}$$

Where δ = pure time preference, percent per year;
   η = income elasticity of the marginal utility of income (with sign reversed);
and g = rate of growth of per capita income, percent per year.

The algebra was well set out by Feldstein (1965). The term δ – time preference for marginal utility – defines the extent to which the current population (or its government) cares about future marginal utility. The term ηg measures the extent to which the utility of a marginal dollar declines with increasing income. The STP rate can equally be applied to other monetary numeraires, including public expenditure, so long as all the quantities are expressed in, or converted to, the same numeraire.[22]

Valuation of δ and η is not straightforward. However, there is now enough consensus in the literature to derive practical values for most

---

[20]This is preference in a very uncomplicated sense, without any of the psychologically important factors, such as regret, that may influence *personal* time preference, which as noted in Appendix A has a different literature.

[21]Marglin (1963a) boldly proposed deriving an STP rate from macroeconomic optimization of the growth rate and the level of investment, as these were variables on which politicians could be expected to express policy preferences.

[22]Provided the issues are clearly understood, it can be helpful to use pure time preference alone (the term δ) as a discount rate for quantities measured in a numeraire of utility, such as the Quality Adjusted Life Year (QALY).

Michael Spackman

developed economies. Their derivation, coincidentally implying values for both variables of between 1 and 2, is discussed in Appendix A.

As noted above, financial economists often dismiss STP and wish to apply CAPM instead, but without explaining how the equity market risk premium might apply to publicly financed activities. And in some contexts, the presentational and other administrative attractions of the SOC approach to discounting give that approach considerable weight. However, the STP approach has become fairly widely, albeit not wholly, accepted in welfare economics. Equation (1) was fairly described by Arrow (1995b) as "the well known formula" and was noted several times at the high-powered US workshop on long-term discounting reported in Portney and Weyant (1999) – most clearly in the paper by Cline.

Such controversy as still remains about the STP approach focuses mainly on the value of δ and to some extent the value of η, and on the extent to which conventional discounting, even with declining rates over time, is appropriate for very long-term impacts such as those of climate change (e.g., Weitzman, 2008).

International Practice

There appears to be no readily available international data on government practices with respect to the appraisal of private financing.[23] However, this section records some international practice with respect to government discounting in general.

Recent practice on government discounting in ten OECD countries is summarized in Table 1. There is some geographical pattern.

In the United States, the academic powerhouse of welfare and financial economics, the welfare economists appear to have concluded by the early 1980s that the theoretical issues had been sufficiently explored[24] and chose not to become embroiled in administrative debate about federal (OMB) government practice. They were content that the government borrowing rate was near enough to an STP rate for practical use and content to see a

---

[23]The author would be most grateful for any advice on this or on international practice on public sector discounting generally.

[24]The subject came to academic life again only with the growing prominence from the 1990s of the very long term, especially in the context of comate change.

Table 1: Government Discount Rates in Some OECD Countries (2006)

Country	Central Guidance	Standardization across Government	Discount Rate	Theoretical Basis of Discount Rate
Australia	Commonwealth finance ministry issues *Handbook of Cost-Benefit Analysis*, Jan. 2006	Varies across states. Commonwealth specifies SOC rate for CBA, long-term bond rate for cost-effectiveness, STP rate if only consumption, risk-free rate for financing	SOC rate (10%) annually reviewed (but higher than STP or bond rate). STP rate 3%, but rarely used	SOC rate is "true opportunity cost of capital" and "ensures that resources are used efficiently". Also recommends CAPM for property ownership and divestment
Canada	Treasury Board Secretariat issues "Benefit Cost Analysis Guide" July 1998, modified Dec. 2002	Applied throughout national government	10% real	Based on traditional SOC (tracing sources of finance from foreign borrowing, forgone private sector investment and forgone consumption), with some weight given to CAPM
France	Expert committee makes recommendations to *Commissariat General du Plan*	Each sector draws up its own methodology using the specified discount rate	Real discount rate set since 1960. Set in 1985 at 8% real; in 2005 at 4%	1985 working group estimated cost of capital at 6%, but discount rate was set at 8% to keep a balance between public and private sector investment. 2005 regime based on STP with decreasing schedule of rates after 30 years
Germany	Federal finance ministry publishes guidance	Applied at federal level	1999: 4% real; 2004: 3% real	Based on federal refinancing rate, which over late 1990s was 6% nominal. Average GDP deflator (2%) was subtracted, giving 4% real
Italy	Central guidance to regional authorities, 2001	Regional investment	5% real	Apparently based on STP

Michael Spackman

New Zealand	Finance ministry issues "Cost Benefit Analysis Primer" (version 1.12, Dec. 2005), supported by a Working Paper (2002)	Project appraisal on departmental basis following central broad methodology, but many discount rates used	Formally 10% real as a standard rate unless another sector rate is agreed	Based on CAPM, using private sector comparators to estimate betas. But STP accepted as appropriate "in principle". The policy was in late 2006 being re-examined
Norway	Government-wide recommendations	Departmental interpretations of central guidance	1978: 7% real; 1998: 3.5% real	Appears to be based now on government borrowing rate
Spain	Central guidance set by sector		6% real for transport; 5% for environmental; 4% real for water	Based on STP, having regard to EC conventions
United Kingdom	Finance ministry issues guidance to all central government	Central guidance, plus consistent guides written by spending ministries	1967: 8% real; 1969: 10% real; 1978: 5% real; 1989: 6% real; 2003: 3.5% real	Traditional SOC until early 1980s; thereafter STP. Until 1973, applied only in nationalized industries. The 2003 regime specifies a decreasing schedule of discount rates after 30 years
USA	OMB issues discount rates for federal programs: Circular A-94 (Appendix C on cost-effectiveness revised Jan. 2006)	Departments take note of OMB guidance but also have their own standards and guidelines	Cost effectiveness: 2.5–3.0% real, depending on period discounted. CBA: 7% real from 1992 (previously 10%)	Cost-effectiveness rate equal to federal borrowing rate. CBA rate derived from pre-tax return to private sector investment in 1970s/80s. Pre-1992 rate based on private return in 1960s

higher rate (reduced in 1992 from 10% to 7%) for CBA. The latter appears to be higher for a mix of unpublished political and administrative reasons, such as helping to offset systematic optimism bias in CBA cost and benefit estimates. The US academic *financial* economics community does not appear to have expressed views on public sector discounting since the inconclusive exchanges of the late 1960s and early 1970s.

In Europe, there appears to be increasing acceptance of the technically more rigorous use of an explicit STP rate, which is generally a little higher than government borrowing rates (although in Germany, the rate of 4%, used as a borrowing rate until 2004, could equally well be an STP rate) (Spackman, 2007). The current STP rate specified by the European Commission (EC) is 3.5% for developed European Union (EU) member states and 5.5% for "Cohesion Fund" states, with their high per capita growth rates (European Commission, 2008).[25]

There appears in Europe to be little academic interest, and no official interest, in the EMH view of the public sector cost of capital and time preference, except for some academic interest in the UK.[26] Perhaps because of the standing of the London Business School, there has long been a small UK literature by economists schooled in CAPM. The issues were considered in some depth in the UK Treasury in the late 1980s, but the EMH case was rejected. Academic interest in quantifying the elements of STP appears today to be mainly centred in the UK, as referenced in Appendix A.

In other developed economies, notably Australia, Canada, and New Zealand, there appears to be more debate at the official level, with EMH/CAPM advocates more influential than in other countries and the SOC approach to discounting also sometimes carrying significant weight. The concept of STP, while accepted by many with a welfare economics background, finds limited acceptance in these countries as a practical tool.

International organizations other than the EC, as noted on page 88, appear generally to adopt the SOC approach for the CBA of projects that they might support, perhaps for reasons similar to those ascribed above to the OMB.

---

[25]This is based unconventionally on a growth rate and associated elasticity for public expenditure rather than per capita income growth, but this appears to be quantitatively important.

[26]An exception is a Dutch paper (van Ewijk and Tang, 2003), which promotes the conventional EMH view. It also explains that the Dutch government discount rate was "based on the historic average of the real yield on long-term government bonds" and was at that time 4%, as in Germany.

Discounting and the Cost(s) of Capital with Private Financing

The explicit handling within public sector appraisal of private financing costs has become prominent in the context of PPPs, where, in principle, publicly financed options are being compared with privately financed alternatives. This is discussed below.

The explicit analysis of private financing costs can also be important in some other circumstances in developed economies, in appraisal to support government decision making that affects specific private sector investments. This discussion begins on page 103.

Comparisons of Public and Private Financing

First principles

Governments have for 50 years or more been comparing public with private financing for public service assets in the context of lease versus buy, mainly for property. The UK Treasury's first formal guidance on discounting (HM Treasury, 1973) recognized, as "one common exception" to use of the standard rate, "the choice of methods of financing investment once the actual decision to invest has been taken". It recommended the use in this financing case of the government borrowing rate.

Nearly 20 years later, Lind suggested the same approach as obvious: "[For] a lease or buy decision ... clearly, the government's borrowing rate is appropriate [for discounting] in a world where crowding out is not a significant problem. From the taxpayer's point of view, it will minimize their cost whether they choose to pay it now or defer it to the future through government borrowing" (Lind, 1990, p. S-23).[27]

---

[27]Lind's rationale was that financial markets had become so globalized that marginal extra borrowing by the state had no material effect on access to capital by the private sector. This was fairly widely accepted at that time and increasingly so in the subsequent decades. But this does not, of course, mean that governments can therefore be relaxed about borrowing. As noted on page 88, the taxation ultimately needed to fund most public spending imposes distortions, so dollars of public spending should be given more weight than dollars of consumption. And the widely accepted difference between STP rates and (lower) government borrowing rates presumably reflects the fact that increasing debt, or decreasing savings, incurs costs in terms of reputation or reduced insurance against difficult times, for governments

For most practical cases, this technically simple (if in some contexts potentially contentious) approach may often suffice. But formally, it overlooks or unduly plays down two significant issues.

First, it overlooks taxation, to the extent that tax applies differently to public and private financing. The government borrowing rate, after an upward adjustment to avoid a bias from the inclusion in private financing costs of corporation tax, provides a rigorous comparator with the private sector cost of capital.

Second, the three variables noted above – STP, the public cost of capital, and the private cost of capital – are *all* relevant. Simply discounting at the government borrowing rate overlooks any difference between STP and the public cost of capital. However, if this adjusted government borrowing rate differs from the government time preference rate, the public interest is not strictly best served by also *discounting over time* at the borrowing rate.

A rigorous procedure

A rigorous calculation would estimate the alternative financing streams of depreciation and "return on capital" payments over the project lifetime, for the publicly financed and the privately financed option, and then discount both at the STP rate.[28]

The principle is partially illustrated by the highly stylized example in Table 2 below, which shows its application to private financing alone for a capital expenditure of $100. Applied to *public* financing, with a tax-adjusted government borrowing rate of, say, 2.5% in real terms, discounting at an STP rate of 3.5% would produce a present value of *less than* $100. Discounting private and public financing costs at an STP rate understates both of their full social costs, but it does accurately measure the present value of the *difference* between the two sets of financing costs. This understating of both social costs should be unsurprising, as the fact that STP

---

and consumers as for commercial enterprises. The problems for governments are starkly illustrated by the state of UK finances in 2009 and the problems for commercial enterprises even more starkly by the banking crisis of 2008, to which excessively high gearing was a contributor.

[28]There are few, if any, other circumstances where it is appropriate to discount at the STP rate the financing stream of a private investment, which will nearly always incorporate a return on capital (including an equity risk premium) higher than the STP rate. However, it provides a rigorous comparison of the social costs, *ceteris paribus*, of public and private financing (unless, of course, it is maintained that a substantial "equity risk premium" is incurred also with public financing).

Table 2: Illustrative Calculation of the Social Cost of Private Financing Costs ($)

Year	0	10	20
Capital spending	100		
Capital repayment		50	50
Cumulative return @ 6.5% (or 4.5%)		88 (or 55)	44 (or 28)
Total payment of capital + return		138 (or 105)	94 (or 78)
Discount factor @ 3.5%		0.709	0.503
Present value in year 0		98 (or 74)	47 (or 39)
Total present value in year 0	145 (or 113)		

rates are higher than government borrowing rates is rarely contentious; but it is not something easily explained to or accepted by a senior, non-technical audience.

A typical procedure in practice today for PPPs is to discount the costs of the private finance option at the government discount rate. The present value is then compared with the present value of expenditure on the publicly financed option, where the latter includes public capital spending directly, *not* as depreciation and financing costs. If this procedure is applied with a discount rate materially higher than the government borrowing cost, it will be biased in favour of private financing. The bias will be greater the higher the discount rate used. The procedure is applying an implicit cost of capital to public financing equal to this discount rate rather than equal to the cost of government borrowing.

Practical realities

Appraisal priorities. The devotion of much time to discounting and costs of capital can be a distraction from more important issues.

A government may be seeking private financing to postpone the public accounting consequences for public debt or taxation, or as a political measure to reduce the activity, if not the expenditure, of government, or in some developing or transitional economies, as a means of financing that aid agencies consider desirable at that stage of development. In this case, precise comparison with hypothetical public finding may divert attention from the serious issues of establishing sensible incentives and tight and fair contracts.

Even if a fair comparison is required between public and private financing, this should not divert attention from the effects of alternative types of financing on likely cost and time overruns, and how the impacts of these would be distributed among users, taxpayers, and suppliers. Effects of this kind may be much more important than the difference in the cost of capital.

Administrative acceptability and data availability. Standard appraisal procedures, even in the most sophisticated governments, need either to be very simple or to be heavily policed. Occasionally, an issue may achieve such a high policy profile, and such resources for policing, that some complexity is sustainable.[29] But the analytical comparison of public and private financing is not such an issue.

Thus, the procedure outlined on pages 100-101, that employs not only a discount rate but also the costs of capital to the public and private sectors, is unlikely to be feasible in any country as a standard, rigorous procedure. It would not be accepted by senior administrators and ministers, and if it were, it would be routinely challenged by suppliers and would not be applied competently in the field. It might possibly be applied by a strong ministry of finance (or even a strong international agency) to an occasional high-profile case, but no more.

In terms of data, the capital costs and return to capital embedded in a PPP tender are in any case rarely, if ever, available to the client. The best that the government client can usually do is to be equipped to make informed judgments about the contractor's capital and operating costs, and the financial terms the contractor is likely to have obtained from the financier, and to negotiate on that basis a fair distribution of costs and risks.

Comparing public and private financing in practice. As set out above, the appropriate procedure depends upon whether or not the government's STP rate is close to or significantly higher than a tax-adjusted government borrowing rate.[30]

- If the STP rate is close to a tax-adjusted government borrowing rate, the public spending flows on both the public and the private finance options

---

[29]As in the UK with the shadow pricing of CO_2, and some fine details of regulatory costs.

[30]The tax adjustment, to allow for the fact that privately financed enterprises pay corporate taxes, is obviously country-specific, but is probably always fairly small. In the UK, it is an addition of no more than a one-percentage point to the actual real borrowing rate.

can be discounted in the normal way, with no need to identify financing costs. The procedure outlined on pages 100–101 is in this case being applied, but painlessly.

- If the STP rate is significantly higher than the government borrowing rate, then, as a run-of-the-mill procedure, using the *government borrowing rate* as a discount rate is likely to give a reasonably fair comparison between publicly and privately financed options. This would follow the US OMB guidance. The time preference will not be quite right, but the comparison of the financing costs would normally be broadly correct.

If, in this second case, the government wished to use a higher discount rate to compare the later benefits from the investment with the costs, there would still be sense in using the government borrowing rate for the public/private financing comparison.

General Handling of Privately Financed Capital in CBA

Sometimes privately financed investment needs to be handled within government CBA when data is available on the capital costs but not directly on the financing costs. This is unlikely to arise in a developing or transitional economy, but in a developed economy can arise from:

- The CBA of regulatory proposals (e.g., environmental or safety) that would require substantial investment from private enterprises.
- The CBA of some major private sector investment proposals that are subject to government approval because of planning or other require-ments.

The same principles apply as in "Comparisons of Public and Private Financing" above, but with the simplification that there is no publicly financed option. The requirement is simply for the capital asset costs to be properly included in the CBA. To do this, informed judgments are needed about the relevant cost of capital for the asset in question and about how the return will be distributed over time.

As a highly stylized numerical example, suppose that:

- the (gross of tax) cost of capital for the private asset is 6.5% or, as an alternative assumption, 4.5% in real terms;

- the STP rate, also in real terms, is 3.5%;
- the capital is repaid (typically by consumers) in two equal instalments after 10 years and 20 years, each time with the accumulated cost on capital.

If the initial capital investment is $100 in year 0, the present value, including financing costs, can then be derived as in Table 2 (where the illustrative rates of return and discount rates are real rates as opposed to nominal rates).

Thus, in this example, the financing cost adds 45% to the social cost of the investment with a private cost of capital of 6.5% and adds 13% with a private cost of capital of 4.5%. These extra costs would, of course, be less if the capital were repaid more quickly. As noted on pages 100-101, discounting financing costs in this way generally somewhat *understates* the full social cost of the investment and its financing, but any further adjustment for the difference between the government borrowing rate and STP would seem impractical.

If a rigorous comparison were being made with public financing, the same procedure would in principle need to be carried out with the public cost of capital, as described on pages 100-101.

Conclusion

The Opportunity Cost of Public Expenditure

A marginal dollar of taxation imposes more costs on society than the loss of a marginal dollar of consumption. This arises partly from the opportunity cost of productive activity displaced by taxation and partly from other costs that taxation imposes by distorting supply side incentives in many ways. However, it is most usefully described as an opportunity cost. It justifies the application of a shadow price to public expenditure (net of revenues such as user charges).

Government Time Preference

Three main approaches, as follows, have over the years been proposed for the handling of time preference in government. The first two are based on rates of return achieved from privately financed sector investment. The third derives an STP rate derived not from market data, but from other behavioural data and ethical judgment.

- The CAPM approach: Many financial economists propose that the cost of capital and hence time discount rate applied to publicly financed expenditure should be the same as that for mainly equity-financed private sector investment of a similar activity. This may imply use of the government borrowing rate to discount public expenditure but considerably higher rates to discount consumption benefits in CBA.

  This approach, derived from the EMH, appears to be universally rejected by welfare economists. This is mainly for the persuasive reason that the equity risk premium appears to be largely a feature of equity markets, and no mechanism has ever been advanced to explain how it could be generated by a publicly financed investment. (The equity risk premium in private financing arises from covariance of returns to the equity and the average equity market return. There is an analogous effect with public financing in that the costs or benefits are often correlated with national income; but this effect is extremely small because national income fluctuations are so small relative, in particular, to fluctuations in equity markets.)

- The SOC approach: A popular approach in public administrations in the 1960s and 1970s was that of taking the cost of capital and hence the time discount rate for publicly financed expenditure to be broadly equal to the average rate of return achieved in the private sector. This was based on the principle that public investment displaces private investment and should therefore be costed in the same way.

  This approach has more recently carried less weight, for a number of persuasive technical reasons. One is that the SOC of public spending is now more widely seen as attributable to the wide range of distortionary impacts of taxation, including, but not confined to, the displacement of private capital investment; indeed, the displacement of private investment is today probably small. The opportunity cost is also now generally seen as the present value (at an STP rate) of the consequent stream of lost consumption rather than as an annual rate of return. Another reason, as noted above, is that the risk premium element of private sector returns to equity is now generally seen in welfare economics as irrelevant to the social cost of publicly funded expenditure.

  Much of the work invested in developing this approach might usefully be subsumed in work to develop the rather thin literature of the opportunity cost of public expenditure, as outlined on page 104.

- The STP approach: STP is generally derived from the equation $STP = \delta + \eta g$, where δ is pure time preference for marginal utility, g is the growth rate of per capita income, and η is the elasticity of marginal utility with respect to income (with sign reversed).

  This appears to be the approach now most widely accepted in the literature for handling time preference in government and has over many years become increasingly accepted in public administrations.

Time Preference and Opportunity Cost: Practical Application

- In practice, a procedure that explicitly applies both STP and the SOC of public expenditure at the same time will be, for most if not all public administrations, too complicated for application as standard practice. However:
  - For cost-effectiveness analysis, the opportunity cost of public expenditure is irrelevant, as it applies equally to all the figures that are being compared.
  - For CBA, where public expenditures are being compared with impacts valued in terms of consumption, a benefit/cost ratio can be estimated with public expenditure as the denominator. The opportunity cost of public expenditure then defines a floor below which approval should not be considered.
- If, for political or administrative reasons, a government is unable to adopt the concept of STP, the government borrowing rate will usually be the best of the available alternatives.
- In the United States, the OMB adopts the government borrowing rate for cost-effectiveness analysis, including public private comparisons such as lease versus buy. This appears to be the best that is achievable given the constraints within US federal administration, although US academic opinion appears now to accept the concept of STP as long since uncontroversial. The more explicit adoption of (somewhat) higher STP rates appears to be achievable fairly widely in European administrations.
- The OMB and some international organizations adopt much higher rates for CBA, where public expenditures are being compared with consumption costs and benefits. These high rates are explained in terms of private sector returns (i.e., the SOC approach to discounting); but they appear to be set high to take account of other factors, such as concern about optimism bias and perhaps the opportunity cost of public spending. Setting a high rate is a very crude mechanism for handling such factors,

but appears to be the best that can be done in the circumstances of these bodies.

Comparing the Costs of Public and Private Financing

- The comparison of public and private financing costs requires inputs that at least implicitly include these two financing costs, the public financing cost being defined by the cost of government borrowing. In a rigorous analysis, the public financing costs would be adjusted slightly upward to offset the corporate tax charged on private returns. The difference between these two streams of financing costs over time would then be discounted at the STP rate.
- This rigorous analysis would generally be too complex to be a standard procedure. However, if the government uses a discount rate that is similar to the government borrowing rate, then discounting the private financing costs at this rate and comparing these with the public capital spending is generally sufficient. In practice, developed countries adopting STP discount rates do now generally derive rates that are reasonably close to government borrowing rates.
- If the government applies this simple procedure using a discount rate materially higher than the cost of government borrowing, the present values will be biased in favour of private financing. How much this matters depends upon the context. Concern about this bias should not unduly displace concern about other crucial issues such as optimism bias and contract design and enforcement.

Appendix A: The Estimation of δ and η to Derive a Value for STP

Pure Time Preference (δ)

The value of pure time preference for marginal utility – the term δ in equation (1) – is mainly an ethical choice about the relative weighting of the marginal utility of today's population and future populations. However, there is no solid empirical data on people's preferences in this respect.[31]

Pigou (1920) and Ramsey (1928), like a minority of later authorities,[32] considered that discounting future marginal utility was irrational for individuals and ethically unsatisfactory for governments. This was applied in the *Stern Review* (Stern, 2006) and attracted much criticism (which appears to have been accepted by Stern). As set out by Schelling (1995), people in general have concern for future generations (and for those in other countries), but this is evidently less than their concern for those with whom they have a closer affinity.

No profession has a special claim to pronounce on this ethical judgement. Kopp and Portney (1999) comment on the coverage of discounting by the Intergovernmental Panel on Climate Change: "The [IPCC's] prescriptive approach is premised on the view that there is an ethically or morally 'correct' rate of discount to use in project evaluation – a rate that is independent of the views of the present generation (save, of course, those who get to determine what the morally just rate is). Yet those of us who teach benefit-cost analysis and advocate its use … we argue that BCA is attractive because it is based in the preferences of all those around today." Eckstein (1957, p. 75), expressly refuting Ramsey, made the same point 50 years ago: "I assume [discounting of future utility] because I believe that a social welfare function based on consumer sovereignty must accept people's tastes, including their intertemporal preferences." Marglin (1963a) says similarly: "I consider it axiomatic that a democratic

---

[31]Much work has been done on *personal* time preference (e.g., Frederick, Loewenstein, and O'Donoghue, 2002), generally yielding values at least approaching double figures and often very much higher, but there are reasons to doubt the relevance of these measures to preferences about how the government should weight the future.

[32]Including the distinguished names of Harrod, Koopmans, Solow, Broome, and Cline.

government effects only the preferences of the individuals who are presently members of the body politic."

A more pragmatic, but powerful, objection to a zero rate of pure time preference is that it implies a patently unrealistic level of saving and investment. This was first noted by Ramsey (1928, p. 548), set out in qualitative terms by Hayek (1936, p. 46), and explained clearly by Arrow (1995b, p. 16).[33]

Aside from those who believe that pure time preference should be at or very close to zero, there may be some consensus in the literature on a value, over a few decades, of around 1.5% per year, if an element is included for the risk of some natural or man-made catastrophe, eliminating many of the prospective benefits, beyond the range of risk factors normally considered in specific appraisals.[34]

---

[33]Dasgupta (2006) applied the implausible savings rate argument in another way. He argued that with a pure time preference rate of effectively zero, a plausible savings rate could be obtained only with a high elasticity of marginal utility, η. He notes (p. 7) that values of δ=0.1% and η=3 imply a "reasonable" savings rate of 25% of net output. This presumably reflects a personal ethical view that policy distributions of marginal utility should be strongly egalitarian over time for households of a given income, but strongly biased in favour of lower-income households.

[34]Few authors, apart from those advocating a zero rate, commit themselves to an explicit estimate of δ. Little and Mirrlees (1974, p. 266), while expressing sympathy with the zero rate view, suggest that "in any case it would probably not mean an addition [to time preference] of more than 2% or 3% per year". More widely quoted is Scott in the references cited below, who supposed that, in periods of stable inflation, STP has been indicated by the post-tax return on low-risk savings. Scott and Dowley (1977), on the basis mainly of data for the half-century before World War I, estimate a value for δ of 0.5%, but suggest, "since the risk of total destruction of our society has increased", "a best estimate" for δ of 1.5.%. Subsequently, using post-WW II and pre-WW I data on post-tax returns to equity, Scott (1989, pp. 230-231) estimates a value for δ of 1.3% and also examines (p. 233) the higher value for δ of 2.5% suggested by Stern (1977). Arrow (1995b, p. 17) suggests that "very tentatively, it would seem that the pure rate of time preference should be about 1%".

The Elasticity of Marginal Utility (η)

The Moral Dimension

Whereas the term δ in equation (1) is essentially ethical, the term ηg as usually applied is wholly utilitarian, ignoring any moral aspect of transfers from poorer to richer populations. Yet many might argue that "fairness" or "egalitarian" concerns would justify rather less redistribution of marginal utility (and certainly no more) from poorer to richer than implied by the simple utilitarian criterion of maximizing the sum of individual utilities. This would imply for STP purposes a higher value of η.[35]

Derivation of η from the Personal Tax Regime

Derivation of η from personal tax regimes conventionally assumes that the schedule of income tax rates against income is based on the principle of "equal absolute sacrifice" (i.e., an equal loss of utility for each marginal dollar of tax paid). Combining this principle with a constant-elasticity utility function yields an implicit value for η.

Strengths of this approach are its conceptual simplicity and measurability, and that it may also include concern about fairness as well as marginal utility; but it has important limitations.[36] Social concern about contemporary inequality might differ from concerns about inequality over time; and personal taxation in many countries is influenced by concerns about incentives and personal freedom as well as fairness. Concern about incentives will bias downward estimates of η based on the assumption of equal absolute sacrifice. Problems also surround the inclusion or exclusion of the standard personal allowance or other allowances, and the significance

---

[35]As noted above, Dasgupta argues for a value for η of about 3. This contrasts with a comment by Newbery (1992, p. 11) that "[HM Treasury's] preferred value of [η] is 1.5, which is quite egalitarian, and one might quite reasonably defend a value of 1.0 or even less". However, despite the implication in the latter comment that the Treasury value of η incorporated an ethical judgment, this was not part of the Treasury's logic at that time.

[36]Many other qualifications apply to this and to all other methods of estimating η. One which applies to many methods is the assumption that the utility function is additively separable.

of other policy instruments geared to income distribution, as discussed by Evans (2005).

Cowell and Gardiner (2000) use this method to derive UK values for η in the late 1990s of 1.42 if applied just to income tax, and of 1.29 if applied to income tax and National Insurance Contributions (NICs).[37] Evans and Sezer (2005), Evans (2005), and Evans (2007) present results for a large number of OECD countries, deriving an average value close to 1.4, with a perhaps surprisingly narrow spread of about ± 0.2.

The derivation by Stern (1977) for the UK income tax regime in 1973–74, before concerns about tax incentives became so prominent, may give a better measure of social judgments about the utility of marginal income across the income distribution. Stern derived a value for η of 1.97, although Evans (2005) suggests that Stern's inclusion of the standard personal tax allowance gives a strong upward bias to η at relatively low levels of income. For US income tax from 1948 to 1965, Mera (1969, p. 469) found that "for a major portion of the income range", the rates implied a value for η of 1.5.

Derivation of η from Personal Savings Behaviour

Many studies of household savings behaviour over the life cycle estimate the inter-temporal elasticity of substitution of household consumption. Under fairly restrictive assumptions, as set out by Cowell and Gardiner (2000, Appendix A3), the reciprocal of this quantity is equal to the household elasticity of marginal utility. Cowell and Gardiner consider some of this work, in particular Blundell, Browning, and Meghir (1994) on UK data. They note that the two principal models in Blundell, Browning, and Meghir imply, for η, values of 1.2 to 1.4, or of 0.34 to 1.0 (both sets of values increasing with income). However, as noted by Evans (2005), the sample period of 1970–1986 ends in the year in which UK retail financial markets were deregulated. It is unclear what either model would produce with data for the deregulated environment.

---

[37]Evans (2005) suggests that NICs should be ignored because the notionally insurance-based rationale for such deductions is "completely different" from that underlying income tax rates. In practice, the contributions are widely seen to serve in effect as a (politically convenient) form of income tax, but, as Evans implies, it is hard to believe that the regime was ever designed other than to minimize disincentives for a given total NIC revenue. This, however, has for many years been increasingly the objective of income tax regimes as well!

Barsky *et al.* (1997) measure the inter-temporal elasticity of substitution directly by means of survey questions from the US Health and Retirement Study. They obtain a mean value of 0.18, which implies a very high value for η of 5.6.

The savings ratio, together with assumptions for δ and for the long-run rate of return, yields an implicit value for η. Stern (1977, p. 220) records that taking plausible figures for the UK in the 1960s, and $\delta = 2.5\%$, the implicit value of η was approximately 5 (or higher for lower values of δ).

These studies suggest, however, that personal savings behaviour has little relevance to the effect on the marginal utility of income to society of increases in income over time.

Derivation of η from Direct Evidence of Personal Risk Aversion

Barsky *et al.* (1997) report empirical measures of η (defined in this case as relative risk aversion) of US respondents between the ages of 51 and 61. The authors give most weight to measures of the reciprocal, which they define as relative risk tolerance, for which the arithmetic average value was 0.24, implying a value for η of 4.2. This high value relates, however, to very significant risks to income, where factors such as the potential for regret would be expected to increase risk aversion.[38] They found no correlation across individuals between their risk aversion and their inter-temporal elasticity, as described above.

Derivation of η from Income and Price Elasticities

An approach with a long history (Fisher, 1927; Frisch, 1932, 1959) estimates η from the income and price elasticities of a preference-independent good such as food (i.e., a good that contributes an additively separable component to the users' utility). Frisch (1959, equation 64) shows that $\eta = -E_i(1 - a_i E_i)/(e_{ii} + a_i E_i)$, where E_i is the income elasticity of demand for the *i*th good, a_i the budget share, and e_{ii} the own (uncompensated) price elasticity.

---

[38]They may, therefore, be more relevant to the equity risk premium.

Brown and Deaton (1972, p. 1206) report studies by other authors of data from several countries, together with work of their own on UK data for 1900-1970 that gave a value of η of 2.8. They conclude that "though estimates obtained this way [from linear expenditure systems] fluctuate considerably and some are very large, an average value of -2 for [$-\eta$] seems consistent both with most such studies and with the results from fitting other models".

Kula (1984) reports values for η derived in this way for the US of 1.89 and for Canada of 1.56. For the UK, Kula (1985) derives a markedly lower value of 0.71. More recently, Evans and Sezer (2002) derive for the UK a value of 1.6. Subsequently, Evans (2004a) has examined alternative specifications, deriving values for the UK of 1.6 (as above) by a constant elasticities model (CEM) and 1.2 by an almost ideal demand system (AIDS); and for France, values of 1.8 and 1.3 (Evans, 2004b).

The validity of assumptions such as the constancy of the relevant demand functions over time and income is difficult to assess, and there are problems of data and definitions. The substantial effect of the model specification sounds a note of caution. This approach has nonetheless the merit of being a direct measure of η and it has been subject to empirical studies in many countries and over different goods.

Derivation of η from International Happiness Data

Recent years have seen the development of the new literature, now evolving into several strands, on the measurement and determinants of happiness. Much work has been done on international measurement. Layard, Mayraz, and Nickell (2007) use data from six surveys to derive a combined estimate for η of 1.26, with highest and lowest values of 1.34 and 1.19. The results are similar for subgroups in the population.

Derivation of η from Intuition

A value for η of 1 implies that an extra \$1 to someone with an income of \$x gives twice the extra utility provided by an extra \$1 to someone with an income of \$2x. Values for η of 1.5 and 2 would imply factors of, respectively, 2.8 ($2^{1.5}$) and 4 (2^2). However, although the judgment required is conceptually fairly simple, there are few points of reference by which to judge what is plausible.[39]

Scott and Dowley (1977) advance the argument, maintained in Scott (1989), and which they report has the support of Little and Mirrlees and of Stern, that "it is reasonable to suppose that there is a maximum level of utility which anyone can derive from income", in which case "*[η]* must exceed one at least above some income level …".[40]

Expert Views on η

In the American literature, there is some consensus around values for η, in the context of STP, of about 1.5. For example, Eckstein (1958) considers a range of 0.5 to 2.0 and Feldstein (1965) a range of 1 to 2; Cline (1993) opts for 1.5; Boscolo, Vincent, and Panayotou (1998, p. 7) conclude that "the few available estimates suggest that the elasticity of marginal utility [ranges] from 1 to 2"; and Arrow (1995a, p. 6) suggests, on the basis of "rather thin evidence", 1.5 to 2.0.

In the UK literature, Stern's review of 1977 concludes that the evidence then pointed to the range of 1 to 10, with measurements based on consumer behaviour pointing to the middle of the range and those based on government behaviour to around 2. Scott (1989, and Scott and Dowley, 1977), working back from market rates, estimates a value of 1.5. Little and Mirrlees (1974, p. 240) suggest that "on admittedly extremely inadequate evidence, we guess that most people would put *[η]* in the range 1-3". Cowell and Gardiner (2000) conclude that the evidence supports a value in the range of 0.5 to 4, within which they give most weight to the range of 1.2-1.4, derived, as explained above, from the personal tax regime of the late 1990s. Evans (2005) regards a figure of 1.4, derived from the personal tax regimes of a large number of countries, and not inconsistent with derivations from food income and price elasticities, as plausible for many countries.

---

[39]Although Stern's (1977, p. 243) comment that a value "of around 5 does not seem ludicrously large" might for most applications be questioned.

[40]One obvious counterargument is that the ultra-rich may gain utility from knowing that they are relatively richer even than the super-rich. However, it is hard to imagine that this is material to the personal utility impact of a marginal change in taxation; and in any case, such comparative concerns apply more weakly to a nation as a whole than to individuals within it.

References

Arrow, K.J. 1965. "Criteria for Social Investment", *Water Resources Research* 1(1), 1-8.

_____. 1966. "Discounting and Public Investment Criteria", in A.V. Kneese and S.C. Smith (eds.), *Water Research*. Baltimore, MD: The Johns Hopkins University Press for Resources for the Future.

_____. 1995a. "Discounting Climate Change Planning for an Uncertain Future", Lecture given at *Institut d'Economie Industrielles*, Université des Sciences Sociales, Toulouse, 24 April.

_____. 1995b. "Intergenerational Equity and the Rate of Discount in Long-Term Social Investment", International Energy Agency World Congress, December 1995, *Stanford University Economics Department Working Paper* 97-005.

_____. 2000. "A Comment on Cooper", *The World Bank Research Observer* 15(2), 173-175.

Arrow K.J. and R.C. Lind. 1970. "Uncertainty and the Evaluation of Public Investment Decisions", *American Economic Review* 60, 364-378.

Arrow, K.J. and M. Kurz. 1970. *Public Investment, the Rate of Return, and Optimal Fiscal Investment*, Baltimore, MD: The Johns Hopkins University Press for Resources for the Future.

Bailey, M.J. and M.C. Jensen. 1972. "Risk and the Discount Rate for Public Investment", in M.C. Jensen (ed.), *Studies in the Theory of Capital Markets*. New York, NY: Praeger.

Barsky, R.B., F.T. Juster, M.S. Kimball, and M.D. Shapiro. 1997. "Preference Parameters and Behavioral Heterogeneity: An Experimental Approach in the Health and Retirement Study", *The Quarterly Journal of Economics* 112(2) (in memory of Amos Tversky), 537-579.

Birdsall, N. and A. Steer. 1993. "Act Now on Global Warming – But Don't Cook the Books", *Finance and Development* 30(1), 6-8.

Blundell, R., M. Browning, and C. Meghir. 1994. "Consumer Demand and the Life-Cycle Allocation of Expenditure", *Review of Economic Studies* 61, 57-80.

Boardman, A., D. Greenberg, A. Vining, and D. Weimer. 1996. *Cost-Benefit Analysis: Concepts and Practice*, Upper Saddle River, NJ: Prentice Hall.

Boscolo, M., R.V. Vincent, and T. Panayotou. 1998. "Discounting Costs and Benefits in Carbon Sequestration Projects", *Development Discussion Paper* No. 638, Harvard Institute for International Development, Harvard University.

Bradford, D.F. 1975. "Constraints on Government Investment Opportunities and the Choice of Discount Rate", *American Economic Review* 6, 887-899.

Brealey, R.I., A. Cooper, and M.A. Habib. 1997. "Investment Appraisal in the Public Sector", *Oxford Review of Economic Policy* 13(4), 12-28.

Brealey, R.A. and S.C. Myers. 2003. *Principles of Corporate Finance*. Boston, MA: McGraw-Hill/Irwin.

Brown, J.A.C. and A. Deaton. 1972. "Models of Consumer Behaviour", *Economic Journal* 82(328), 1145-1236.

Cline, W.R. 1993. "Give Greenhouse Abatement a Fair Chance", *Finance and Development* 30(1).

Cooper, R.N. 2000. "International Approaches to Climate Change", *The World Bank Research Observer* 15(2), 145-172.

Cowell, F.A. and K. Gardiner. 2000. "Welfare Weights", *Economic Research Paper* 20 (oft282.pdf), London, Office of Fair Trading.

Currie, D. 2000. "Funding the London Underground", London Business School, *Regulation Initiative Discussion Paper* 35.

Dasgupta, P. 2006. "Comments on the Stern Review's Economics of Climate Change", comments for a seminar organized by the Foundation for Science and Technology at the Royal Society, London, on November 8, at http://www.econ.cam.ac.uk/faculty/dasgupta/STERN.pdf.

Department for Transport. 2004-6. "Guidance on Value for Money" (December 2004, modified January 2006), at http://www.dft.gov.uk/stellent/groups/ dft_about/documents/pdf/dft_about_pdf_033477.pdf.

Department of Finance and Administration. 2006. *Handbook of Cost-Benefit Analysis*, Commonwealth of Australia, January.

Eckstein, O. 1957. "Investment Criteria for Economic Development and the Theory of Intertemporal Welfare Economics", *Quarterly Journal of Economics* 71, 56-84.

_____. 1958. *Water Resource Development: The Economics of Project Evaluation.* Cambridge, MA: Harvard University Press.

_____. 1961. "A Survey of the Theory of Public Expenditure Criteria", in *Needs, Sources and Utilisation: A conference of the Universities National Bureau Committee for Economic Research, 1960.* Princeton University Press, 439-504.

Economic Commission for Europe. 2003. *A Set of Guidelines for Socio-economic Cost Benefit Analysis of Transport Infrastructure Project Appraisal.* New York and Geneva, United Nations.

European Commission. 2008. "Guide to Cost-Benefit Analysis of Investment Projects", Final Report, 16 June. At: http://ec.europa.eu/regional_policy/sources/ docgener/guides/cost/guide2008_en.pdf.

Evans, D.J. 2004a. "The Elevated Status of the Elasticity of Marginal Utility of Consumption", *Applied Economics Letters* 11(7), 443-447.

_____. 2004b. "A Social Discount Rate for France", *Applied Economics Letters* 11(13), 803-808.

_____. 2005. "The Elasticity of Marginal Utility of Consumption for 20 OECD Countries", *Fiscal Studies* 26(2), 197-224.

_____. 2007. "Social Discount Rates for the European Union: New Estimates", Chapter 12 in M. Florio (ed.), *Cost-Benefit Analysis and Incentives in Evaluation: The Structural Funds of the European Union.* Cheltenham: Edward Elgar.

Evans, D. and H. Sezer. 2002. "A Time Preference Measure of the Social Discount Rate for the UK", *Applied Economics* 34(12), 1925-1934.

_____. 2005. "Social Discount Rates for Member Countries of the European Union", *Journal of Economic Studies* 32(1), 47-59.

Feldstein, M.S. 1964. "The Social Time Preference Discount Rate in Cost Benefit Analysis", *Economic Journal* 74, 360-379.

_____. 1965. "The Derivation of Social Time Preference Rates", *Kyklos* XVIII(2), 277-287.

_____. 1970. "Choice of Technique in the Public Sector: A Simplification", *The Economic Journal* 80, 985-990.

_____. 1973. "The Inadequacy of Weighted Discount Rates", in R. Layard (ed.), *Cost–Benefit Analysis: Selected Readings,* Harmondsworth: Penguin Books Ltd.

_____. 1997. "How Big Should Government Be?" *National Tax Journal* 50(2), 197-213.

Fisher, I. 1927. "A Statistical Method for Measuring Marginal Utility of Justice of a Progressive Income Tax", in J.H. Hollander (ed.), *Economic Essays Contributed in Honor of John Bates Clark.* New York: Macmillan, 157-193.

Frederick, S., G. Loewenstein, and T. O'Donoghue. 2002. "Time Discounting and Time Preference: A Critical Review", *Journal of Economic Literature* 40, 351-401.

Frisch, R. 1932. *The New Methods of Measuring Marginal Utility.* Tübingen: Mohr.

_____. 1959. "A Complete Scheme for Computing all Direct and Cross Demand Elasticities in a Model with Many Sectors", *Econometrica* 27(2), 177-196.

Grout, P.A. 2003. "Public and Private Sector Discount Rates in Public-Private Partnerships", *The Economic Journal* 113, C62-C68.

Hayek, F.A.V. 1936. "Utility Analysis and Interest", *The Economic Journal* 46(181), 44-60.

Hirshleifer, J. 1966. "Investment Decision under Uncertainty: Applications of the State-Preference Approach", *Quarterly Journal of Economics* 80, 252-277.

HM Treasury. 1973. *Use of Discounted Cash Flow and the Test Discount Rate in the Public Sector,* Management Accounting Unit.

Kirman, A. 1995. "The Behaviour of the Foreign Exchange Market", *Bank of England Quarterly Bulletin* 35, 286-293.

Klein, M. 1997. "The Risk Premium for Evaluating Public Projects", *Oxford Review of Economic Policy* 13(4).

Kopp, R.J. and P.R. Portney. 1999. "Mock Referenda for Intergenerational Decisionmaking", in P.R. Portney and J.P. Weyant (eds.), *Discounting and Intergenerational Equity.* Washington, DC: Resources for the Future, 87-98.

Kula, E. 1984. "Derivation of Social Time Preference Rates for the United States and Canada", *Quarterly Journal of Economics* 99(4), 873-882.

_____. 1985. "An Empirical Investigation on the Social Time-preference Rate for the United Kingdom", *Environment and Planning A* 17, 199-212.

Layard, R., G. Mayraz, and S.J. Nickell. 2007 (revised July 2008). "The Marginal Utility of Income", London School of Economics, *Centre for Economic Performance Discussion Paper 784.*

Lind, R.C. 1990. "Reassessing the Government's Discount Rate Policy in Light of New Theory and Data in a World Economy with High Degree of Capital Mobility", *Journal of Environmental Economics and Management* 18, S8‒S28.

Little, I.M.D. and J.A. Mirrlees. 1974. *Project Appraisal and Planning for Developing Countries.* London: Heinemann Educational Books Ltd.

Mandelbrot, B.B. and R.L. Hudson. 2004. *The (Mis)behaviour of Markets: A Fractal View of Risk, Ruin and Reward.* London: Profile Books.

Marglin, S.A. 1963a. "The Social Rate of Discount and the Optimal Rate of Investment", *Quarterly Journal of Economics* 77(1), 95‒111.

_____. 1963b. "The Opportunity Costs of Public Investment", *Quarterly Journal of Economics* 77, 274‒289.

Mera, K. 1969. "Experimental Determination of Relative Marginal Utilities", *Quarterly Journal of Economics* 83(3), 464‒477.

Newbery, D.M. 1992. *Long Term Discount Rates for the Forest Enterprise*, Department of Applied Economics, Cambridge University, for the UK Forestry Commission, Edinburgh.

OMB. 2003. *Guidelines and Discount Rates for Benefit-Cost Analysis of Federal Programs,* Section 8 and Appendix C (revised January 2003): *Discount Rate for Cost-Effectiveness, Lease Purchase and Related Analyses,* OMB Circular No. A-94, Office of Management and Budget.

Pigou, A.C. 1920. *The Economics of Welfare,* 1952 (4th edition). London: Macmillan.

Portney, P.R. and J.P. Weyant. 1999. *Discounting and Intergenerational Equity.* Washington, DC: Resources for the Future.

Ramsey, F.P. 1928. "A Mathematical Theory of Saving", *Economic Journal* 38, 543‒359.

Ruggeri, G. 1999. "The Marginal Cost of Public Funds in Closed and Small Open Economies", *Fiscal Studies* 20(1), 41‒60.

Schelling, T.C. 1995. "Intergenerational Discounting", *Energy Policy* 23(4/5), 395‒401.

Scott, M.F.G. 1989. *A New View of Economic Growth.* Oxford: Oxford University Press.

Scott, M.F.G. and M. Dowley. 1977. "The Test Rate of Discount and Changes in Base Level Income in the United Kingdom", *Economic Journal* 87, 219‒241.

Spackman, M. 2001. "Risk and the Cost of Risk in the Comparison of Public and Private Financing of Public Services", *Topics 23,* London, National Economic Research Associates.

_____. 2007. "Social Discount Rates for the European Union: An Overview", Chapter 11 in M. Florio (ed.), *Cost-Benefit Analysis and Incentives in Evaluation: The Structural Funds of the European Union.* Cheltenham: Edward Elgar.

Stern, N. 1977. "The Marginal Valuation of Income", in M.J. Artis and A.R. Nobay (eds.), *Studies in Modern Economic Analysis.* Oxford: Basil Blackwell, 209‑258.

_____. 2006. *The Economics of Climate Change: The Stern Review.* Cambridge University Press.

van Ewijk, C. and P.J.G. Tang. 2003. "How to Price the Risk of Public Investment?" Notes and Communications, *De Economist* 151(3), 317‑327.

Wadhwani, S.B. 1999. "The US Stock Market and the Global Economic Crisis", *National Institute Economic Review* 1/99(167), 86‑105.

_____. 2008. "Insight: Policymakers Should Have Known Better", *Financial Times* 16 December.

Warlters, M. and E. Auriol. 2005. "The Marginal Cost of Public Funds in Africa", *World Bank Policy Research Paper* 3679.

Weitzman, M.L. 2008. "On Modeling and Interpreting the Economics of Catastrophic Climate Change", *Review of Economic Statistics*, Final Version, 7 July, at http://www.economics.harvard.edu/faculty/weitzman/files/REStatFINAL.pdf.

Summary of Discussion

Glenn Jenkins: Michael has given a very good review of the alternative approaches to the discounting problem, and he comes down pretty much to saying we should be using the social rate of time preference. That's based on a number of things. First is the idea that with capital mobility, we really just get all our capital from the United States. Well, capital mobility runs both ways. We beggar the neighbour, and the neighbour beggars us.

So the issue is that we'd better not be accepting 3% projects if our neighbours are going to be pulling capital out on what we would have earned 10% on. But there's an issue here that represents a failure to distinguish between stocks and flows. We have a stock equilibrium. How fast the capital moves in a given day is really irrelevant. What matters is the magnitude of the shift from the initial equilibrium to the final equilibrium.

What's very interesting is that if you look at many countries, the proportion of total capital stock that's financed by domestic sources versus foreign sources remains remarkably stable. And countries that try to move it a lot get into deep trouble, as we know in the developing countries. The thing you're thinking is: You've got the cost of funds is the blip on the screen that comes from New York; that's what comes in the front door. But what goes out the back door?

The first project I ever worked on was the lobbyists came to town in Toronto down in the late sixties, when we had a recession, and they wanted to make all the roads out of concrete rather than asphalt. The cement lobby was in town. And they were right as long as the cost of funds was 2% or less. The same thing happened with AECL. For AECL, the heavy-water technology will never dominate the other nuclear technology unless the discount rate is less than the cost of funds of 2.5%.

The other kind of basic unease is that if we have high-return projects available that will pass the criteria of a higher discount rate, why shouldn't we do them? The reality is that policy makers don't spend their time *maximizing* the NPV; they accept projects that have a positive NPV. Using a low discount rate allows the bureaucrats to come up with positive NPVs and ignore higher NPVs. Or ignore higher technologies that perhaps would have a higher return.

Now, I'm going to put some numbers on the board on the gross rate of return on reproducible capital for South Africa for the period 1994-2004. The numbers are calculated from national accounts data. They exclude economic rents in the mining sector and are based upon the best estimates of the replacement cost of the capital stock. The annual rate of return averaged 13.90%. That's the national accounts measure of the rate of return. It's not the stock market rate of return.

During the previous decade, with low commodity prices and all hell was breaking loose in South Africa, the rate of return was still 9.1%. In the decade before that, it was 10.87%, and the decade before that was 13.78%. So the numbers are there – there's no magic. Now I understand, part of the rate of return is a risk premium.

On the social rate of time preference, I realize there's been a tremendous academic consensus. But let's think a little bit about what that concept really is. The first component is called the pure rate of time preference and it's kind of a spiritual number, right? We're not going to be able to tie that one down; we're going to let the government tell us what that is. That's OK. The next one is n, representing the marginal utility of income. I have a little more of a problem with this one.

We're worrying about this generation versus next generation. The issue is that the next generation's going to be better off, so income's not going to be worth as much. So if per capita consumption is growing at 2% a year and you have a value of n equals 2, that says that if we give up $1 today, we have to generate $4 to keep social welfare unchanged.

If that's the way the world works, why is that just a future-generations problem? In fact, people derive the data from looking at the current generation's preferences. My brother always earned about twice as much income as I did. Evidently, our family would have been so much better off if he'd just given me some of his money. I loved my brother; my brother loved me. The worst thing I could ever do was to ask him for a dime or for him to offer me a dime.

Is that the way society works? And yet we blatantly say that it's an academically accepted principle. It doesn't make any sense to me as a way to produce a social-welfare improvement, because there'd be blood in the street if we even tried it. So Mike, what is the basis of it?

The other thing is that if you want to use an STP, you've got to use a shadow price. But with respect, everyone backs off that because it's complicated. Also, it's never quite clear from the discussion whether it's a shadow price of investment or a shadow price of the cost of raising funds? Are we really talking about the welfare cost of taxation, or are we talking about the shadow price of investment?

It does pose a problem because Michael is absolutely right in that it's a shadow price of public expenditure. Therefore, we've got to apply it to the nurses' salaries as well as to the investment in a road. So a nurse's marginal product has to be 30 to 40% more than her wage rate before we are willing to hire her. That makes sense if you're looking at the cost of taxation. But it also applies to the same things that we've raised money for, for general expenditure.

All I'm saying is that I worry about some of the problems that arise in thinking that the social rate of time preference as something that is generally accepted and is based on good economics. I have considerable trouble with that.

Also, Michael states in his paper that using a higher discount rate than the STP rate would create a bias towards private-sector finance. That's really because he is applying it to the after-financing cash flows. If you apply an economic discount rate to the fundamental cash flows, that is not a bias.

I guess the bottom line is, in looking at this paper, where Michael comes out, he's in the right direction in saying: We use an approximation of the government borrowing rate, and then we're going to add something to it. But because the government borrowing rate is a reflection of this spiritual number I feel much more comfortable starting the other way around, starting from actually observable data and then cutting it down to some sort of consensus.

Michael Spackman: On the issue of whether using the STP rate ignores high return investments, the answer is they haven't been ignored. A little while ago, in a World Bank paper, a professor of International Economics at Harvard produced a very fine paper on climate change but used a discount rate of 10% representing the rate of return in the private sector. Arrow was invited to comment and used a very magisterial riposte. He made the point that the higher taxes used to finance a project displace consumption rather than investment, so the high rate of return on investment is irrelevant. On the issue of the elasticity of the marginal utility of consumption, it is a concept that people see in different ways. It isn't terribly controversial. The issue of whether there should be an altruistic element to it is an interesting one on which people differ. Certainly, during all my time in the Treasury in the United Kingdom we were absolutely clear that there was no altruism element in that particular variable at all. We were strictly concerned with what was the marginal utility that someone with a higher income got relative to someone with a lower income. There are all sorts of ways that you can approach it, some with more limitations than others.

Richard Leon and others have recently come out with using the happiness status data being collected around the world. So you've got some cross-sectional data that are looking at different countries. And they've come up with the same sort of number of about 1.4 or something like that. It's simply a piece of positive economics. If different communities on different incomes at a point in time can be treated as different generations with different incomes at different points of time, we can use the number in calculating the STP.

On the appropriate shadow price, yes, it's the shadow price for public expenditures, for the raising of funds. That's the only one that makes any sense to me. I don't think the shadow price of investment displaced is worth bothering about.

Frank Milne: Questions and statements from the floor.

Jack Gibbons: I have a question for Michael. You're talking about a discount rate for governments to apply to public projects. I'm wondering, would you think the government should apply different discount rates to different public-sector projects depending on the risk? That is, should riskier projects have a higher discount rate than less risky projects? I ask this question because it's a very real question right here in Ontario. I want to give you an example.

We have an agency called the Ontario Power Authority. It's a public agency, and it's responsible for long-term planning of our electricity sector and selecting the generation mix. To meet our needs, there are many generation options. There's nuclear, there's water, there's wind, there's solar, there's hydroelectric. And the Ontario Power Authority, in their analysis, is proposing to use the same discount rate for all of these projects, all these generation options.

It's my view that some of these generation options have much higher risks than others, much higher technological risks. Some projects are much more likely to go over budget than others, and for some, there's a much higher probability that they actually won't work or won't achieve the capacity utilization factors that their proponents promised.

So I'm wondering, should the Ontario Power Authority be using a risk-adjusted discount rate, and for the higher-risk projects require a higher return on capital and a lower return on capital on the lower-risk projects?

Michael Spackman: "No" would be my answer. I mentioned the fast-meter reactors as one example. Sure, big projects have a terrible history. But the history of some big projects is that they turn out just fine. Attention to what the risks are on nuclear versus coal, solar or wind is profoundly important, probably more important than fretting about the discount rate. And it is conceivable that sometimes you have a particular kind of risk that does have a sort of exponential form. A capital overrun wouldn't have this form, it seems to me. A capital overrun risk should be handled by adjusting the cost estimates.

The UK Treasury actually commissioned some work some while ago to produce default factors for certain categories of investments, and the ones you mentioned would fit into some particular category. These factors could be 30% or 40% or even more for some novel, big IT project, and they would be applied to the initial estimate of capital costs. And there is good evidence that the capital costs are reliable.

It's just possible, though, that the private sector does do this in a big way, even setting aside all the systematic risk, the CAPM stuff, the private sector also generally adds on a premium for risk because their risks are often marketing risks. A new project, a new product – you're not quite sure when its lifetime's going to end. A lot of the risks are such that they get more and more down side as time goes on. And it seems to me quite reasonable to build that into a discount rate in the private sector.

But in the public sector, on the whole, risks don't follow that sort of form. If they do, I see nothing wrong with having an extra component on the discount rate. But it must be very clearly ascribed to some particular form of risk that you in the Ministry of Finance or Treasury feel is a reasonable adjustment for the likely downside risk of this particular technology. The basic discount rate, though, should be the same; I'd be with the Ontario power board on that.

Jack Gibbons: So if I've heard you right, then, you're not against them having a risk-adjusted rate of return, but there are other ways to deal with it?

Michael Spackman: Yes, if I had to say yes or no, I would be against building risk into the rate of return. What I'm saying is that they should certainly adjust for risk. There are some risks that maybe do have an exponential form, in which case a specific extra adjustment of that kind might be appropriate. But for *most* risks, it seems to me, in these sorts of technologies, they're not of that form; they're much more in terms of – either they simply don't deliver, or they simply go 300% over costs or time.

Christopher Shugart: I agree with Michael. I'll just add one thing that since you're clearly not talking about systematic risk, you're talking about downside risk of some sort. I really think it's much more transparent to deal with all of these new cash flows, even if it's an exponential, you can see what's going on if you model it and do a Monte Carlo simulation, then use the same discount rate. To me, it's much more transparent, it shows you what is really going on in the risks, and you can understand it and deal with it better that way. I would reserve the contentious question, which will come up again and again, as what to do with the zero-main, non-diversifiable, systematic risks, but those aren't the kind you're talking about. So I would deal with them in the cash flows.

Jack Gibbons: I hear you. Maybe that's another way of doing it. But I want to know whether you've got a fundamental theoretical objection to what I'm proposing. What I'm proposing my way, and I think there's a problem with yours is, I think in your paper you talked about optimism bias. And here in Ontario, the public sector is making decisions about generation mix for 50 years. And there's a profound optimism bias. My friend from the C.D. Howe Institute said there couldn't be optimism bias in the public sector because those people would be fired. But that doesn't happen in Ontario. They've had failure after failure for 50 years, and they've never learned. And they're as optimistic now as they were in the 1950s, when they said nuclear would be too cheap to meter.

So here we have upcoming hearings before the Ontario Energy Board as a regulator. They'll have the optimist advocates from the public sector saying: Everything's going to be fine in the future. They'll have me saying: You should learn from history. And how do they judge? Whose words do they take? I think it would be much more transparent to use the information about required rates of return in the market. Wall Street will tell you that the capital markets demand a higher return on capital for nuclear projects versus hydroelectric. And there's some real data that can be taken there. I'm trying to be practical, and get market data to support my contention as opposed to being just a boring expert relying on paper studies and different views of optimism.

Michael Spackman: I think Chris and I are both pro-transparency. Unfortunately, as soon as you push into this, you lose transparency. A high rate is wanted by all three alternatives to nuclear because of fiscal risks, mainly. This is getting into another, different sort of field.

Part II

Theoretical Approaches to the Discounting of Benefits and Costs

3

Toward a Reconciliation of Alternative Views on the Social Discount Rate

David F. Burgess

Introduction

The appropriate discount rate for evaluating public investment decisions has been a matter of heated debate for over 40 years. The central focus of this conference – the appropriate discount rate for evaluating public private partnerships (PPPs) – provides a convenient opportunity to review the issues surrounding the determination of the social discount rate and to consider its relevance for evaluating projects undertaken in the private sector under government contract or under regulatory approval. My plan in this paper is first to examine three criteria for project assessment that are prominent in the literature and, in the process, remove some of the divergence in viewpoint. This would seem to be a useful exercise in light of the remarkably wide range of opinion about the appropriate numerical value for the social discount rate that exists among economists who are generally regarded as experts in the field.[1] Then, in

---

[1]Weitzman (2001) asked 50 acknowledged experts (after explaining that all benefits and costs had been converted into consumption equivalent real dollars for that year): "What real interest rate do you think should be used to discount the (expected) benefits and costs of projects being proposed to mitigate the possible effects of global climate change?" He received responses ranging from 0% to 15%.

the penultimate section, I will draw some inferences about the appropriate discount rate for evaluating PPPs. I conclude by emphasizing the importance of ensuring that the social discount rate reflects the economic opportunity cost of capital.

The SOC Criterion

The first criterion – associated with Harberger (1972) and Sandmo and Dreze (1971) – is that the appropriate social discount rate should reflect the rate of return forgone in the private sector when resources are withdrawn from the capital market to fund the project. In a closed economy, the funding for any project must come at the expense of consumption or investment. Taxes and other distortions drive a wedge between the marginal rate of productivity of capital and the marginal rate of return to those who own the capital. The social discount rate is a weighted average of the marginal rate of productivity of investment in new capital and the marginal rate of time preference (consumption rate of interest), with the weights reflecting the proportions of funding drawn from investment and consumption, respectively. Thus, if ρ represents the marginal rate of productivity of capital, r represents the consumption rate of interest, and α represents the proportion of funding that comes at the expense of investment, the social discount rate is

$$SDR = (1-\alpha)\, r + \alpha\, \rho = w$$

According to this view, the social discount rate is unique and common to all projects undertaken in the public sector. Even if a proposed project is to be financed by a special tax, the revenue raised could be used to pay down the debt instead of funding the project, so the marginal source of funding for all projects is the capital market. It should also be emphasized that the social discount rate does not depend upon whether the project is undertaken by a government agency or by a firm in the private sector. The funding for the project has the same economic opportunity cost in either case.

There is little disagreement that in a closed economy, a dollar of funding from the capital market will come mostly at the expense of investment because investment is more interest rate sensitive than consumption.[2] If the marginal rate of productivity of capital is well approximated by the pre-tax rate of return to capital in place, the social discount rate is in the order of 10% for an economy that is closed to international borrowing and lending.[3]

So far, nothing has been said about risk. Assuming that individuals are risk-averse, if there are efficient markets for hedging risk and if all risk is diversifiable, the analysis is perfectly valid. If some risks are not diversifiable, then part of the pre-tax (and after-tax) rate of return will reflect a premium for bearing risk. Whether this premium should be netted out in determining the appropriate social discount rate depends upon whether the government can pool and spread risk so as to eliminate it. If the government's ability to pool and spread risk is no better than the private sector's, there is no justification for adjusting the rate of return forgone in the private sector to arrive at a lower social discount rate.

If the economy is well integrated into the international capital market, a significant proportion of funding will come from abroad as net exports are displaced instead of investment or consumption. The social discount rate then becomes a weighted average of ρ, r, and the marginal cost of incremental funding from abroad. The cost of incremental foreign funding – the *marginal* cost – is difficult to estimate because the rate of return that foreign savers demand to provide additional funding may depend upon the country's net indebtedness. A plausible estimate of the *average* cost of foreign funding for OECD countries is in the order of 5%. It represents the rate of return that accrues to foreign investors net of taxes paid to host governments. However, despite an increasingly integrated global capital market, countries continue to exhibit "home bias" in the investment of their saving. The famous Feldstein-Horioka

---

[2]Estimates of the elasticity of demand for investment with respect to the cost of capital are typically in the range of -1.0, whereas estimates of the compensated elasticity of supply of saving to the rate of return are in the range of 0.2. The debt that is issued to finance the project is perceived as net wealth by the private sector. Interest payments on the debt are financed by revenue from the project or by a lump sum tax increase that is more than offset by the project's benefits.

[3]Under competitive conditions and constant returns to scale, the pre-tax rate of return to capital in place will equal the marginal rate of return on investment, but if there is monopoly power in product markets and increasing returns to scale, this equality will not hold. The pre-tax rate of return may overstate or understate the marginal rate of return depending upon whether there is pure monopoly or monopolistic competition.

(1980) puzzle has inspired many studies that report cross-country regressions of national investment rates on national saving rates, and the results continue to suggest that at least half of an exogenous increase in national saving will finance investment within the country rather than investment and consumption elsewhere (see, e.g., Helliwell, 1998). This leads to the conclusion that the social discount rate for most OECD countries must be in the order of 7.5% and perhaps even higher.

Thus, according to the social opportunity cost (SOC) criterion, the appropriate way to evaluate a project, given estimates of the constant dollar values of expected benefits and costs at various dates, $\{Bt\}$ (measured by willingness to pay) and $\{Ct\}$ (assumed to reflect real resource costs), is to discount them at the SOC rate. A project is judged as worthwhile provided that

$$\sum (Bt-Ct)/(1+w)^t > 0 \qquad (1)$$

High discount rates – certainly discount rates of 7.5% or more – make benefits and costs that occur in 50 years almost insignificant in present value terms. If we care about future generations, should we abandon the conceptual framework behind the SOC criterion and look for alternative approaches? Certainly we should question the methodology if we have reason to believe that it is flawed in some way, but to abandon it because we don't like what it implies about the importance of distant benefits and costs is clearly wrong.

The Shadow Price Algorithm

The second criterion that is prominent in the literature is the shadow price algorithm first proposed by Eckstein (1957), and refined and extended by Marglin (1963), Feldstein (1972), Bradford (1975), and Lind (1982). This approach claims that a weighted average discount rate commits an aggregation error by combining two distinct prices – the price of future consumption in terms of current consumption and the price of investment in terms of consumption – into one discount rate. The appropriate way to evaluate a project is to convert its constant dollar values of costs and benefits into "consumption equivalents" by shadow pricing all investment displaced or induced by the project and then discounting these values at the social rate of time preference, or STP rate.

David F. Burgess

The STP rate has been interpreted as both a positive and a normative concept. I will restrict attention to the positive interpretation that the STP rate is the consumption rate of interest. In other words, the STP rate reflects the rate at which individuals are willing to trade present for future consumption rather than the policy-maker's subjective valuation of the importance of future consumption.[4]

Thus, given estimates of a project's benefits (measured by willingness to pay) and costs (project expenditures) at various dates, the first step is to convert these values into their consumption equivalent. No shadow pricing is required if the benefits will be "fully consumed" when they are produced, but for many projects, the benefits will induce the private sector to alter its inter-temporal consumption plan. For example, if the benefits are marketable, there is reason to believe that the private sector will treat the benefits as income and respond by saving and investing a portion. The portion invested must be multiplied by the "shadow price of capital" to convert it into units of consumption. Similarly, the project's costs must be converted into their consumption equivalent by determining the proportion of funding that displaces investment.

Let β represent the proportion of a dollar's worth of benefits that are saved, and let α represent the proportion of a dollar's worth of costs that displace investment. Also, let SPC represent the shadow price of capital, which is the present value of the stream of consumption that a dollar of private investment would generate, discounting at the STP rate. These parameters may be time-dependent, but suppose they are not. If the project's benefits in period t are worth Bt, the consumption equivalent value of benefits in period t is $(1-\beta + \beta\,SPC)\,Bt$, and if the project's costs in period t are Ct, the consumption equivalent value of costs in period t is $(1-\alpha + \alpha\,SPC)\,Ct$.

The project is worth doing according to the shadow price algorithm if the stream of consumption that the project induces is more valuable than the stream of consumption that is forgone in financing the project. Formally, a worthwhile project satisfies

$$\sum[(1-\beta + \beta\,SPC)\,Bt - (1-\alpha + \alpha\,SPC)\,Ct]/(1+r)^t > 0 \qquad (2)$$

---

[4]The STP rate will reflect the consumption rate of interest only if all individuals are savers rather than borrowers and face the same marginal tax rate on capital income. Otherwise, there will be aggregation errors in using the STP rate to evaluate multi-period benefits and costs.

Proponents of the shadow price algorithm argue that future benefits receive the proper weight (unlike the SOC criterion) because they are discounted at a rate that reflects society's willingness to trade present for future consumption. At the same time, the rate of return on any private investment that is displaced in financing the project, or induced by the project itself, is taken into account by applying the appropriate shadow price. Aggregation errors in using a "weighted average" discount to reflect both time preference and opportunity cost are thereby avoided. For these reasons, the shadow price algorithm seems to have become the criterion of choice among academic experts.[5]

Two further observations are worth making at this point. First, the shadow price algorithm allows projects to be financed in different ways. If different methods of financing have different displacement effects, a project with a given stream of benefits and costs will be judged differently depending upon how it is financed. For example, if consumption taxes are used to finance the project, α might be close to zero, whereas if the project is debt-financed, α will reflect the interest responsiveness of investment versus saving and be close to one. Raising (lump sum) taxes to finance the project will draw a greater proportion of funding from consumption than debt financing if the private sector fails to discount the future tax liability associated with the debt. If α is higher under debt financing than under tax financing, a project that fails to pass muster under debt financing might be acceptable under tax financing. A basic tenet of the SOC criterion — that the capital market is the marginal source of funds for all projects — is rejected by proponents of the shadow price algorithm.

Second, a well-known paper by Sjaastad and Wisecarver (1977) showed that the shadow price algorithm and the SOC criterion produce identical results for a project with an initial cost C that generates a perpetual stream of benefits worth B. However, these authors implicitly assumed that the project's benefits are treated as income and that they are fully anticipated. In fact, the shadow price algorithm, as it is conventionally applied, assumes that the private sector is myopic with respect to the project's costs as well as its benefits.

For example, consider a project with initial cost C that generates a stream of benefits worth B beginning in period T and continuing

---

[5]Weitzman (2001) takes it as a given that the appropriate procedure is to convert benefits and costs into consumption equivalents before discounting. The major textbooks also recommend the shadow price algorithm.

David F. Burgess

thereafter. The SOC criterion judges the project as worthwhile if $-C + B/\rho(1+\rho)^{T-1} > 0$. Benefits are treated as income and discounted at the SOC rate, which exceeds the STP rate that reflects the private sector's willingness to trade present for future consumption.

The shadow price algorithm judges the project as worthwhile if $-C(\rho/r) + B\ (\rho/r)/r\ (1+r)^{T-1} > 0$. The project is debt-financed and crowds out private investment, dollar for dollar, if ρ is exogenous. The shadow price of capital is ρ/r if the private sector consumes the annuity value of wealth, so the first term represents the present value of consumption displaced in financing the project.[6] The second term is the present value of the stream of consumption that the project generates. Since the project's benefits are treated as income, each dollar of project benefit is a dollar of government revenue that will be injected into the capital market and "crowd in" private investment, dollar for dollar. The consumption equivalent value of each dollar of project benefit is therefore ρ/r dollars.[7]

It is easy to see that the SOC criterion is more stringent than the shadow price algorithm. The project must have an internal rate of return of ρ to be worthwhile, whereas the shadow price algorithm requires that the internal rate of return be at least r. To appreciate the extent of the divergence, assume that the SOC rate $\rho=.1$, the STP rate $r=.03$, and the project delivers benefits beginning in 50 years, so $T=50$. The SOC criterion would judge the project as worthwhile provided that $B/C > 10.6$, whereas the shadow price algorithm would judge the project as worthwhile provided that $B/C > .128$. Thus, if the project costs $1 billion today, it would be worthwhile, according to the SOC criterion, if annual benefits beginning in 50 years are worth $10.6 billion or more. According to the shadow price algorithm, the annual benefits would have to exceed just $128 million.

---

[6]The present value calculation is performed at discount rate r, reflecting the rate at which the representative agent is willing to trade present for future consumption. A dollar of investment generates ρ dollars of income in perpetuity. This represents ρ dollars of consumption if individuals consume the annuity value of wealth. The present value of the consumption forgone is therefore ρ/r.

[7]In this formulation, project benefits coincide with government revenue from the sale of the project's output. This revenue is injected into the capital market, where it impacts the private sector by an equal amount per dollar, but opposite in sign, to the financing.

Examples like this have led many to reject the SOC criterion on the grounds that it is biased against projects with deferred benefits and therefore insensitive to the well-being of future generations.

The MCF Criterion

The third criterion is the marginal cost of funds (MCF) criterion recently proposed by Liu (2003) and Liu, Rettenmaier, and Saving (2004). The MCF criterion is an extension to a multi-period context of the static welfare criterion for worthwhile public expenditure in a tax-distorted economy. Thus, for a project with costs $C0$ and benefits $B0$ occurring in the same period, the project is worthwhile provided that $B0 > MCF.C0$, where MCF is the marginal cost of raising a dollar of funds to finance the project.[8] If we extend this criterion to a multi-period context and assume that the benefits (measured by willingness to pay) are fully consumed while the costs are incurred only in the initial period, we have the criterion

$$\sum Bt/(1+r)^t - MCF.C0 \qquad (3)$$

The project is worthwhile according to the MCF criterion if the present value of its benefits discounted at the STP rate (equal to the consumption rate of interest) exceeds the project's expenditure requirements, multiplied by the marginal cost of raising a dollar of funds to finance the project.

If we generalize to projects with deferred costs and with benefits that are not fully consumed, the MCF criterion becomes

$$\sum Bt/(1+r)^t - MCF \sum [Ct-IRt]/(1+\rho)^t \qquad (4)$$

Notice that deferred costs are discounted at the SOC rate ρ rather than the STP rate r. This is because the costs are incurred by government on behalf of the private sector. Even if the government can borrow at rate r to finance the project (e.g., when interest on government debt is tax-exempt), each dollar of debt will crowd out a dollar of private investment

---

[8]See, for example, Wildasin (1984). Note that according to this interpretation the MCF does not equal one plus the marginal excess burden.

David F. Burgess

that earns a rate of return of ρ. Therefore, each dollar of project expenditure that is deferred for a period has a present value cost of $1/(1+\rho)$ dollars. It is the economic opportunity cost of capital that is relevant for project analysis, not the financial cost of capital.

In addition, if the project's benefits are not fully consumed, it will affect the private sector's inter-temporal consumption plan and thereby affect the amount of capital income tax revenue collected at the pre-existing tax rate. IRt represents the "indirect revenue effect" of the project in period t.

Proponents of the MCF criterion claim that both the SOC criterion and the shadow price algorithm are flawed. The SOC criterion expressed in equation (1) is flawed because it discounts benefits at too high a rate (ρ rather than r), because it ignores indirect revenue effects, and because it assumes that the marginal cost of funds is unity for a lump sum tax. The shadow price algorithm expressed in equation (2) is flawed – even for projects whose benefits are fully consumed (i.e., no indirect revenue effects) – because it discounts costs at the STP rate rather than at the SOC rate and because it measures the consumption equivalent value of a dollar of project costs incorrectly (by failing to recognize that the MCF for a lump sum tax exceeds one). According to the MCF criterion, when the government spends a dollar on a project, it must finance the spending by increasing lump sum taxes either now or later. Whenever taxes are increased, part of the tax increase will reduce saving and capital income tax revenue in subsequent periods, so a dollar increase in lump sum taxes will raise less than a dollar of revenue.

Toward a Reconciliation

The purpose of this section is to attempt to reconcile at least some of the divergence in viewpoint about the appropriate social discount rate that is apparent in these three criteria. Part of the problem reflects a misunderstanding about what is being assumed about the nature of the benefits – whether they are fully consumed or treated as income. But there are also differences in assumptions about the degree of foresight of the private sector with respect to the project and the cost of implementing it.

I will compare one criterion with another under two different assumptions about the project's benefits: when the benefits of the project are fully consumed and when the benefits are treated as income. I begin by comparing the shadow price algorithm to the MCF criterion when the benefits are fully consumed, then compare the SOC criterion to the MCF criterion and the shadow price algorithm when the benefits are treated as income, and finally compare the SOC criterion to the MCF criterion when the benefits are fully consumed. The ordering that I have chosen may appear somewhat arbitrary, but it yields four propositions that I think are useful. It can be shown that the MCF criterion correctly identifies all welfare-improving projects, so if the SOC criterion and the shadow pricing algorithm differ from the MCF criterion, they fail to meet this standard (see Liu, 2003; and Burgess, 2008).

Shadow Price Algorithm versus MCF Criterion When Benefits Are Fully Consumed

If the project's benefits are fully consumed, it has no impact on the private sector's behaviour. Since the project yields no revenue, it must be financed by a tax increase. Assume the tax is a lump sum tax that does not exacerbate existing distortions. The shadow price algorithm judges the project to be worthwhile if

$$\sum Bt/(1+r)^t - \sum Ct(1-\alpha+\alpha\ SPC)/(1+r)^t > 0 \qquad (5)$$

Each dollar of project expenditure is financed by an equal dollar increase in taxes, results in a proportion α of project expenditure displacing investment. Each dollar of private investment displaced has a consumption equivalent value of ρ/r if the private sector consumes the annuity value of wealth, so $SPC=\rho/r$.

By comparison, the MCF criterion judges the project to be worthwhile if

$$\sum Bt/(1+r)^t - MCF \sum Ct/(1+\rho)^t > 0 \qquad (6)$$

Notice that since the benefits are fully consumed, there are no indirect revenue effects, so equation (4) simplifies to equation (6). If the project is financed by lump sum taxes, the costs must be multiplied by the MCF for a lump sum tax. The MCF is defined as the increase in lump sum tax divided by the present value of the increase in tax revenue (discounted at the SOC rate). In a model in which the private sector consumes the annuity value of wealth, the MCF for a lump sum tax is equal to $\rho(1+r)/r(1+\rho)$.[9]

A comparison of the two criteria reveals that while they both treat the benefit stream in the same way − benefits are discounted at the STP rate − the shadow price algorithm overstates the consumption equivalent value of the costs, and it does this for two reasons. First, it fails to recognize that a lump sum tax creates an excess burden when there is a capital income tax in place. This is because a lump sum tax increase in period t will reduce saving and capital income tax revenue in subsequent periods. The result is that financing a dollar of project expenditure will require more than a dollar increase in lump sum taxes. By understating the required tax increase, the shadow price algorithm understates the amount of consumption displaced per dollar of project expenditure and thereby overstates the amount of private investment displaced.[10] Second, the shadow price algorithm discounts deferred costs at the STP rate rather than at the SOC rate (which reflects the economic opportunity cost of capital). Essentially, it treats the private sector as myopic with respect to the project's costs, as if the project entailed a sequence of un-anticipated expenditures requiring equal-dollar lump sum tax increases. In contrast, the MCF criterion assumes that the private sector has the same foresight as the planner.

The consequence of these differences is the following: *For projects whose benefits are fully consumed, the shadow price algorithm is more stringent than the MCF criterion. The MCF criterion correctly identifies all welfare-improving projects, whereas the shadow price algorithm is sufficient, but not necessary, for a welfare improvement.*

---

[9]The MCF is the ratio of the increase in lump sum taxes to the increase in the present value of tax revenue. Formally, $MCF = 1/[1-\alpha\tau\rho/(1+\rho)]$, where α represents the marginal propensity to save. If individuals consume the annuity value of wealth, α will equal $r/(1+r)$, which produces the result. See Burgess (2008).

[10]If the funds for the project are obtained by increasing lump sum taxes in an economy in which individuals consume the annuity value of wealth, then $\alpha=1/(1+r)$. The consumption equivalent value of a dollar of expenditure is therefore $r/(1+r)+\rho/r(1+r)$. On the other hand, the MCF for a lump sum tax is $\rho(1+r)/r(1+\rho)$. It is easy to show that when $\alpha=1/(1+r)$, $1-\alpha+\alpha\,\rho/r >MCF$.

SOC Criterion versus MCF Criterion When Benefits Are Treated as Income

The SOC criterion for a project whose benefits are treated as income is to discount benefits and costs at the SOC rate. In general, the SOC rate will be a weighted average of ρ and r, but if the pre-tax rate of return is exogenous, each dollar of funding will displace a dollar of private investment, so the SOC rate is just ρ. According to the SOC criterion, when $w = \rho$ in equation (1), the project is worthwhile if

$$\sum (Bt\text{-}Ct)/(1+\rho)^t > 0 \qquad (7)$$

In words, the project must have an internal rate of return at least equal to the rate of return forgone in the private sector when resources are withdrawn from the capital market to fund the project.

By comparison, the MCF criterion requires that benefits be discounted at the after-tax rate of return r, and costs minus indirect revenue effects be discounted at the pre-tax rate of return ρ, but multiplied by the marginal cost of funds. The project is worthwhile if

$$\sum Bt/(1+r)^t - MCF \sum [Ct\text{-}IRt]/(1+\rho)^t > 0 \qquad (8)$$

Since the benefits are treated as income, the project will have indirect revenue effects when applying the MCF criterion because its benchmark is a project whose benefits are fully consumed. Costs minus indirect revenue effects must be discounted at the SOC rate because the SOC rate represents the economic opportunity cost of capital.

Proponents of the MCF criterion claim that the SOC criterion is flawed for three reasons: it discounts benefits at too high a rate (ρ rather than r); it fails to incorporate indirect revenue effects; and it fails to recognize that the marginal cost of funds for a lump sum tax exceeds one when there is a pre-existing capital income tax. These claims are misguided. What is not appreciated is that the SOC criterion takes as its benchmark a project whose benefits are equivalent to income. There are no indirect revenue effects to take into account because indirect revenue effects reflect the *compensated* impact of the project on capital income tax revenue rather than the uncompensated impact. Moreover, it is appropriate to discount benefits at the SOC rate because benefits are treated as income and do not necessarily represent net increments to consumption. Finally, there is no need to multiply project expenditures by the marginal cost of funds because a dollar of financing has the same effect on capital income tax revenue as a dollar of project benefits.

The indirect revenue effects that enter into the MCF criterion measure the *uncompensated* impact of the project on capital income tax revenue. If the project's benefits are equivalent to income, the indirect revenue effects will be equal to the impact of a sequence of lump sum transfers equal to the private sector's willingness to pay for the project's benefits. If this substitution is made in the MCF criterion, it simplifies to the SOC criterion (see Burgess, 2008).

In terms of implementation, the SOC criterion has an advantage over the MCF criterion because it is unnecessary to estimate indirect revenue effects, and it is also unnecessary to estimate the marginal cost of funds. While the example of an exogenous pre-tax rate of return makes the calculation of the weighted average discount rate trivial, in the more general case, all that is necessary to implement the SOC criterion is estimates of the proportions of capital market funding that are drawn from investment and consumption. These proportions are project-independent.

To summarize, we have the following result: *For projects whose benefits are equivalent to income, there are indirect revenue effects to take into account in applying the MCF criterion. If these indirect revenue effects are incorporated, the MCF criterion is equivalent to the SOC criterion. Both criteria correctly identify all welfare-improving projects.*

Shadow Price Algorithm versus SOC Criterion When Benefits Are Treated as Income

Since the SOC criterion is equivalent to the MCF criterion when the project's benefits are treated as income, it is only necessary to compare the shadow price algorithm with the SOC criterion in this situation.

When the benefits are treated as income, each dollar of benefits is converted into its consumption equivalent by multiplying by $1-\beta + \beta SPC$ where β represents the marginal propensity to save. If the project is tax-financed, each dollar of project expenditure is converted into its consumption equivalent by multiplying by this same conversion factor. The result is the Arrow-Bradford rule: A project whose benefits are equivalent to income will be worthwhile if its benefits minus its costs are positive when discounted at the STP rate. This criterion is obviously less stringent than the SOC criterion (and its MCF equivalent).

What if the project was debt-financed? Under perfect foresight, tax and debt financing would have the same displacement effects, but the shadow price algorithm treats the private sector as myopic. Under debt financing, each dollar of project expenditure displaces a dollar of private investment and therefore has a greater consumption equivalent cost than under tax financing.

The implication of this lack of foresight by the private sector is the following: *For projects whose benefits are equivalent to income, the shadow price algorithm may be more or less stringent than the SOC criterion depending upon how the project is financed. Therefore, satisfying the shadow price algorithm is neither necessary nor sufficient to ensure a welfare improvement.*

SOC Criterion versus MCF Criterion When Benefits Are Fully Consumed

Finally, let us return to the case where the project's benefits are fully consumed and compare the SOC criterion to the MCF criterion. Proponents of the MCF criterion claim that the SOC criterion is flawed because it discounts benefits at too high a rate (ρ rather than r), and while it correctly discounts costs at the SOC rate, it fails to multiply costs by the marginal cost of funds. These claims are correct if the practitioners of the SOC criterion fail to incorporate indirect revenue effects. However, since the benchmark for the SOC criterion is a project whose benefits are equivalent to income, there will be indirect revenue effects to take into account when the project's benefits are fully consumed. The SOC criterion treats the capital market as the marginal source of funds for all projects, but if a project's benefits are fully consumed, it will generate no revenue (either from the sale of the output or from the impact of the project on capital income tax revenue). This must be taken into account in applying the SOC criterion. The SOC criterion for a worthwhile project whose benefits are fully consumed becomes

$$\sum (Bt - Ct + IRt^c)/(1+\rho)^t > 0 \tag{9}$$

Here IRt^c measures the *compensated* effect of the project on capital income tax revenue in period t. This is the effect on capital income tax revenue of the project, accompanied by a sequence of lump sum tax increases equal to the private sector's willingness to pay for the project.

Once the indirect revenue effects are properly accounted for, the SOC criterion is equivalent to the standard MCF criterion expressed in equation (5)[11]

$$\sum Bt/(1+r)^t - MCF \sum Ct /(1+\rho)^t \qquad (6)$$

Therefore, we can conclude the following: *For projects whose benefits are fully consumed, there are indirect revenue effects to take into account in applying the SOC criterion. Once these indirect revenue effects are incorporated, the SOC criterion is equivalent to the MCF criterion. Both criteria correctly identify all welfare-improving projects.*

When the project's benefits are fully consumed, the MCF criterion has an implementation advantage over the SOC criterion because there is no need to incorporate indirect revenue effects. Benefits are discounted at the STP rate, and costs are discounted at the SOC rate, but costs are multiplied by the MCF, which is project-independent.

However, I would argue that situations where a project's benefits are fully consumed are rare.[12] Space exploration might be an example. Whatever the benefits of space exploration are, do these benefits affect the private sector's inter-temporal consumption plan in any predictable way? More precisely, if the *timing* of the benefits were altered, would this affect the private sector's inter-temporal consumption plan in any predictable way? The answer is far from clear, but perhaps this simply indicates that the benefits of space exploration are difficult to conceptualize. Individuals might derive satisfaction from knowing that space exploration is going on and therefore be willing to sacrifice real income to have it continue. The benefits are nebulous — satisfying one's intellectual curiosity about outer space, or serving as a symbol of national pride in scientific achievement — and perhaps best represented

---

[11]See Burgess (2008). Harberger (1997) states that if the project does not generate enough revenue to pay for its costs, both benefits and costs should be multiplied by "the shadow price of fiscal funds" whenever raising revenue causes an excess burden. However, this will not suffice to eliminate the difference between the SOC criterion and the MCF criterion because benefits are discounted at the SOC rate using the SOC criterion, not the STP rate.

[12]Larson (1993) maintains that if a project induces no change whatsoever in an individual's behaviour, it cannot be of significant value to the individual.

by project expenditures rather than by any tangible output, such as new energy sources or improved communication systems.[13]

Be that as it may, I would argue that most projects fit into the category of having benefits that are treated as income. It is reasonable to assume that projects with marketable benefits are treated as income because the project substitutes for goods or services that the private sector might otherwise produce. Even for projects whose benefits are not marketable, as in the case of infrastructure projects, like flood control, or projects that improve the environment, such as cleaner air or water, individuals may respond by reducing their spending on defensive measures like air purifiers or water filters. To this extent, these projects produce marketable benefits that are equivalent to income. In each of these situations, the standard SOC criterion is appropriate.

Evaluating Projects with Intergenerational Benefits

So far, I have restricted attention to what can be described as intra-generational projects: those who incur the costs also enjoy the benefits, or treat the well-being of those who enjoy the benefits as their own. If the benefits accrue to future generations to whom the current generation is unwilling to make bequests, the justification for discounting these benefits at the STP rate (whether or not it reflects the rate at which individuals currently living are willing to defer current consumption for future consumption) depends upon a particular social welfare function that not everyone would accept. The advantage of both the SOC criterion and the MCF criterion is that they do not depend upon intergenerational comparisons of utility. Instead, they require that the Kaldor-Hicks compensation test be passed before approving any project: it must be possible for everyone to be at least as well off with the project as without it, and at least someone must be better off.

If we apply the shadow price algorithm to projects whose benefits are intergenerational, we introduce the possibility that a project satisfies the algorithm but fails to satisfy the Kaldor-Hicks compensation test. This means that by redistributing income, everyone could be made better off

---

[13]If the benefits of space exploration are in the nature of new energy sources or improved communications systems, these benefits are marketable and better regarded as equivalent to income than being fully consumed.

David F. Burgess

without the project than they would be if the project were undertaken. Even if we deem the Kaldor-Hicks compensation test to be unnecessary for a social welfare improvement (because we are prepared to burden ourselves to improve the well-being of future generations), by approving a project that satisfies the shadow price algorithm while failing the Kaldor-Hicks compensation test, we would be improving the well-being of future generations at greater cost to ourselves than is necessary.

To emphasize these points, let us consider a project that costs $C0$ and yields benefits worth $B1$ to the next young generation, who will treat the benefits as income. Individuals live for two periods: working in the first period and consuming principal plus interest on their saving in the second. They care about their own well-being and about the well-being of the next generation, but they are not prepared to sacrifice their well-being to improve the well-being of the next generation, who is expected to be at least as well off. A dollar of saving by the young generation that is invested in the private sector yields a pre-tax return of $1+\rho$ dollars in old age and an after-tax return of $1+r$ dollars.

According to the SOC criterion, the project is worthwhile provided that

$$B1/(1+\rho) -C0>0 \qquad\qquad (10)$$

Thus, the project must have an internal rate of return in excess of ρ, the economic opportunity cost of capital, to be worthwhile. The project will be debt-financed to avoid burdening those currently alive. If the project's benefits are more valuable to the next generation than the burden imposed on them by the additional debt, then it is worth undertaking. Notice that the SOC criterion is invariant to the model: it discounts intergenerational benefits at the same rate as it discounts intra-generational benefits, and it does not shadow price these benefits even though they are treated as income and therefore partially invested.

According to the MCF criterion, the project is worthwhile provided that

$$B1/(1+\rho) - MCF[C0 - IR/(1+\rho)]>0 \qquad\qquad (11)$$

Notice that because the benefits accrue to future generations, they are discounted at the SOC rate, not the STP rate. This is because the MCF criterion, like the SOC criterion, requires that worthwhile projects satisfy the Kaldor-Hicks compensation test. Also, since the benefits are treated as income, there will be indirect revenue effects to take into account.

Specifically, the next young generation will save a proportion β of the project's benefits, which will generate additional tax revenue worth $\beta\tau\rho B/(1+\rho)$ valued in terms of its working period income. The indirect revenue effect of the project is $IR = \beta\tau\rho B/(1+\rho)$. As far as costs are concerned, even though the project must be debt-financed to avoid burdening the current generation, taxes must ultimately be increased to redeem the debt. Whenever taxes are increased, a fraction β will come from saving, so capital income tax revenue will decrease by $\beta\tau\rho$ in the following period. The marginal cost of funds is the ratio of the increase in lump sum tax to the increase in present value of revenue collected, which is equal to $1/(1 - \beta\tau\rho/(1+\rho))$. If we substitute for IR and for MCF in the formula above, it reduces to the SOC criterion.

The project is worthwhile according to the shadow price algorithm if

$$B1[1-\beta+\beta (1+\rho)/(1+r)]/(1+r) -C0 (1+\rho)/(1+r) >0 \qquad (12)$$

Since the project is debt-financed, it crowds out private investment dollar for dollar, and a dollar of private investment displaced has a consumption equivalent value of $(1+\rho)/(1+r)$ dollars because it generates consumption worth $1+\rho$ dollars in the next period. Also, since the benefits are treated as income, a fraction β of benefits will be saved and invested. However, the shadow price algorithm discounts consumption equivalent values at the STP rate, whether these values pertain to those currently alive or to future generations.

It is easy to verify that the shadow price algorithm is weaker than the SOC criterion. Since the SOC criterion is necessary and sufficient for a Pareto improvement to be possible, the shadow price algorithm fails to meet this standard. Undertaking the project when it satisfies the shadow price algorithm but fails to satisfy the SOC criterion will make the next generation worse off.

So far, we have assumed that the project's benefits will be treated as income by the next generation. What if the project's benefits will be fully consumed?

The shadow price algorithm becomes

$$B1/(1+r) -C0 (1+\rho)/(1+r) >0 \qquad (13)$$

No shadow pricing of the benefits is required because they will be fully consumed.

The MCF criterion becomes

David F. Burgess

$$B1/(1+\rho) - MCF\ C0 > 0 \qquad (14)$$

There are no indirect revenue effects because the benchmark for the MCF criterion is a project whose benefits are fully consumed.

The SOC criterion becomes

$$(B1 + IR^c)/(1+\rho) - C0 > 0 \qquad (15)$$

Here IR^c is the *compensated* effect of the project on capital income tax revenue. Since the project's benefits will be fully consumed, it will not induce the next generation to save and invest. The capital income tax revenue that would be generated if the benefits were treated as income (the benchmark in applying the SOC criterion) will not materialize. The capital income tax revenue that is lost because the project's benefits are fully consumed is the indirect revenue effect in applying the SOC criterion, so $IR^c = -\beta\tau\rho B/(1+\rho)$.

If we substitute for IR^c in the SOC criterion, it is easy to verify that the SOC criterion and the MCF criterion are equivalent. It is also easy to verify that the shadow price algorithm is weaker than the MCF criterion. Since the MCF criterion correctly identifies all Pareto-improving projects, the SOC criterion meets this standard, but the shadow price algorithm does not. Once again, there are projects that satisfy the shadow price algorithm but fail to satisfy the MCF (and SOC) criterion, while the converse is not true.

Finally, what if the project is tax-financed rather than debt-financed? Debt-financing is necessary to ensure that the current generation is not burdened to benefit the next generation. Debt-financing is therefore necessary for the Kaldor-Hicks compensation test to be passed. However, if we reject this test as a necessary condition for a project to be worthwhile, we can still ask whether there would be a "social welfare" improvement if the project were financed by lump sum taxes imposed on the current generation.

A project with costs $C0$ and benefits $B1$ that are treated as income will be worthwhile according to the shadow price algorithm if

$$B1(1-\beta+\beta\ (1+\rho)/(1+r))/(1+r) - C0\ (1-\beta+\beta\ (1+\rho)/(1+r)) > 0 \qquad (16)$$

Costs and benefits are multiplied by the same conversion factor because successive generations are assumed to have marginal propensity to save. The project is therefore deemed to be worthwhile provided that

$$B1/(1+r) -C0 > 0 \qquad (17)$$

This is the Arrow-Bradford rule for worthwhile projects whose benefits are treated as income. Even though a proportion β of the cost of the project displaces private investment that earns a rate of return of ρ, the project is deemed to be worthwhile as long as it earns a rate of return marginally greater than r. However, unless the project satisfies the SOC criterion (i.e., unless it earns a rate of return of ρ), it will fail to satisfy the Kaldor-Hicks compensation test, which means that the project is an inefficient use of resources. Future generations would be better off if the current generation used the tax revenue to pay down the debt instead of undertaking the project.

There are three conclusions to draw from this analysis.

- The SOC criterion and the MCF criterion are equivalent whether the benefits are treated as income or fully consumed. Both criteria correctly identify Pareto-improving projects.
- The shadow price algorithm can recommend projects that either make future generations worse off or that benefit future generations at greater cost to the current generation than is necessary.
- The SOC criterion has an implementation advantage because (unlike the MCF criterion) the discount rate is invariant to the model, there are no indirect revenue effects to incorporate when the project's benefits are treated as income, and in situations where the project's benefits are fully consumed, indirect revenue effects can be incorporated by multiplying costs by the marginal cost of funds, thereby making the SOC criterion just as easy to implement as the MCF criterion.

Implications for Evaluating PPPs

What implications follow from the above analysis for the evaluation of PPPs? A PPP is a contractual arrangement that engages the private sector in some or all stages of a project, whether it be design, build, finance, maintain/operate, or all of the above. One way to evaluate a PPP is to compare the estimates of the real resource costs incurred by the private partner to the estimates of the real resource costs incurred under purely

David F. Burgess

public sector provision. If the time stream of benefits can be taken as given and identical for the two options, and if the project's non-diversifiable risk is the same whether it is performed in the public sector or the private sector, we have a "choice of technique" problem in which it is only necessary to compare the costs. The issue is: which is the most efficient way to deliver the benefits?

Proponents of the shadow price algorithm claim that if the shadow price of capital and the marginal propensity to consume are both unchanged over time, the coefficient that converts a dollar's worth of project expenditure into its consumption equivalent will be the same for every dollar of project expenditure. If the marginal source of funding for each option (whether it is in the private sector or the public sector) is the capital market, each dollar of project expenditure will have the same consumption equivalent. Therefore, the efficient option has the lowest present value of costs discounting at the STP rate (see Feldstein, 1970).

However, we have seen that as long as the expenditure requirements for a project are fully anticipated by the private sector (which will be true if the private sector is fully informed about the project's costs), the consumption equivalent value of a dollar of project expenditure will not be independent of when that dollar is spent. What is true is that the *present value* of every dollar of project expenditure (discounting at the economic opportunity cost of capital) will have the same consumption equivalent. It follows that a dollar of project expenditure in period 0 (when the project is initiated) has a greater contemporaneous consumption equivalent than the contemporaneous consumption equivalent value of a dollar of project expenditure that occurs (as anticipated) T periods later. This difference arises because the government's discount rate reflects the economic opportunity cost of capital (the SOC rate), whereas the private sector's discount rate reflects the after-tax rate of return. The MCF criterion tells us that the appropriate way to evaluate the costs of any project is to multiply them by the marginal cost of funds and discount them at the SOC rate. Projects with the same benefits will have the same indirect revenue effects, so to compare two projects with the same benefits, it is only necessary to compare the costs. Since the MCF is project-independent, the efficient project has the lowest present value of costs discounted at the SOC rate.

So far, we have assumed that we have reliable estimates of the real resource costs of each option. However, we may only have information about the private partner's bid price to undertake the project. This will typically take the form of a stream of contractual payments that the government would be expected to make to the private partner in order to secure the benefits. It is this stream of contractual payments that may have to be compared to the real resource costs incurred under purely public provision. We know that the present value of the stream of contractual payments (discounted at the private partner's cost of capital) will be equal to, or exceed, the present value of the underlying real resource costs. The more competitive the bidding, the smaller will be the rent or surplus in the contract. If the SOC rate is less than the private partner's cost of capital, the present value of the stream of contractual payments (discounted at the SOC rate) will *overstate* the present value of the underlying real resource costs plus any anticipated surplus. This is because the contractual payments are deferred relative to the real resource costs (which will be front-end-loaded as a result of the initial capital cost). It follows that if the present value of the stream of contractual payments (discounted at the SOC rate) is less than the present value of the real resource costs under purely public provision, the PPP is the efficient option.

If the SOC rate is greater than the private partner's cost of capital, the present value of the stream of contractual payments will *understate* the present value of the underlying real resource costs plus anticipated surplus. In this situation, if the present value of the contractual payments (discounted at the SOC rate) exceeds the present value of the real resource costs under purely public provision, the PPP option should be rejected (unless there are other compelling factors to be taken into consideration).

Concluding Remarks

If we agree that worthwhile projects must be capable of achieving Pareto improvements, the SOC criterion and the MCF criterion meet this standard, but the shadow price algorithm does not. If the benefits of a project are treated as income, the SOC criterion has a clear implementation advantage because all that is required is information about the pre- and post-tax rates of return and the proportions of funding that are drawn from investment, consumption, and (in an open economy) net exports when the government or private firm borrows to finance the project. All this information is project-independent. By comparison, the MCF criterion requires information about pre- and post-tax rates of return, indirect revenue effects, and the marginal cost of funds. The indirect revenue effects depend upon the project. While the marginal cost of funds is project-independent, it is model-dependent; it depends upon whether the private sector behaves as an infinitely lived agent or as a finite lived agent that cares only about its own well-being. In applying the SOC criterion, it is irrelevant whether the benefits accrue to individuals currently alive or to future generations, whereas this information is crucial in applying the MCF criterion: intra-generational benefits are discounted at the STP rate, but intergenerational benefits are discounted at the SOC rate.

If the benefits of a project are fully consumed, indirect revenue effects must be taken into account in applying the SOC criterion, but not the MCF criterion. This would seem to give the MCF criterion an implementation advantage, but the discount rate for benefits depends upon whether they are intergenerational or intra-generational (unlike the SOC criterion).

The claim that is made by proponents of the shadow price algorithm that the SOC criterion introduces an "aggregation error" by combining two distinct prices into one is incorrect. While it is true that a weighted average discount rate requires information about the proportions of funding drawn from various sources – displaced private investment and consumption and, in an open economy, incremental funding from abroad – these proportions are project-independent. Thus, the SOC rate has a clear implementation advantage over the MCF criterion despite empirical challenges in determining the weights.

The claim made by proponents of the shadow price algorithm, that for cost-effectiveness analysis (e.g., comparing the real resource costs of a PPP to a public sector comparator (PSC), it is only necessary to compare the cost streams discounted at the STP rate, is false. The economic opportunity cost of debt-financed public expenditure is the SOC rate even if the government can borrow at a lower rate, because each dollar of borrowed funds must not only pay interest to bondholders; it also displaces private investment and thereby reduces capital income tax revenue.

Throughout the paper, I have assumed that the STP rate coincides with the consumption rate of interest, reflecting the rate at which individuals are willing to trade present for future consumption. Proponents of the shadow price algorithm claim that the consumption rate of interest overstates the "social" rate of time preference if individuals are myopic, i.e., suffer from a "weakness of the imagination", in the words of Frank Ramsey (1928). The STP rate then reflects the ethical preferences of the planner toward the well-being of future generations. Some argue that for projects whose benefits accrue to generations yet unborn, the social discount rate should be lower than it would be if the benefits accrued to those currently alive who bear the costs. According to the analysis of this paper, the rate at which future benefits (and costs) should be discounted is the same whether those benefits are intra-generational or intergenerational, and that rate is the SOC rate. Paradoxically, we make future generations worse off if we undertake projects that pass muster at the social rate of time preference but not at the economic opportunity cost of capital.

References

Arrow, K.J. 1966. "Discounting and Public Investment Criteria", in A.V. Kneese and S.C. Smith (eds.), *Water Research*. Baltimore, MD: The Johns Hopkins University Press for Resources for the Future.

Bradford, D.F. 1975. "Constraints on Government Investment Opportunities and the Choice of Discount Rate", *American Economic Review* 65 (December), 887–899.

Burgess, D.F. 2008. "Removing Some Dissonance from the Social Discount Rate Debate", *EPRI Working Paper* 2008-2, University of Western Ontario, June.

Eckstein, O. 1957. "Investment Criteria for Economic Development and the Theory of Inter-temporal Welfare Economics", *Quarterly Journal of Economics* 71, 56–85.

Feldstein, M.S. 1970. "Choice of Technique in the Public Sector: A Simplification", *Economic Journal* (December), 985–990.

_____. 1972. "The Inadequacy of Weighted Discount Rates", in R. Layard (ed.), *Cost-Benefit Analysis*. Harmondsworth, UK: Penguin.

Feldstein, M.S. and C. Horioka. 1980. "Domestic Saving and International Capital Flows", *Economic Journal* 90, June.

Harberger, A.C. 1972. "The Opportunity Costs of Public Investment Financed by Borrowing", in R. Layard (ed.), *Cost-Benefit Analysis*. Harmondsworth, UK: Penguin.

_____. 1997. "New Frontiers in Project Evaluation? A Comment on Devarajan, Squire, and Suthiwart-Narueput", *The World Bank Research Observer* 12(1), 73–78.

Helliwell, J.F. 1998. *How Much do National Borders Matter?* Washington, DC: Brookings.

Larson, D.M. 1993. "On Measuring Existence Value", *Land Economics* 69(4), 377–388.

Lind, R.C. 1982. "A Primer on the Major Issues Relating to the Discount Rate for Evaluating National Energy Options", in R.C. Lind (ed.), *Discounting for Time and Risk in Energy Policy*. Washington, DC: Resources for the Future.

Liu, L. 2003. "A Marginal Cost of Funds Approach to Multi-period Public Project Evaluation: Implications for the Social Discount Rate", *Journal of Public Economics* 87, 1707-1718.

Liu, L., A. Rettenmaier, and T. Saving. 2004. "A Generalized Approach to Multigenerational Project Evaluation", *Southern Economic Journal* 71(2), 377-396.

Marglin, S.A. 1963. "The Opportunity Cost of Public Investment", *Quarterly Journal of Economics* 77, 274-289.

Ramsey, F.P. 1928. "A Mathematical Theory of Saving", *Economic Journal* 38, 543-559.

Sandmo, A. and J. Dreze. 1971. "Discount Rates for Public Investment in Closed and Open Economies", *Economica* 38, 395-412.

Sjaastad, L. and D. Wisecarver. 1977. "The Social Cost of Public Finance", *Journal of Political Economy* 85, 513-548.

Weitzman, M.L. 2001. "Gamma Discounting", *American Economic Review* 91, 260-271.

Wildasin, D.E. 1984. "On Public Good Provision with Distortionary Taxation", *Economic Inquiry* 22, 227-243.

Summary of Discussion

Al Harberger: I think David has done a wonderful job of sorting through the literature and coming up with some very sensible and straightforward answers. I don't know that any nitpicking on my part would be appropriate at this stage. So I'd like to elaborate on the link between using the consumer's rate of time preference and the weighted average economic opportunity cost of capital. From the beginning, in Marglin's paper it was recognized that we had corporation income taxes, etc. striking the earnings that would take place in the future on displaced investment and that we had personal taxes on the personal income of people.

I'm going to try to go with the same story we had last night. We're drawing $1,000 from the capital market, $750 is displaced investment, $250 is incremental saving. The rate of return on the investment is 12%, so we're giving up $90 forever. And on incremental saving we're going to get a return of 4%, which is $10 forever. So we're going to forego $100 a year.

This $10 representing the after-tax rate of return – these guys were earning 6% on their savings, but they pay a third of that to the government, so they're only getting $4. That's the after-tax rate of return. And this then barely compensates them for having to forego consumption. The $750 is earning 12%, but half of that goes to corporate income taxes. Then by the time you get it back to the personal level, you lose a third of the remainder, so everybody's getting 4% on their money after all taxes are paid.

What we do is, we say: You see this $100, and you see that $1,000? That's 10%. If our project yields 10%, they're able to pay these necessary costs for as long as it takes, and we're home. What Marglin and others say is: We like to use that 4% discount rate because we learned something about consumption in our 101 class, and we shouldn't discount at any other rate than at the consumption rate of interest.

They say that all of this is true. This is the cost to society. But the present value of that cost equals this $100 of annuity divided by 0.04 equals $2,500. So they get a SPIF – shadow price of investment funds – of 2.5. And they say: We'll discount everything at 4%, but every dollar of expenditure we're going to multiply by 2.5. I say that's stupid if you try to argue with the Secretary of Agriculture who only sees the $1,000 going out and you say: Oh, no, you've got to count that $1,000 as if it were $2,500. He'll probably kick you out the door.

That aside, for investments that are perpetuities these two things are equivalent. For a one-year investment, they're also equivalent. I don't have time to show you that, but that's the story. Sjaastad and Wisecarver talked about this, as David noted. But I get so mad at them because they have a deep, beautiful paper that is so arcane and difficult that nobody gets the message out of it. And the message is exceedingly powerful, exceedingly powerful. They entitle their paper something like "The Social Cost of Public Finance", as distinct from "The Social Cost of Public Investment".

What one has to realize is that the government has gone into the capital market and sucked this $1,000 out, displacing consumption and investment in these proportions. Nothing about that says, I'm going to build a road, or I'm going to build an airport. I might be doing it to pay teachers, or to pay retirement benefits for what I committed a long time ago. Therefore, it is not a shadow price of investment funds; it is a shadow price of public funds.

Once you've got that, if you're going to go down their road, you've got to say, Every project has to produce 2.5 times its cost in order to compensate the future sacrifices that people have been exposed to. That means that when I pay policemen I have to be sure that the benefit from the policemen is 2.5 times their cost. When I pay teachers or garbage collectors the benefits must be 2.5 times their cost. There are enormously powerful implications here. This argument about using the STP rate is always made by big-government, or semi-big-government people – certainly Marglin was a big-government person. Most people who want to use the low discount rate want to approve projects. And yet here is the much-more-than-Friedman small government, because if your funds cost $2.5 per dollar you're going to have to insist that current projects have this huge rate of return in order to compensate. So I think that is the most important.

The second comment that I would make with David is that I think David has followed the march, so to speak, in this literature. And damn it all, whenever they talk about an after-tax rate of return as the social rate of time preference and all of that, they think of it as one number. The logic of all of what they do consists of one number. But as we said last night, if you go to the economics that lies behind it all, we're talking about each individual's own after-tax rate of return, including the 18% rate on the credit card of the guy who's always owing on his credit card. These are the relevant marginal rates of time preference that apply to different people. And we know they vary hugely across citizens, even of very developed countries with very developed capital markets. So the idea of using a representative consumer model with just one rate, I think, misses a very important point of reality.

I go down two roads. One road, I say Marglin ultimately didn't care about this. He is ready to have a planning commission give you a social rate of time preference, and the hell with what you observe in the market and all of that. I don't endorse it, but I can't fight it either, intellectually. That's an assumption, and what can you do? But I think the minute you get into the sensitive price-theory kind of story, where the marginal rate of time preference of a person is that after-tax rate of return that that person faces at the market, then you get into the problem of not two different discount rates, or three different rates, but hundreds, thousands, millions of different discount rates. And all the impossible problems that that gives rise to, most particularly what I mentioned last night, that when you have two different rates you value two projects at two different rates. You discount to one point in time and you find one better than the other, and you accumulate to another point in time and you find the other better than the one. I just don't know where to go with that.

In comparison, R, the economic-opportunity cost of capital is going to be a weighted average of rates of return in all sectors. There can be a million of these weights; it doesn't create a problem. I'm not discounting separately by them. And I have a very good reason for what I'm doing.

I'm going to do this with two stories here. Here, we have two investment stories. Here we have two savings stories. When any entity enters this capital market, it raises this market interest rate a little bit – let me get into the whole picture. Let's have these subject to tax. So here we raise this interest rate a little bit, we lose this. Here we have a tax and we raise this interest rate a little bit, and we lose that. Here we have a tax down this way, and we raise the interest rate and stimulate this. And here we have a different tax; we raise the interest rate, and we stimulate that.

All we're doing is adding up all of these externalities, and I don't have to have this R being similar to this R or any other R. I don't have this row being similar to this row or any other row; I can have different intrinsic rates of return; I can have different taxes and other distortions in each of these places. I think that this gives you a very easy way out of what otherwise is a terribly messy problem.

The thing that I have consistently been complaining about is why the guys who created this literature about using the 4% discount rate based upon time preference never have more than one marginal rate of time preference in their story, as if they don't see this bridge and ever want to cross it. And they're very happy, going along, and feeling content. But I think the minute you introduce that bridge, you've got to do something about it. And I think the social opportunity cost way, first of all, gives you a straightforward answer, is compatible with Hicks-Kaldor and is not only easy, but also easy to swallow.

Thanks very much, David. This is for my reading list.

4

The New (but Old) Approach to the Economic Opportunity Cost of Capital

Graham Glenday

Introduction

In the practice of the conduct of the economic appraisal or cost-benefit analysis of projects and programs in the public sector, the approach of defining the economic opportunity cost of capital (EOCK) as a national parameter has become widely used. This approach estimates the real (or inflation-adjusted) opportunity cost of capital as a weighted average of the economic value of the forgone domestic investments and the economic cost of additional domestic and foreign savings supplied to the economy as a result of the capital markets responding to a project using more capital funds over some future, long time horizon.[1] This approach

This paper has benefited from comments from Glenn Jenkins, Chun-Yan Kuo, Fernando Fernholz, and other members of the Public Finance Group at the Duke Center for International Development. All opinions, errors and omissions remain the responsibility of the author.

[1]The issues of the appropriate approach to estimating the EOCK in this paper is purely in the context of the "Harberger" framework for the conduct of cost-benefit analysis of investment projects – the weighted average economic opportunity cost measured in domestic currency units as the accounting numeraire. It is not raising any of the issues of other frameworks using other numeraires, such as consumption values. See, for example, Jenkins and Harberger (2002, Chapter 12) for different discount rates applied in different analysis frameworks.

has had the strength of encouraging the use of one EOCK for all public sector project selection. It simplifies communication, control, and calculation of the EOCK in the public sector of a country. As long as the bulk of projects that are being evaluated are not self-financing (ultimately paid for by the revenues their services generate, as in the private sector), but rather are financed out of the general revenues, this approach appeared sound as the marginal funds for these projects arguably are sourced through the government going to the capital markets for added public sector borrowing.

The criticisms of the national parameter approach primarily focus on the lack of risk adjustment of the single EOCK for the differential costs of risk of a project on the economy, thereby either penalizing less risky projects or favouring more risky ones. The EOCK as a single national parameter has come under greater pressure of criticism as more governments have decentralized public sector investments. This results in greater private sector involvement in the risks and returns from public sector investment through various partnership and regulatory approaches that include private investment in public sector ventures. The criticism also predated the growth in recent decades of the public private partnership approach to the extent that governments were investing in commercial ventures, actively or passively, or were taking decisions to affect the viability of commercial businesses through guarantees, regulations, or tax preferences. At the same time, in the field of corporate finance, models and methods used to identify and measure risk premiums have developed and become more widely used. This led to the realization that the variation in the size of risk-adjusted discount rates for investments in different sectors and countries was large and a significant, and often dominant, factor in evaluating investments.

While these criticisms of the national parameter approach have been recognized for some time, the difficulty in moving away from this single-value EOCK has been as much a practical estimation difficulty as a conceptual one. What is a feasible method to correct the EOCK for the risk and other characteristics of the particular project?

This paper presents a new approach to estimating the EOCK in a country for a specific project that can be readily adopted and is consistent with, and even strengthens, the overall framework for undertaking the appraisal of public sector projects and programs. The new approach will also be shown to be "old" in that it uses techniques that have been adopted over recent decades at the advocacy of Professor Harberger for dealing with similar problems in the estimation of the economic opportunity cost of labour, where wage rates can be affected by job-related risks as well as other differentials arising from job and location conditions. The new approach will also provide a formulation of the EOCK that is consistent with all economic pricing: namely, any economic price equals the market price plus externalities. The paper first lays out the issues that cause concern with the single national parameter; second, discusses the alternative approaches; third, gives the suggested approach and discusses its application in different situations; and finally, shows its strengths in improving the distributional analysis of investment projects.

Issues with a Single-Valued EOCK

There are three issues that raise concerns with the national parameter or single-valued EOCK:

Costs of Risk of Project

The first and largest in magnitude, as already mentioned above, is the lack of risk adjustment for the risk factors related to a specific project, particularly the systematic market or sector risk in the case of self-financing projects.[2] The lack of appropriate costing of risk can result in either overestimating the economic value of a high-risk project or undervaluing a low-risk project. It is noted that the typical estimate of the EOCK excludes the costs of risk on the incremental savings (except country risk on foreign savings) but includes the risk premiums implicit in the forgone product of capital investments displaced. This means that the typical EOCK contains some element of market risk such that it overcharges less risky public sector projects in situations where most of the capital is ultimately drawn from forgone investments.

---

[2]Self-financing projects are projects where the revenues from the sale of the project services are adequate to cover the full costs of the project over its life. This includes private or commercial ventures, or regulated utilities or infrastructure projects, funded out of user charges, irrespective of whether a project receives tax assistance or some public subsidy. In such cases, the revenues will be subject to demand risks and possible real price fluctuations.

Transactions Cost of Supplying Capital to Project

A second issue, but usually of less consequence, is the issue of the differential transactions costs in raising capital for a project. Raising capital has mobilization costs that are contained in the market costs of capital. To the extent that a project has markedly higher transaction costs implicit in its costs of capital, as would typically be the case in projects financed by the micro-finance sector, for example, then using an EOCK that assumes that these costs have not been incurred by the economy overstates the value of the project. For most large-scale projects, the differentials in the costs of capital may be closer to the market average except where large upfront expenditures may be required to organize project finance arrangements. In such cases, however, these soft costs may be built into the upfront capital investment cash flow costs and not be captured in a cost of capital premium. While these transaction cost differentials may typically be of less consequence, the new approach is designed to capture them.[3]

Distribution of Gains and Losses in Economy

The third issue that arises from a national parameter EOCK is in the context of conducting the distributional analysis of a project. Conceptually, the net present value (NPV) of an investment from an economic perspective captures the aggregate net gain or loss experienced by all stakeholders in the project. The distributional analysis identifies these gains and losses to the stakeholders. The financiers of a project are always key stakeholders, and the gain or loss that they expect is the NPV based on their weighted average risk-adjusted discount rate. At the same time, the capital invested in the project needs to generate positive externalities to offset the externalities forgone by the economy by investing capital in this particular project. When the EOCK does not capture the costs of risk and transaction costs actually borne by the financiers, then the difference between their cost of capital and the

---

[3]Note that the focus here is on transaction cost differentials within a country. Large transaction cost differentials exist among countries, reflecting the technical efficiency and regulatory cost differences between the capital markets of countries. Much of these differentials are often captured as part of the country risk premium of a particular country relative to the least risky countries.

Graham Glenday

EOCK does not capture properly the externalities forgone by the project that need to be offset by the project externalities. For example, if the real private cost of capital is 15%, say, because of high risk and capital mobilization costs, this cost may exceed a national EOCK of 11%, say, which contains the tax and other externalities incurred by the economy. The meaning of the difference between the private and economic costs of capital is then not clear. This issue will be returned to once the new method has been discussed further below.

Two Approaches to Adjusting the EOCK

Two approaches can be taken to adjusting an economic price when market prices differ because of compensating differentials for risk, transaction costs, and other related features between two market situations, as often occurs in labour and capital markets. For example, the market wages at the factory gate for two jobs may differ because of different risks inherit in doing the two jobs, the relative attractiveness of the different work or location conditions, or the different costs of commuting to the two jobs, and so on. Similarly, the cost of capital can vary between financial investment opportunities because of differences in risks or capital mobilization costs. In labour markets, one approach to estimating the economic cost of labour is to systematically make adjustments for all the differential conditions plus the fiscal externalities (taxes, and unemployment and social security contributions and benefits) between the new jobs and jobs from which labour is sourced.

The second and more elegant approach to estimating the economic opportunity cost of labour is referred to as the *supply price of labour approach*. See, for example, Harberger (1976, Chapter 7) and Harberger and Jenkins (2002, Chapter 13). In this approach, the competitive market gross wage rate for the new project job is taken as the starting point. As long as this market wage can be taken as the wage rate that is just sufficient to attract workers to the new job, it must offset all the compensating differentials between the new job and labour market alternatives internalized in the workers' decisions. If it is a riskier and more unattractive job, then the higher wage rate required to attract workers should be just sufficient to offset these added costs of the job. By contrast, if the job has more attractive features, the minimum wage rate required to attract workers may be lower than those in the alternatives. The minimum supply wage, therefore, offsets for all the different features among jobs and leaves workers indifferent among them. Hence, a lower supply wage can be taken as economically equivalent to forgoing a higher-paying job because of the compensating differentials between the jobs. To incorporate the economic costs of hiring workers into the new job, the supply price approach takes this minimum supply wage and then adjusts it for the fiscal differentials (or tax, unemployment, and social security differentials) between the project job and the alternative jobs from which workers are ultimately sourced. Another way of stating this *economic cost of labour* is that it is the *minimum or competitive supply wage* plus *the economic externalities.*

In the capital markets, the first approach of making all the adjustments for compensating differentials plus other externalities could be followed. This requires subtracting out all the cost of risk saved on investment forgone and adding them to the added savings induced into the market plus the added costs associated with the specific project financed. One such approach is to derive a weighted average EOCK, removing the systematic risk saved on the forgone investments and adding back the systematic risk associated with the project. This approach leads to a "risk adjusted" national EOCK to which the systematic risk has to be added.[4] It is not entirely satisfactory as it does not deal with the full range of costs of risk or capital mobilization costs associated with a project.

The second approach of the minimum supply price plus externalities holds more promise of generality, flexibility, and practicality. As with the economic opportunity cost of labour, the minimum supply price in capital markets is the minimum cost of capital required in a competitive market by the financiers of the investment project. This minimum required rate of return by financiers would adjust for all the differential costs of risk and capital mobilization that would make them indifferent between financing the project and alternative investments in the economy or withdrawing their savings from the capital market of the economy. Hence, it implicitly captures all the compensating differentials for the specific project without explicitly having to analyze and account for them. On the other hand, in the case of a long-run investment, given the general fungibility of funds over the long run, the externality associated with the long-run investment of capital in an economy can be taken to be more a function of the characteristics of the economy rather

---

[4]This approach is discussed in Glenday (2003).

than the project itself. Hence, the externality per unit of capital invested over the long run can be thought of as a national parameter. This approach to estimating the EOCK captures the specific characteristics of the project financed as well as the general externalities arising from the long-run use of capital funds by the project. The EOCK then differentiates between non-self-financing projects, which are financed by general government revenues, and self-financing projects in different sectors of the economy and the other project-specific characteristics that may cause added costs to the financiers. At the same time, explicit recognition is made of the externalities arising from using capital funds. The formulation is also consistent with the general specification of economic prices, namely, they are the sum of the financial or market prices of the project plus externalities per unit.

Simple Derivation and Specification of EOCK

The supply price approach can be seen to be consistent with the standard economic pricing model in competitive markets with a single price – that is, markets that contain no compensating differentials for the market good or resource traded. Consider a capital market with all costs of capital equal to a single market interest rate, i_m.[5] Capital investments are subject to a uniform income tax on their returns at tax rate t_c such that all investments have to generate a gross-of-tax return on investment of $\pi_c = i_m/(1 - t_c)$. If $i_m = 7\%$ (real or inflation-adjusted rate) and $t_c = 25\%$, $\pi_c = 9.33\%$. On top of this gross-of-tax return, the products of capital investment yield indirect taxes that have to be paid for by the consumers or users of the products. These indirect taxes become part of the economic return on the investment, so that the gross return on investments becomes $\pi = i_m/(1 - t_c) (1 + t_i)$, where t_i is the effective indirect tax rate expressed relative to the gross-of-tax return on investment.[6] If $t_i = 15.4\%$, then $\pi = 10.77\%$. Alternatively, this gross

---

[5] All interest rates are expressed here on a real or inflation-adjusted basis.

[6] An estimate of t_i can be gained from the share of indirect taxes attributed to capital ((VAK/TVA)*(Indirect Tax)) relative to the net-of-depreciation value added earned by capital (NVAK), or $t_i = ((VAK/TVA)*(Indirect Taxes))/NVAK = VAK/NVAK*(Indirect Taxes)/TVA = (\pi_c + \delta)/\pi_c *(Indirect Taxes)/TVA$,

return to the economy could be expressed as $\pi = (i_m + t_d)$, where t_d is the tax generated per unit of capital invested, or $t_d = i_m (t_c + t_i)/(1 - t_c)$. For the parameter values in this example, $t_d = 2.33\% + 1.43\% = 3.77\%$. Savers in this capital market are willing to supply capital based on their net-of-tax returns, or $r = i_m (1 - t_p)$, where t_p is the income tax rate charged on personal savings. If $t_p = 15\%$, then $r = 5.95\%$. Alternatively, this can be expressed as $r = (i_m - t_s)$, where t_s is the tax generated per unit of capital saved, or $t_s = i_m t_p = 1.05\%$. The EOCK of the capital used by a project under the standard weighted average formulation is the economic cost of share of capital coming from forgone investments, where ω^d is the share from forgone investments that would have earned π, and the economic cost of the share coming from savings, where $\omega^s = (1 - \omega^d)$ is the share from added savings at the cost r, or

$$
\begin{aligned}
EOCK \;=\;& \omega^d \pi + \omega^s r \\[2mm]
=\;& \omega^d i_m \frac{1+t_i}{1-t_c} + \omega^s i_m (1 - t_p) \\[2mm]
=\;& \omega^d (i_m + t_d) + \omega^s (i_m - t_s) \\[2mm]
=\;& i_m \;+\; \omega^d t_d + \omega^s (-t_s)
\end{aligned}
\tag{1}
$$

The expressions for the EOCK in (1) show the equivalence of different ways of expressing the EOCK given the assumptions about the capital market in the economy made above. The initial expression of $\omega^d \pi + \omega^s r$, or the weighted average of the economic value of the forgone product of capital and the cost of additional savings supplied, characterizes the traditional approach to estimating EOCK as a national parameter. Taking $\omega^d = 0.75$, then EOCK = 0.75*10.77% + 0.25*5.95% = 9.6%. The final equivalent expression of $(i_m + \omega^d t_d + \omega^s (-t_s))$ gives the same value of EOCK, or EOCK = 7% + (0.75*3.77% + 0.25*-1.05%) = 7%+ 2.6% = 9.6%, but breaks out the components in a different way is important both from an estimation point of view and from a "reinterpretation" of the meaning of the components of the EOCK to allow for the direct re-entry of issues of the costs of risk and transaction costs into the estimation of the EOCK. Importantly, the final expression

---

where δ = depreciation rate and TVA = total value added or GDP at factor cost. If (Indirect Taxes)/TVA = 10%, δ = 5%, and π_c = 9.33%, then t_i = 15.4%.

breaks out the private market cost of capital or interest rate from the economic externalities of using capital in a project. In addition, the two components are expressed as a rate per unit of capital – in the simple example, 7% for the private market cost of capital and 2.6% as the economic externality per unit of capital, which, in this simple case, represents the net forgone taxes in the rest of the economy by using the capital in the particular project under consideration. The proposed new approach focuses on each component separately, namely, the minimum required rate of return by the investors and the economic externality.

Minimum Required Private Rate of Return

First, the expressions above assume that all capital is the same and earns the same return, or costs the same, per unit. This is clearly a gross over simplification of capital markets which mobilize capital at varying costs and invests across many investments with varying costs of risk arising from a variety of factors: liquidity of the investment, inflation and exchange rate or currency risk, industry or systematic risk, project-specific risk, and country risk. All these risk factors result in persistent and large differences in rates of return across investments and countries. At the same time, any particular investment is typically financed by a set of different financiers through different types of debt and equity instruments, which bear different shares of the risk inherent in the project. In a competitive market, it is expected that suppliers of capital, both domestic and foreign, will seek the highest returns on supplying capital to investments with given risk characteristics, while project owners or sponsors will be seeking the lowest cost of capital and will seek out the lowest cost of mix of capital. In a competitive market, on the marginal investment, we expect the return and the cost of capital to converge. In addition, we expect all the players in the market to be reallocating their investments across all the investment opportunities to their own net benefit given the returns and risks perceived across all investment opportunities. Hence, when a new project is brought into the market to be financed, existing financiers have to make their judgments about the risk characteristics of the new project and how it fits into their portfolios, and based on this, decide how they trade off the new with existing investment opportunities. Hence, they decide what minimum returns they require from the new project for different types of debt and investment instruments available to invest in the new project. The importance of this competitive private capital market assumption is that this trade-off and pricing process results in investors internalizing or taking into account all the risk and transaction cost differentials between the new and existing investment opportunities. Hence, the minimum price of capital that private investors require to be willing to supply capital to a project takes into account the costs of investing in the particular project and leaves them at least as well off as investing in the alternative opportunities. From an economic perspective, this allows the minimum supply price of capital terms to capture the economic cost borne by the private investors, including differentials in costs of risk and transactions.

The implications of the above is that the competitive or minimum required rate of return becomes the first component of the EOCK, and this component captures the added costs of risk and transaction costs of supplying capital to the project. Importantly, from an economic perspective, the capital invested is the total capital investment. The relevant cost of capital is, therefore, the weighted average cost of capital (WACC), where all the components are being priced at their minimum supply prices. For a project being financed in a competitive market, the actual WACC[7] can be used in the EOCK. This includes an estimate of the minimum return required by equity holders, which may require some sophisticated or difficult estimate of the cost of equity for projects outside of well-developed capital markets. There are four cases that should be noted where the interpretation of i_m as the competitive WACC needs some added considerations.

a) If *capital funds are raised by the project in a non-competitive situation* (possibly a regulated market or non-arms length investment) such that the whole or parts of the WACC are above the minimum required by private investors, then the price premiums should be removed from the WACC in the economic and financial analyses, unless higher costs of capital arise from added risk or transaction cost incurred by the specific investors. In the former case, the financiers gain a windfall, but in the latter, the economy loses by the added costs of uncompetitive financing. This case is elaborated on below in the distributional analysis.

---

[7]Note that WACC here includes the full, or gross-of-tax, interest rates. It is not adjusted for any tax shield from tax deductibility of interest expenditures, which are already taken into account in the cash flows.

b) If part of the *capital funds are subsidized or at concessional rates,* then unless these are external funds that are completely tied to the particular project (i.e., they have no possible alternatives available or uses in the economy), the subsidy element should be added back into the WACC in the economic analysis, but not in the financial analysis. In the distributional analysis, this will be recognized as a transfer to the project owners from the payers of the subsidy (typically the government).

c) If the *project is financed by and wholly owned by a government* such that the *marginal capital finance is coming from the general budget,* then aside from the considerations in b), where a share of the investment is financed with a concessional loan, the financial opportunity cost of capital for a government is taken as the long-term borrowing cost of the government, which would contain the country risk premium on sovereign debt. The economic opportunity cost of such budget-financed projects would effectively become the long-term borrowing cost of the government plus the economic externality of capital. *This implies an effectively constant EOCK for budget-financed public sector projects.* Where the government is assuming large risks relative to the size of its resources, however, then project risk premiums should also be included or the cash flows adjusted to reflect these risks.

d) If a *public sector project receives user charges,* then a market systematic risk (beta) premium should be included in the minimum supply price of capital. As betas are typically estimated for the cost of equity, the equity beta should be adjusted for (i) the share of equity financing or $(1-d)$, where d is the share of debt financing to obtain an asset beta, and (ii) the share of the total cost covered by the user charge, or u, or the share of the market premium included should be $(1-d)u\beta$, where β is the equity beta for the type or sector of the project. For pure budget-financed projects, then, $u=0$ and case c) above occurs, whereas for fully commercialized projects, $u=1$, and the full premium for systematic risk becomes included.

Economic Externality per Unit of Capital

The second component of the EOCK is the aggregate economic externality arising from the use of capital funds in the project. From an economic perspective, the capital funds used by a project come from three basic sources: a share of the capital is sourced from forgone investments (ω^d) as the market cost of capital increases; and shares come from increased domestic savings (ω_d^s) and from increased foreign savings (ω_f^s) in response to higher market returns. Compared to the simple assumptions presented in (1) above, it is recognized that within these sources of capital are market segments with different degrees of responsiveness to changes in the rates of return and that different segments face different tax rates. The estimation of these weights, and the different tax and other distortions, essentially follows the same logic and methodology as used in the traditional estimates of EOCK, as shown in the first expression in (1) above, except that here, the externalities are separated out from the economic returns of forgone investments and economic costs of the added domestic and foreign savings. The unbundling of the externalities in some situations simplifies and some complicates estimation of the externalities, but importantly, once an estimate has been made of the economic externalities, it can be considered a national parameter. While different investment projects generate different risks and different investment instruments bear different amounts of risk, given the long-run fungibility of money and the interconnectedness of capital markets, that aside from the differential premiums that are paid for using capital in different uses, the long-run response of the economy to removing marginal capital funds into a project is independent of the use of the funds. This means that the economic externality per unit of capital from using capital funds can be regarded as a national parameter. Given that this is an external cost suffered by the economy, the use of the funds in the project needs to earn internal and external surpluses sufficient to offset this loss. This balance is discussed further in the distributional analysis below.

The estimation of the economic externality per unit of capital needs to follow the same structure as the traditional estimation of the EOCK except that the focus is only on adding up the net economic externalities arising from using capital funds over the long term. The added savings are drawn from different sources, S_i, which is the existing value of savings of that type that responds to increasing returns according to a long-run (or stock adjustment) price elasticity of supply, ε_i^s. Savings could be drawn from national sources (personal, corporate and government savings) and from foreign sources as debt or equity. S is the total savings available in the economy. Similarly, capital is drawn from forgone investment in different sectors, I_j, depending on how responsive investment in a sector is to increases in the cost of capital, as captured by the long-run (or stock-adjustment) price elasticity of demand for investment, η_j^d. Investment could be displaced from private, corporate and non-corporate investment in the primary, secondary and tertiary sectors or from public sector investments. I is the total investment in the economy and equals S. If the externalities in each savings and investment sector per unit of capital are e_i and e_j, respectively, then the EOCK can be expressed as

$$EOCK \; = \; i_{min}^p \; + \; \frac{\displaystyle\sum_{i=1}^{m} \varepsilon_i^s (S_i / S)\, e_i - \sum_{j=1}^{n} \eta_j^d (I_j / S) e_j}{\displaystyle\sum_{i=1}^{m} \varepsilon_i^s (S_i / S) - \sum_{j=1}^{n} \eta_j^d (I_j / S)}$$

$$(2)$$

or

$$EOCK \; = \; i_{min}^p \; + \; \sum_{i=1}^{m} \omega_i^s e_i + \sum_{j=1}^{n} \omega_j^d e_j$$

where

$$\omega_i^s = \frac{\varepsilon_i^s (S_i / S)}{\displaystyle\sum_{i=1}^{m} \varepsilon_i^s (S_i / S) - \sum_{j=1}^{n} \eta_j^d (I_j / S)}$$

$$\omega_j^d = \frac{-\eta_j^d (I_j / S)}{\displaystyle\sum_{i=1}^{m} \varepsilon_i^s (S_i / S) - \sum_{j=1}^{n} \eta_j^d (I_j / S)}$$

$$(3)$$

Here, i_{min}^p is the minimum competitive supply price of capital or WACC of the project. On the demand side, the externality in any sector, e_j, allowing for income tax rate, t_c, tax-deductible taxes on property values of t_{prop} per unit of capital, and indirect taxes earned on the gross-of-tax return on capital at the rate of t_i,[8] then the externality per unit of capital investment is

$$e_j = t_{dj} = \frac{t_{prop}(1+t_i)(1-t_c)+i_m(t_i+t_c)}{1-t_c} \qquad (4)$$

Note that here, the tax rates in all investment sectors are taken to be equal. In practice, tax rates may vary by sector. In addition, in some countries, significant monopoly premiums may be earned in sectors where entry is regulated or restricted, or some sectors may receive significant subsidies either as financial transfers, tax breaks, or under-priced or subsidized inputs. Monopoly premiums per unit of investment would need to be added to the unit externality but removed from the supply price of capital, while subsidies per unit of investment would be subtracted from the unit externality generated by a sector.

On the supply side, two major sources of capital are national and foreign savings. Taking private savings out of total national savings as being price-responsive to returns on its investment opportunities, the externality is the tax gain (hence, a reduction in the EOCK) or the average return on market investments (r_m^{av}) multiplied by the effective tax rate on these investments (t_p). Foreign savings that are responsive to changes in the domestic market returns (these exclude unresponsive capital flows such as concessional loans to governments or fixed interest rate loans) can generate tax gains to the extent that withholding taxes are charged on repatriated funds but they can also generate losses to the country to the extent that foreign savers earn higher returns on their infra-marginal savings as interest rates rise in the domestic market in response to the added demand for capital funds. The marginal economic cost of foreign capital becomes $i_m^f(1-t_{wh})(1+\phi/\varepsilon_f^s)$ where i_m^f is the market price of foreign savings, t_{wh} is the effective withholding tax rate, ϕ is the price-responsive share of foreign savings, and ε_f^s is the price

---

[8]With taxes on the capital value of property at the effective rate of t_{prop} and with these taxes being deductible from income taxes, the gross-of-income and property tax return earned by investments becomes

$$\pi_c = (i_m + t_{prop}(1-t_c))/(1-t_c)$$

       Graham Glenday

elasticity of supply of foreign savings. Hence, the externality has two parts: a tax gain, $(-t_{wh}i_m^f)$, and the loss of surplus to foreign savers, $i_m^f(1-t_{wh})\phi/\varepsilon_f^s$. Importantly, this externality *declines* as the price elasticity of foreign savings increases, but at the same time, the share of the overall economic externality of using capital that arises from the cost of added foreign savings *increases*. In an open economy faced with a fixed price of foreign savings, this share approaches 100% and dominates the EOCK, which in the limit becomes $i_m^f(1-t_{wh})$, assuming i_m^f includes any project-related risks and transaction costs. At the other extreme, in a closed or high-risk country, this external cost of foreign savings per unit of capital *rises* as ε_f^s declines, but its share of the overall externality also *declines*. In such cases, the externalities related to forgone investments tend to dominate.

Some hypothetical examples of estimates of the economic externality per unit of capital invested are provided below in Table 1 for three countries in different country risk ranges. To estimate the externalities three market WACCs are used: 6% for a very low-risk country, 9% for a moderate- to low-risk country, and 12% for a high- to very high-risk country.[9] For the sake of simplicity, all countries are assumed to have the same effective tax rates: $t_c = 25\%$, $t_{prop} = 0.5\%$, $t_p = 15\%$, $t_{wh} = 5\%$, and indirect taxes of 10% of total value added.[10] In the investment sectors, 85% of investment is taken to be responsive to changes in market costs of capital at a price elasticity of demand of -1. On the savings side, 70% of total savings is national savings that is responsive to rates of return with a price elasticity of supply of 0.3. For a high-risk country, 20% of foreign savings is responsive to market rates of return at a price elasticity of supply of 1; for the moderate-risk country, 40% is responsive to market rates of return at a price elasticity of supply of 3; and for the very low-risk country, 60% is price-responsive at a price elasticity of supply of 6. This means that high returns to foreign savers result in an externality being earned by foreign savers in the high-risk country of some 2.3% per unit of capital, but these high returns form only 16% of

---

[9]In the examples in Table 1, in each type of country, $WAAC = i_m = i_m^f$.

[10]Following footnote 6, t_i is 15.01% for a very low-risk country, 13.95% for a moderate- to low-risk country, and 13.01% for a high- to very high-risk country.

Table 1: Hypothetical Illustrative Examples of Estimates of Economic Externality per Unit of Capital

Country Risk	High/ Very High	Moderate/ Low	Very Low
Market WAAC	12%	9%	6%
Elasticity of supply of foreign savings	1	3	6
Shares of capital from			
investment:	67%	38%	18%
National savings	17%	9%	5%
Foreign savings	16%	53%	77%
Sector externality:			
Investment taxes	6.6%	5.2%	3.8%
National savings taxes	-1.8%	-1.4%	-0.9%
Foreign savings taxes	-0.6%	-0.5%	-0.3%
Foreign savers' surplus	2.3%	1.1%	0.6%
Tax externality	4.1%	1.6%	0.4%
Foreign savers' externality	0.4%	0.6%	0.4%
Economic externality per unit of capital	**4.4%**	**2.2%**	**0.8%**

the source of capital, or an externality of only 0.4% per unit of capital invested. By contrast, in the very low-risk country, the foreign savers' externality falls to 0.6%, but foreign savings form 77% of the source of capital, or 0.4% per unit invested. The very low-risk country is taken to have an open capital market that is highly integrated into the global capital market; this results in high international capital mobility in response to changing rates of return. By contrast, the high-risk country has an open capital market but is poorly integrated into the global capital market, causing limited capital mobility.

In the high-risk country, tax externalities are a positive 6.6% of forgone investments, but they are -1.8% from taxes on added national savings and -0.6% on added taxes on foreign savings. The combined tax externality is 4.1% per unit of capital. In the very low-risk country, the tax externality on forgone investment is 3.8%, while on added national savings it is -0.9%, and on added foreign savings it is -0.3%, giving a combined tax externality of 0.4% per unit of capital invested.

For the three hypothetical countries, the combined economic externalities are 4.4% per unit of capital invested in the high-risk country, 2.2% in the moderate- to low-risk country, and 0.8% in the very low-risk country. This illustrates the importance of openness and country risk in determining the economic externality from capital investment. In practice, actual countries will have somewhat different economic, tax, and capital market structures, which will yield their own estimates of the national parameter that measures the *economic externality per unit of capital invested* in projects in the country. This national parameter, however, can also be expected to change over time as the economic structure, tax policy, tax effectiveness, and capital markets develop and, as such, should be estimated on a prospective basis.

The economic externality from capital investment is then added to the minimum supply price of total capital, or the minimum competitive WACC of the project, $i_{\min}^p$, to obtain the EOCK for the project, as in expressions (2) or (3) above, to estimate the EOCK as:

$$EOCK = i_{\min}^p + Economic\ externality\ per\ unit\ of\ capital \quad (5)$$

The minimum supply price of capital to the project ($i_{\min}^p$) will capture the country risk, project risk, and industry or market risk premiums and transaction costs in mobilizing capital for the project. If the project is a non-self-financing project – that is, it is financed out of the general budget revenues – then the supply price of capital would be the long-term cost of market borrowing by the government, which would include any country risk premium on sovereign debt. Where projects are very large relative to the revenue capacity of a country, then project risk should also be reflected either in $i_{\min}^p$ in the EOCK or as risk adjustments to the cash flows. If a project is self-financing or commercial, then the systematic industry risk premium needs to be included in $i_{\min}^p$.[11]

---

[11]Bailey and Jensen (1972) developed a risk-adjusted version of the Harberger weighted average EOCK that is somewhat analogous to the formulation presented here, but it also has some fundamental differences. Bailey and Jensen proposed an EOCK composed of a risk-free EOCK plus a risk adjustment component that reflected the systematic risk of the new investment

Implications of New Approach to Distributional Analysis

Distributional analysis is critical to understanding the gains and losses to the various stakeholders or parties involved in or affected by the operations of a project. Economic analysis aggregates all the winners and losers to give an aggregate net benefit or net present value (NPV) for all these stakeholders or interested and affected parties. Distributional analysis, by contrast, breaks out the net benefits or NPV of each group of stakeholders. Key stakeholders include the financiers (the equity holders or sponsors and the debt holders), government as a tax collector and provider of subsidies, consumers, suppliers, labour, and other parties positively or negatively affected by environmental impacts, as examples.

Distributional analysis typically expands the net economic benefit that is internalized in the project accounts to an economic perspective. It takes the net benefits accruing to the debt and equity holders and adds in the external net benefits accruing to the government, consumers, and other stakeholders. On an annual basis, the economic net benefits (ENB) can be taken to be equal to the financial or private net benefits (PNB) of the project, plus the sum of all the external costs and benefits, or in any year t:

$$ENB_t = PNB_t + \sum_i external\ NB_{t,i} \tag{6}$$

Given that this identity holds in every year, then it holds if all of its components are discounted to the present by the same discount rate or EOCK. In that case, the present value of the present value of the ENB discounted at the EOCK gives the NPV of the project from the economic perspective (NPV_{EOCK}^{econ}), or

---

project. This formulation results in the capital market externalities in the EOCK from the new project absorbing capital funds from other uses being a function of the riskiness of the new project rather than being independent of the riskiness of the new project. The new approach presented in this paper separates the forgone externality of using capital funds from the riskiness of the new project. It also allows for a wider range of types of risk and transactions costs (not just systematic or market risk) to be recognized in the supply of capital to the new project. See Bailey and Jensen (1972).

$$NPV_{EOCK}^{econ} \quad = \quad NPV_{EOCK}^{tot\,cap} \quad + \quad \sum_{i} PVExt_{EOCK,i} \qquad (7)$$

The first right-hand term gives the financial net cash flows to the total capital investment discounted by the EOCK; the second term sums up the external costs and benefit flows arising from the project discounted by the EOCK. Typically, these externalities would include the added consumer surplus captured by project beneficiaries (particularly in public sector projects delivering services at no or low prices) as well as the tax externalities from the direct taxes paid by the project and the indirect taxes arising from the net production of foreign exchange or the net products or services delivered by the project. Now, while this expression for the distribution of the aggregate losses and gains is correct and useful in checking the consistency in the overall analysis, it does not show the actual gains and losses to certain key stakeholders. Critically, the actual gains and losses of the financiers can only be captured if their actual values are included. To do this, (7) is transformed first by adding and subtracting the NPV expected by the project financiers from the expected total cash flows of the project discounted by their WACC ($NPV_{WACC}^{tot\,cap}$). Initially, assume the financiers are operating in competitive capital markets and their WACC is the minimum private supply cost of capital funds, i_{min}^{p}. Hence, (7) becomes

$$NPV_{EOCK}^{econ} = NPV_{i_{min}^{p}}^{tot\,cap} + (NPV_{EOCK}^{tot\,cap} - NPV_{i_{min}^{p}}^{tot\,cap}) + \sum_{i} PVExt_{EOCK,i} \quad (8)$$

The first right-hand term now captures the actual net benefits (surplus or loss) going to the financiers. What is the meaning of the second term, the difference between the same project cash flows from the total capital perspective discounted by the EOCK and by i_{min}^{p}? From the expression for the EOCK in (5) above, this difference in the second term measures the forgone economic externalities caused by investing capital in the project. This precise interpretation of this term only arises under the new approach to the EOCK that adjusts the EOCK for the costs of risk and capital mobilization transaction costs related to the project investment. It is a useful result as it allows the forgone externalities (typically, largely taxes) to be compared with the surplus made by the project and the externalities captured by the government (often largely taxes) and by consumers and other stakeholders. For example, in cases where a project gets a tax holiday it allows a comparison of this tax forgone by the government (both directly through the tax holiday and indirectly by the use of capital) with the surplus captured by the project and the direct and indirect tax externalities going to the government. This allows important questions to be answered, such as whether the tax holiday was needed by the project or whether the government suffers a net loss of tax revenues. To go further and explore the distribution of the gains and losses from a project that provides public services at no or low user charges as well as cases where project financiers are not facing competitive market conditions (by, for example, having access to low-interest rate debt), further expansion of expression (8) is desirable, but before doing that, it is useful to gain insights into this expression for simple private sector investments.

Private Sector Projects

Consider an investment of 100 in a commercial project that yields perpetuities of 6 to the private financiers and direct tax externalities of 4 (all in constant price terms). The private cost of capital is 6%, and the economic externality per unit of capital investment is 4% (primarily forgone taxes), and hence, EOCK = 10%. Clearly, this project is marginal from both private and economic perspectives, or $NPV_{i^p_{min}}^{tot\ cap} = -100 + 6/6\% = 0$ and $NPV_{EOCK}^{econ} = -100 + 10/10\% = 0$. The private financiers are just indifferent to taking on this marginal investment.

If the distribution of the gains and losses is explored using the consistency expression (7), then it is not clear that the private investors actually break even. According to (7),

$$NPV_{EOCK}^{econ} = (-100 + 6/10\%) + (4/10\%) = -40 + 40 = 0$$

whereas expression (8) shows that the private investors break even, that the economy forgoes 40 in externalities by investing 100 in the project, but the project generates 40 in direct tax externalities so that the economy also breaks even. To gain further insights into the second term in expression (8), it is useful to express this simple investment in more general terms.

Let p equal a private perpetuity captured by the private financiers, *ext* equal the annual direct economic externality generated by the investment, and e gives the rate of forgone economic externalities, or $e = EOCK - i_{\min}^p$ in terms of expression (5) above. Now expression (8) for the 100 investment becomes

$$NPV_{EOCK}^{econ} = (-100 + p / i_{\min}^p) + [-100 + p / EOCK$$
$$- (-100 + p / i_{\min}^p)] + (ext / EOCK)$$

or

$$NPV_{EOCK}^{econ} = (-100 + p / i_{\min}^p) + [(p / i_{\min}^p)(-e / EOCK)] \qquad (9)$$
$$+ (ext / EOCK)$$

Now for a marginal private investment, $p / i_{\min}^p = 100$ or $NPV_{i_{\min}^p}^{tot\,cap} = 0$, then

$$NPV_{EOCK}^{econ} = +(-100\,e / EOCK) + (ext / EOCK) \qquad (10)$$

or the project needs to generate direct externalities (such as added direct taxes) at a rate as fast as economic externalities are forgone (or $ext/100 \geq e$) for it to be economically attractive or $NPV_{EOCK}^{econ} \geq 0$. In the simple example above, the forgone externalities are −40, which are offset by the direct externalities generated of 40.

If the private investors expect to capture a surplus or $NPV_{i_{\min}^p}^{tot\,cap} > 0$ such that $p / i_{\min}^p > 100$, then the forgone externalities $((p / i_{\min}^p)(-e / EOCK))$ increase over those in (10), as the economy now loses access to the surplus captured by the private investors. These forgone externalities are offset by both the surplus captured by the private investors and the direct externalities. To illustrate, staying with the same simple investment as an illustration, assume that the private perpetuity increases from 6 to 7.2, but otherwise generates the same perpetual externality of 4. From (9)

$$NPV_{EOCK}^{econ} = (-100 + 7.2/6\%) + (7.2/6\%)(-4\%/10\%) + (4/10\%)$$
$$= \quad (20) \quad + \quad (-48) \quad + \quad (40) \qquad\qquad (11)$$
$$= \quad 12$$

Note that the forgone externalities have increased from –40 to –48, but in this case, the private gains are 20 and more than offset this increased external loss of 48. Importantly, the external loss on the capital invested increases by the financiers' surplus of 20 times the externality forgone per unit of capital, or $20*4\% = 8$.

What if the government offered the marginal investor a tax break that increased the private perpetuity by 2.4 from 6 to 8.4, but this tax break cut the direct annual externality generated by the project by the same amount from 4 to 1.6? Again using (9),

$$NPV_{EOCK}^{econ} = (-100 + 8.4/6\%) + (8.4/6\%)(-4\%/10\%) + (1.6/10\%)$$
$$= \quad (40) \quad + \quad (-56) \quad + \quad (16) \qquad\qquad (12)$$
$$= \quad 0$$

In this case, the tax break transfers added 40 to the private investors' gains, raising $NPV_{i_{min}^p}^{tot\ cap}$ to 40 at the expense of a loss of direct externalities of 24 (= 40 –16) and indirectly losing an added 16 (= 56-40) such that NPV_{EOCK}^{econ} is reduced to zero (= +40 – 16 – 24)). Note that the added forgone externality on the capital is $40*4\%$, or 16.

Public Sector Projects

In the case of many public sector projects, the project service is delivered at no or a low user charge such that from a financial perspective, the project is financially unattractive and requires significant government subventions from general tax revenues. From the economic perspective, the external gains to the users of the service need to be high enough to offset the financial losses and any other external net economic losses. In such projects, it becomes important to be able to identify the service beneficiaries and how much they gain separately from other externalities, typically due to tax distortions. To do this, expression (8) is expanded to recognize the net benefits or losses by the various external stakeholders, as follows:

$$NPV_{EOCK}^{econ} = NPV_{i_{min}^p}^{tot\,cap} + (NPV_{EOCK}^{tot\,cap} - NPV_{i_{min}^p}^{tot\,cap}) + \sum_j PVExt_{i_{min}^p,j}$$

$$+ \sum_j (PVExt_{EOCK,j} - PVExt_{i_{min}^p,j}) \tag{13}$$

Here, the first and third right-hand terms capture the actual present value of the gains or losses experienced by the financiers and by the external stakeholders, respectively. The second and fourth right-hand terms capture the forgone externalities (mainly tax-related) arising from the capital investment adjusted for the transfers of surplus among stakeholders caused by the project.

A simple water supply project is used as an illustration. A government water agency invests 100 in a water supply project and incurs perpetual annual operating and maintenance costs of 10 each year in constant prices. It supplies the water services free of charge such that the gain to the consumers is a perpetual benefit of 25. This external gain forms the first externality. The operations and maintenance are financed by government revenues, and the economy suffers the external economic cost of raising these public funds annually of 20% of the revenues.[12] This results in the second externality of a perpetual cost of 2 each year. This is the loss in market surplus, or dead weight loss, suffered by the private sector as taxpayers. The private or financial cost of capital (i_{min}^p) is 6%. With forgone economic externalities of 4%, the EOCK is 10%. For simplicity's sake, it is assumed that all the stakeholders have the same discount rate as the project financiers. Table 2 shows this water supply investment project from the financial, economic, and distributive perspectives.

Box A of Table 2 gives the regular financial and economic appraisal of the project. It shows that financially, the government-sponsored water agency invests 100 and incurs perpetual annual costs of 10 to maintain and operate the project. From a financial perspective, the $NPV_{i_{min}^p}^{tot\,cap} = -100 - 10/6\% = -266.7$. From an economic perspective, the $NPV_{EOCK}^{econ} = -100 + (25 - 10 - 2)/10\% = 30$.

---

[12]The marginal economic cost of public funds is taken here to be 20%.

Table 2: Financial, Economic, and Distributional Analysis of a Public Sector Water Supply Project

Private or financial discount rate (priv)	6%				
Economic discount rate (EOCK)	10%			Present values (PV) at	
				6%	10%

	Construction period	Operations period (perpetual)		Financial	Economic
A. Project appraisal					
Benefits					
Economic benefit of free water (Ext 1)		25		416.7	250
Costs					
Capital cost	100			100	100
Operating and maintenance costs		10		166.7	100
Cost of public funds (Ext 2)		2		33.3	20
NPV consumers (Ext 1) - NPV priv sector (Ext 2)				383.3	230.0
NPV water suppliers (total capital investment perspective)				-266.7	-200.0
NPV economic					30
B. Consistency check					
NPV total capital at EOCK					-200.0
NPV Ext (1+2) at EOCK					230.0
NPV econ at EOCK					30.0
C. Distribution of gains and losses					
NPV water suppliers (tot cap) at priv				-266.7	
NPV water suppliers (tot cap) at EOCK - same at priv				66.7	
NPV consumers (Ext) at priv				416.7	
NPV consumers (Ext) at EOCK - same at priv				-166.7	
NPV priv sector (Ext 2) at priv				-33.3	
NPV priv sector (Ext 2) at EOCK - same at priv				13.3	
NPV econ at EOCK				30.0	

	Annual net benefits	Present values
D. Distribution of actual gains and losses		
Consumers (Ext 1)	25	416.7
Private sector (Ext 2)	-2	-33.3
Government as sponsor or agency (investor & operator)	-16	-266.7
Government as receiver of revenue	-4	-86.7
Economy	3	30.0

Box B of Table 2 applies expression (7) to check the consistency of the analysis. The present value at EOCK of the externalities of the project experienced by the consumers and private sector as taxpayers amount to (+25/10% -2/10%) or 230, and the present value of the costs of the water agency amount to (100 + 10/10%) or 200, so that the difference is the $NPV_{EOCK}^{econ} = 230 - 200 = 30$.

Box C of Table 2 applies expression (11) to provide the distributive analysis, while Box D regroups the gains and losses so as to recognize the actual gains and losses. Now, the present value of the actual gain to consumers is 416.7 (which exceeds the gain to the economy of 250). The gain to consumers is reduced by the present values of the loss of the private sector from the economic cost of the public funds used to finance the operations and maintenance (-33.3), the financial loss of the water supply agency (-266.7), and the net economic externality forgone through the use of the capital funds adjusted for the changes in

Graham Glenday

stakeholder surpluses (+66.7−166.7+13.3=−86.7). Again, these add up to the overall present value of the net economic gain of 30. Box D also presents the distribution of these gains and losses as annualized amounts (rather than present values). The annual consumer gain of 25 is reduced by the economic cost of public funds (−2), the rental and operating cost of the water supply agency (−16), and the forgone externality on the capital invested (−4), leaving a net economic gain of 3 per year (or 30 in present value terms).

Uncompetitive Financing

Further refinements can be added to the distributional analysis in cases of uncompetitive financing of a project. Two common situations arise. The first, and possibly more common situation, is that of the project owners or sponsors getting access to low-interest rate loans. Usually, this arises where some national or multinational agency either provides below-market interest rate loans or provides loan guarantees that lower interest rates. The second situation is where the equity holders have above-market costs of capital. This may arise where a government is awarding a contract or concession in an uncompetitive fashion.

Low-Interest Rate Loan

To analyze the effects of a low-interest rate loan case, the first step is to recognize the cash flows to total capital that are allocated to the different equity and debt holders. Typically, where debt is supplied at a competitive market interest rate, it is taken that the debt holders just cover their costs and receive zero NPV (or the NPV of the debt holders' cash flows is zero at the interest rate paid on the debt, or $NPV_{int}^{debt} = 0$). This means that all the residual gains and losses from the project go to the equity holders, or $NPV_{i_{min}^{p}}^{tot\,cap} = NPV_{equity}^{equity}$, or the net cash flows to the equity holders discounted at their discount rate or supply price of equity.[13] In the case of a project receiving guaranteed, concessional, or

---

[13] $NPV_{i_{min}^{p}}^{tot\,cap} = NPV_{equity}^{equity}$ is a useful expression to find the WACC of a project where the structure of debt is complex and the debt-equity ratio varies

subsidized debt, however, the project WACC will be less than i_{min}^p to the extent of the lower cost of debt. Hence, expression (8) needs to recognize this difference between the actual costs of finance in the WACC and the minimum supply price in the EOCK, as follows:[14]

$$
\begin{aligned}
NPV_{EOCK}^{econ} &= NPV_{WACC}^{tot\,cap} + (NPV_{i_{min}^p}^{tot\,cap} - NPV_{WACC}^{tot\,cap}) \\
&+ (NPV_{EOCK}^{tot\,cap} - NPV_{i_{min}^p}^{tot\,cap}) + \sum_i PVExt_{EOCK,i}
\end{aligned}
\tag{14}
$$

The first term remains the surplus accruing to the project owners (which is now larger because of the subsidized debt). The second term is negative ($WACC < i_{min}^p$), as it is the value of the low-interest rate debt captured by the equity holders relative to paying market interest rates. The third term remains the forgone economic externalities on the capital used by the project. One of the externalities is now the present value of the negative cash flow of the cost arising from the low-interest rate loan to the government or funding agency bearing the cost of the low-interest rate loan.

---

over time. If NPV_{equity}^{equity} is estimated, then the WACC or i_{min}^p can be found by finding the value of i_{min}^p that would have the same NPV as NPV_{equity}^{equity} for the net cash flows to total capital. See Glenday and Tham (2003).

[14]Note that $NPV_{WACC}^{tot\,cap}$ in (14) can be disaggregated into the NPVs accruing to the different financiers. Assuming two classes of financier, equity and debt holders, and dividing the cash flow to total capital between them, then $NPV_{WACC}^{tot\,cap} = NPV_{equity}^{equity} + NPV_{debt}^{debt}$. For example, in the case of the perpetuity of 6 to total capital of 100 at a cost of 6%, if debt receives 1.2 from investing 40 at an interest rate of 3%, and equity invests 60 and receives the balance of 4.8, then all parties have NPV = 0, and WACC is 6%. Instead of adjusting the WACC in (14) for subsidized interest rates or other changes in the private costs of capital, if the financiers' NPVs are disaggregated, then the changes in their net benefits can be accounted for directly. If an external agent (such as a government) is funding the change in interest rates, then this external cost is also explicitly recognized in the externalities of the project. The second term in (14) would be similarly disaggregated into the NPVs of the different financiers so that it would capture the gain to the equity holders and loss to the debt holders relative to paying market interest rates on the debt.

A simplified case of a low-interest rate loan can be illustrated using the example in (11) above of a perpetual investment project except that the project is not financially attractive to private investors with market financing because it is generating above-average externalities. Now $p = 5.4$, $WACC = i_{min}^p$, and $ext = 5$, with the same costs of capital such that:

$$
\begin{aligned}
NPV_{EOCK}^{econ} &= (-100 + p/i_{min}^p) + (p/i_{min}^p)(i_{min}^p - EOCK)/EOCK + ext/EOCK \\
&= (-100 + 5.4/6\%) + (5.4/6\%)(-4\%/10\%) + (5/10\%) \\
&= (-10) \quad + \quad (-36) \quad + \quad (50) \\
&= 4
\end{aligned}
\tag{15}
$$

Expression (15) shows that the private financiers lose 10, and the economy gains 4 from the high direct externalities generated by the project relative to those forgone. Now, the government offers a low-interest rate loan, and it costs the government 1.2 each year to finance the low-interest rate loan; this lowers the externalities from 5 to 3.8 each year. With the low-interest rate loan and possibly higher leverage, the WACC falls to 4.8%.[15] Expressing (14) in terms of the perpetuity:

$$
\begin{aligned}
NPV_{EOCK}^{econ} &= (-100 + p/WACC) + (p/i_{min}^p)(WACC - i_{min}^p)/WACC + \\
&\quad (p/i_{min}^p)(i_{min}^p - EOCK)/EOCK + ext/EOCK \\
&= (-100 + 5.4/4.8\%) + (5.4/6\%)(-1.2\%/4.8\%) \\
&\quad + (5.4/6\%)(-4\%/10\%) + (3.8/10\%) \\
&= (12.5) \quad + \quad (-22.5) \quad + \quad (-36) \quad + \quad (38) \\
&= -8
\end{aligned}
\tag{16}
$$

Now the equity holders expect a gain of 12.5 rather than a loss of 10 (or a net improvement of 22.5, as shown in the second right-hand term), but the economy loses 12 in external gains, and the externalities drop from 50 to 38 as it has to finance the forgone interest of 1.2 a year.[16] Note that

---

[15]Without a low-interest rate loan, if equity finances 40% at a cost of 9% and debt the remaining 60% at 4%, then WACC = 6%. If the interest rate is lowered to 2%, then this costs 1.2 per 100 investment in total capital (or 2% * 60% = 1.2%), and the WACC = 4.8%.

[16]A similar net gain could have been passed on to the equity holders of the investment by cutting its tax burden by 1.35 per year. This would also reduce the

this lower interest rate could be achieved by the government financing the interest loss by tax revenues; or by the government using guarantees to some financial institutions to provide the lower cost debt (where the expected cost of the guarantee would be drawn on government revenues)[17]; or if the government received low-interest rate financing from a foreign donor agency, and instead of using this to pay off existing debt at market interest rates, it passes on this low rate to the investment project and forgoes tax savings or benefits from added expenditures. It would only be in the case of the foreign donor agency providing the low-interest rate financing for a specific project that could not be used for alternative uses, and the funding not being available for other purposes, that the interest loss would not be experienced as an externality.

Uncompetitive Equity Supply

Typically, suppliers of equity are not expected to invest if they do not expect to achieve their minimum supply price. They may, however, expect to receive returns above the market minimum supply price or above their own supply price. This may occur where a project is offered an above-market return, as could happen in a regulatory regime guaranteeing a specified return, or where there is a lack of competitive bidding. For example, in the case of bidding for a public concession providing access to income-generating public assets, the government agency may accept a below-market bid. Two difficult-to-distinguish situations may arise − namely, either (a) the equity holders accept a windfall gain ($NPV_{WACC}^{tot\,cap} > 0$) even with $WACC = i_{min}^p$, or (b) the actual WACC exceeds i_{min}^p because the equity holders only have access to high-cost debt and/or have high-cost equity (as may be the case with a

---

external gains from the project by 13.5 such that the economy suffers a loss of 9.5.

[17]Estimating the costs and benefits of loan guarantees is fairly complex in two respects. The gains to the beneficiary requires knowledge of what the supply price of a particular risk-class of debt would have been in a competitive market to the project, the probable costs of default under the conditions of the guarantee, and the amounts of these costs recoverable from the guarantor. The cost to the guarantor becomes these expected claims under the guarantee conditions.

small, undiversified company with risk-averse owners) such that in the extreme the private bidders are, in fact, only just willing to do the project, or $NPV_{WAAC}^{tot\,cap} = 0$. In this latter case, arguably the real added costs of capital are being incurred by the financiers by allowing above-market-cost capital to be used, and following (5), $EOCK_{uc} = WACC + economic$ *externality per unit of capital.* At this higher EOCK, $NPV_{EOCK_{uc}}^{econ}$ is lower than NPV_{EOCK}^{econ} (where EOCK is based on i_{min}^p), and the difference $(NPV_{EOCK_{uc}}^{econ} - NPV_{EOCK}^{econ})$ captures the economic loss from uncompetitive bidding. Taking the example in (11) above, if the project generated a private perpetuity of 7.2 and externalities of 4, then the private gains are 20 with $i_{min}^p = 6\%$, and economic gains are 12 with EOCK =10%. If investors with a minimum WACC of 7.2% were allowed to undertake the project, then $EOCK_{uc}$ becomes 11.2% (7.2% + 4%), and (11) becomes

$$
\begin{aligned}
NPV_{EOCK_{uc}}^{econ} &= (-100+7.2/7.2\%)+(7.2/7.2\%)(-4\%/11.2\%)+(4/11.2\%) \\
&= (0) \quad + \quad (-35.7) \quad + \quad (35.7) \\
&= 0
\end{aligned}
$$

$$(17)$$

Here, the economy loses 12 by allowing high-cost investors to undertake the project. Clearly, in (11) competitive bidding could have extracted an upfront transfer of 20 from the investors with a WACC of 6% to the government (a direct lump sum externality) and left the net economic gains unchanged at 12.

Summary Remarks

In summary, the new, but old, approach to the EOCK as the minimum or competitive supply price of capital to a project plus a national parameter estimate of the economic externality per unit of capital is both flexible and feasible. It unifies the insights and techniques coming from the capital market finance experts of the business school in estimating the minimum supply price of capital with the economic insights of the public finance economist in estimating the economic externalities of using capital. It removes the increasingly weighty criticism of the lack of risk adjustments in the single-valued EOCK, while it contains the EOCK estimate of the cost of public investment funds for the pure public sector project as a special case. In the latter case, however, the EOCK is likely to be somewhat lower than the traditional single-valued estimate as the costs of risk and transaction cost included would only be those included in the cost of long-term public debt. Finally, it allows a more precise disaggregating of the gains and losses to the project financiers, government treasury, public service beneficiaries, and other stakeholders of a project for public sector projects and for projects with private participation under a variety of tax and capital investment incentive arrangements.

References

Bailey, M.J. and M.C. Jensen. 1972. "Risk and the Discount Rate for Public Investment", in M.C. Jensen (ed.), *Studies in the Theory of Capital Markets*. New York: Praeger.

Harberger, A.C., ed. 1976. *Project Evaluation: Collected Papers*. Chicago: University of Chicago Press, Chapter 7.

Harberger, A.C. and G.P. Jenkins. 2002. *Manual on Cost-Benefit Analysis for Investment Decisions*. Kingston: Queen's University.

Glenday, G. 2003. "Economic Opportunity Cost of Capital: Financing Infrastructure in Emerging Markets", a paper prepared for the Inter-American Development Bank, June (mimeo).

Glenday, G. and J. Tham. 2003. "What Weights in the WACC?" Sanford Institute Working Paper Series, Paper No. SAN03-01.

Comment on "The New (but Old) Approach to the Economic Opportunity Cost of Capital" by Graham Glenday

Glenn P. Jenkins and Chun-Yan Kuo

In the above paper by Graham Glenday, he argues that using a single economic opportunity cost of capital as the discount rate in the economic appraisal of a specific project is inappropriate because of the lack of adjustments for the risk factors related to the specific project. These factors can be caused by a lack of liquidity of the investment, exchange rate or currency risk, sector or systematic risk, project-specific risk, and country risk. The claim is also made that a single discount rate does not account for the differential transaction costs in raising capital by the financiers for the project. As a result, the present value criterion using a single economic discount rate for project selection would penalize low-risk projects while favouring high-risk projects.

To rectify these shortcomings, the paper modifies the traditional approach to the estimation of the economic discount rate, which is a weighted average of the economic rate of return on private investment and the time preference rate for consumption. By following the supply price approach to estimating the economic cost of labour, the paper argues that a risk-adjusted discount rate for a specific project can be obtained by taking the minimum supply price of capital in a competitive market by the financiers of the investment project as the initial parameter. It then takes into account the externalities associated with the long-run use of capital acquired for the investment project. These externalities are independent of the use of the project funds, and the externality when based on per unit of capital is considered as a national parameter. By reformulating the risk-adjusted discount rate in this manner, the paper claims to have taken into account risk factors as well as the externalities of using capital in the evaluation of a specific project for the nation as a whole. The paper then further calculates and interprets the implications of the gains and losses to stakeholders under different economic situations by simply rearranging various variables/parameters in computing the net present value of the total net economic benefits as a result of the implementation of a project.

The issue of whether the economic cost of capital for a nation should be adjusted for risk in the economic appraisal of an investment project has been discussed and debated for years in the literature. This issue is not only conceptual but also empirical. The approach suggested by Graham Glenday by adding a national parameter − the externalities associated with the project funds acquired by the specific project − to the minimum supply price of capital in a competitive market by the financiers to form a risk-adjusted discount rate appears to be a neat and interesting concept. It is similar to the commercial evaluation of a project, in which systematic risk must be accounted for. The underlying hypothesis of this approach, however, is to assume that the risk related to the private supply of the project funds is the same as the social risk for the economy. This raises the fundamental question of whether these social risks can well be completely or partially diversified across the nation in the economic appraisal of the project so that no risk premium or just a partial risk premium is called for. For example, a project that is creating systematic risk for the private sector might also create social externalities that are counter cyclical. In addition, the author has not explicitly offered any empirical calculation of the risk premium for a specific project.

Using this risk-adjusted discount rate to discount the returns to financiers as well as the gains and losses received by different stakeholders is not straightforward. This is because the appropriate risk-adjusted discount rates to evaluate the gains and losses by the various stakeholders, including changes in government tax revenues, labour benefits, and consumer surplus, are not all equal. They all certainly do not have the same risk premium and transaction costs that are associated with sourcing of capital by the financiers in the capital market. That being said, after adding and subtracting some variables to various components in the equation of calculating the total net economic benefits − e.g., equation (13) − the author provides some additional and interesting interpretations regarding the net externalities arising from the investment adjusted for the transfers of surplus among stakeholders as the result of the project implementation.

The paper also provides some hypothetical numerical examples to illustrate estimates of the economic externality per unit of capital for three countries with different country risk ranges. The results may be interesting, but they are not surprising, because of changes in the relative shares of project funds sourced from forgone investment, national savings, and foreign savings (Burgess, 1981). However, it would have been a more useful exercise if the paper had presented examples with different levels of project risks within the same country. Glenday argues that the economic discount rate for the project should increase if the financiers viewed the project as being more risky. In a similar fashion, if the externalities of a project were to be enjoyed by a set of stakeholders who had a very low discount rate (the super-rich), then it would appear, following Glenday's approach, that the economic discount rate should be reduced for that project. When one considers the determination of the economic discount rate as a weighted average of the discount rates of the set of stakeholders affected by the project, the elegance of Glenday's approach loses some of its lustre.

The main concern of this paper is how one can deal with the risks associated with all the stakeholders of a specific project. It appears that if one is to put the risk premium explicitly into the discount rate then one must have the appropriate risk adjusted discount rate for each of the stakeholders. This pushes us into the same problem when we use a different time preference rate for each of the stakeholders. Because the various risks are related to a specific project, it would seem preferable if each of the risks were identified and explicitly evaluated. The monetary values of the costs of each of these risks could then be incorporated in the numerator rather than the denominator of the present value calculation of the net economic benefits of the project. After subtracting the costs of risk from the net benefit flows accruing to each of the parties, then the net results for each of these stakeholders can be discounted using a riskless rate of discount.

Reference

Burgess, D.F. 1981. "The Social Discount Rate for Canada: Theory and Evidence", *Canadian Public Policy*.

Summary of Discussion

George Kuo: I enjoyed very much reading Graham's paper, especially when he talks about who is winning and who is losing in the distribution and what is a stakeholder. In the paper he tries to capture the risk of a project in the measure of the economic opportunity cost of capital. The first thing you have to accept is that the risk seen by the investors represents the systematic risk in the society. How do we know that this risk is social risk and not just private risk, or just rent to investors? And why should we apply this risk-adjusted rate to the project's benefits as well as its costs?

Graham Glenday: George has brought up an important point. Governments often end up in non-competitive bidding situations. They award projects uncompetitively. So you do have to distinguish between – and this happens in PPPs, where you use public capital and there's value in that, and governments choose the guy that bids the lowest price. You may not know what his discount rate is, but the one that bids the least to, say, take over the harbour and run it for the next 20 years with all whatever conditions in the contract.

You have an uncompetitive situation. So if our competitive rate was 6%, and now you end up with a situation where somebody effectively seems to be demanding 8%, if you apply the rate of return he's wanting to get on that project from you based on his uncompetitive bid, you have the basic problem of saying: Is this just a transfer to this guy that's being uncompetitive, and we're going to pay him 8 when the market rate is 6? You need to know that, as opposed to, what if it's being uncompetitive, and this guy, if you offered him 7.8 or 7.5, he won't do it. Otherwise, he's saying: My minimum supply price is 8.

You can work out what is the cost of uncompetitive bidding. If you actually go ahead with that project, he's incurring 2. He's telling you, I'm going to bear that cost of risk, and you can then estimate that as well. The cost of having an uncompetitive bidding situation is, you pay 2 extra more, but the economy is not better off in the sense that you've actually caused the economy to bear a premium of 2 on that. That becomes a very important thing.

How you actually find out this minimum supply price, I guess, all these optioning and other kind of techniques, trying to make sure that you actually get a minimum supply price quoted on that. But if you don't, you have this problem of trying to unravel whether this difference is just a transfer to this guy, that his opportunity cost is actually 6%, and you're giving him 8%, or whether you've given it to a high-risk guy and you've actually incurred 2% cost in the economy. That's the puzzle that you have to figure out: are you incurring added costs, or just moving money around in the economy?

Rosalind Thomas: I'm going to open up now to the floor. I know there were questions from earlier on.

Christopher Shugart: I have a question for Graham. I liked your paper very much, but I'm grappling with this one thing. I think it relates to what George was saying. Let me give you an example.

Suppose you have a project, a PPP that's a bridge. And let's say it's going to be used for 30 years. So let's say the people don't pay, but there's obviously a willingness to pay; they get benefits for 30 years. Let's say a private company does it, and they get paid from the Treasury over 15 years. Let's say the particular formula for the way they're paid is risky. Let's say, for some reason they don't pay them just an availability payment. Instead, they do a partial shadow toll where they count the number of people that go across the bridge.

So for 15 years, you have a peculiar risk profile. Therefore, the supply price of the investor takes into account the systematic risk, and he may well say: Look, this is risky in a systematic way, and because of that I'm going to have to add on 2% to my cost of capital.

My problem with what you said – You then look at this extra supply price, this 2% for risk, and you use this in the economic appraisal, where the transfer wipes out. And now you're just using that higher rate, which was based on the transfer, to discount the economic benefits and costs. Why on earth do you do this? The willingness to pay over 30 years is the users' willingness to pay. The risk premium in the discount rate isn't *their* risk aversion; it's the risk aversion of the investor. I think this is my problem, which I haven't quite figured out.

Rosalind Thomas: Do you want to put your second question, and then I can get a couple of additional questions?

Christopher Shugart: OK. This is for David. I'm curious to know how this would play out in terms of your discussion. My understanding of Feldstein's article in 1970, and I may be interpreting it wrong, is that when you're doing cost-effectiveness analysis, only to rank projects, to see which one is better, the opportunity cost of displaced private investment cancels out provided that you are treating all expenditures in both projects exactly the same way in terms of opportunity costs.

If I understand that correctly, the corollary is, if you want to show, in doing cost-benefit analysis, that the opportunity cost of displaced private investment matters, you have to treat certain expenditures in different projects in different ways. First of all, do you agree with that? I think you probably will. But let's see if you agree. And if so, how does that play out in terms of the discussion of the methods you described?

Rosalind Thomas: Let's get a few more questions. Then, I'll ask David and Graham to respond.

Toby Sanger: An interesting paper from David; I hadn't had a chance to read it before, so this is really more of a question. I wasn't clear on how you dealt with differing rates of risk within the public and private sector. It occurs to me that a lot of what government in the public sector does is pool risk, whether it's health care, social insurance, or bailing out Wall Street. And that wasn't clear to me in your paper. It seems that you're treating a dollar of public expenditure as substitutes in different circumstances.

Michael Spackman: Just a clarification of that point. Chris gave the illustration of, say, a toll road. This is one of the reasons why certain UK privately financed toll roads – and the private financing, by the way, is actually costed as if it were a public expenditure. There's no balance sheet. The payments to the private sector are not made for traffic at all; they're made for availability completely, plus a little bit for wear and tear from heavy traffic. But one can get round these corners by clever devices.

With respect to Professor Harberger's remarks, I'm still a bit lost at these very high numbers used for private sector returns – 20%, 15%. That sort of number can only arise under a monopoly, or with optimism bias built into the private sector, or maybe if you've got very high leverage. The fact is, the long-run return to equity we observe is 6 or 7%. Where do these very, very high rates of return come from? What do they mean?

One point does need to be said. David made a very fair point that the shadow price of public expenditure or project funding is rarely, if ever, made explicit. He is absolutely right. I said in my paper that it didn't matter in practice. I'd better say why. One is that when you're talking about cost-effectiveness, as Chris said a moment ago, it cancels out; it applies equally to everything, so it doesn't matter. When you've got cost-benefit analysis, of course it does matter. And if one's going to go down that route, all the figures have to be either public expenditure or public-expenditure savings, or consumption equivalent. That can entail a lot of work.

But when you've done that, and you have your benefit-cost ratio in terms of all the benefits divided by net public expenditure, you can rely on the Ministry of Finance to say, No, you can't have that money. Don't expect anything like a benefit-cost ratio of 1 that is remotely acceptable. We are going to impose a pretty high number. It won't be as high as 2.5. That is unrealistic. In practice, it seems to me, this operates pretty well through a tight budgeting system.

With respect to the very long term, I was very interested in a point that Chris made in his paper about Hicks-Kaldor. When we think about the issue of climate change, we certainly don't observe Hicks-Kaldor, do we? It's universally accepted that climate change, is going to make people in the richer countries worse off. This is simply because we care about the survival of future civilization. So I think when you have a big problem, Hicks-Kaldor is not a fundamental principle.

But more generally, I really don't think discounting is terribly relevant to things like long-term climate change. This is partly because the whole thing is so long-term and partly because we're actually not talking about marginal changes here; we're talking about a willingness to pay to avoid a risk of the end of the world as we know it. And we need lots of information about what climate change would do. But to start working out present values and saying: How much do we in Canada or Europe care about Africans in 50 years' time?

You can't do that; it's not a sensible way to do it. Obviously, it's a huge problem. Obviously, you need to do a lot more than is being done in the world now. But it isn't cost-benefit analysis territory. Economists can, I think, try to stretch cost-benefit analysis too far sometimes.

David Burgess: On the risk question, my paper abstracts from risk. The assumption is simply that the economy generates this annual rate of return year after year and the consumer gets less than that because of taxes.

Let's go to the question of identical benefits. We have these two projects; we can liken it to the discussion earlier about Ontario Hydro's dilemma about the nuclear option versus renewable energy. So we have this benefit stream that both options are going to deliver, and we have to compare the cost streams. The appropriate comparison of the costs is the opportunity costs. That comes out clearly in the MCF criterion discussed in the paper, where you're discounting at the pre-tax rate of return on those costs.

So I'm going to state unequivocally that I believe that Feldstein is wrong about the discount rate for cost-effectiveness analysis, that he should be using the economic opportunity cost of capital and not the lower after-tax rate of return at which the government can borrow. Feldstein's result depends upon the private sector being myopic so a dollar of project spending has the same displacement effects no matter when that dollar is spent. But if people anticipate that the spending will occur they will react differently than if they don't. If the government defers a dollar of spending for a year it doesn't mean that the private sector pretends it will never occur. The economic cost of each dollar spent is the government's borrowing rate plus the taxes lost per dollar of private investment displaced.

As to the long term, and whether we should be discounting benefits realized 100 years from now at 8% or so, which makes them pretty trivial unless we put huge numbers on those benefits. But that's just spelling out opportunity cost. Do we really want to put our money in an abatement project that has a positive NPV at the STP rate if the alternative is debt reduction, which would lead to increased private investment earning 8%? Future generations will be better off with debt reduction.

Graham Glenday: Let me see if I understand Chris's question. You're saying: If I had a public road, and under my formulation I would be discounting at the government's long-term borrowing rate. Now you're saying, if we turned that into a toll road or quasi-toll road, where the private investor has to raise money and bear market risk, do we discount the gains, and the road users' gains would be less because we're now going to take some money out of their pockets, but to the extent they're still getting a consumer surplus out of this, should we discount that at the higher discount rate? Is that what you're concerned about?

Christopher Shugart: A more general point. Why should we use this risk-adjusted rate in the economic analysis?

Graham Glenday: You're saying, now I've put some added costs on those financiers, but we've also got these other guys who're benefiting and *not* bearing those costs. And we'll come back to this in these infrastructure things. I think that in a way, there is an added cost there, but should it be isolated away? That gets down to the issue of whether you bring the cost of risk into the discount rate, or put it into the cash flows? Maybe the only way to isolate it out, and put it back onto the financiers and not onto the consumers, is to put it into the cash flows. That may be the way to go.

5

What Is Risk?

Antal Deutsch

The dictionary definition of risk is the exposure to the hazard of loss. Until risk is quantified, it is an emotion ranging from a specific fear, such as that the plane I am travelling on will crash, to some sort of floating anxiety about unspecified bad things happening in the future. The only thing the economist can do with this emotion is to note that it refers to one or more future events. The future, by definition, is unobservable, thus unknowable and immeasurable.

Risk cannot be managed, or accepted and controlled within bounds, until it can be measured. Because what we need is immeasurable, a large industry has been thriving since the days of Ancient Greece in supplying proxies for the future. The contemporary version of the art is to project the past and allow users to pretend that they have a reasonable − as good as money can buy − version of the future. These calculations would be possible if we had density functions representing the probabilities of events that will occur. Unfortunately, estimates based on past experience do not, on an unknown and unknowable number of occasions, meet this criterion. "Risk budgets" have become a contemporary wealth management tool, based on the record of past price fluctuations. Risk premia attached to project costs, if not purely arbitrary, are based on some distillate of past experience.

Insurance, in its classical essence, is based on the belief, however obtained, of the insurer that the hazard of loss for a large number of exposures is known and stable, but the incidence of the known aggregate loss cannot be predetermined. The insurer then proceeds to sell policies to risk holders at a price that dwarfs the cost of the potential loss to the risk holder but compensates the insurer for its risk, administrative costs, and the profit permitted by market conditions. The only risk that remains with the insured is related to the possible inability of the insurer to meet its obligation. Note the strong requirement of beliefs about the future on the part of both the insurer and the insured for this transaction to take place at any given price.

To the extent that projections of the past serve as proxies of the future, please note the persistent presence of what might be described as two problems. One is the surprise shift of parametric values (shocks?), and the other is the appearance of the effect of omitted variables.

Let me illustrate.

Annuity providers have discovered that their annuitants, in Canada, live longer than expected on the basis of the mortality tables used in writing the annuities. This undoubtedly has many causes, but increased access to more highly developed diagnostic and therapeutic services must loom large in this picture. Research in medicine is a systematic, ongoing activity, but scientific breakthroughs with dramatic results are not. As a result, dramatic increases in life expectancy are unpredictable. Any annuity provider, at least implicitly, has to put a price on unpredictable future scientific breakthroughs each time it provides a quote to a prospective client. To make the exercise look scientific, the actuaries have to make an explicit assumption on the first difference to life expectancy over time, and they do. What they do have is a blind guess.

My second illustration concerns the destruction of the World Trade Center in New York in 2001. The property insurance policies issued to the beneficial owners provided the standard exclusions for war, insurrection, and "the acts of foreign princes". When the dust settled, it became apparent that none of those words covered acts of terrorism; thus, the insurer provided coverage at no premium against a hazard it was unaware of.

The third, and final, illustration concerns the 2007 failure in Canada of asset-backed commercial paper, given top rating by the Canadian Bond Rating Agency. Their public explanation for their rating was the failure of their rating model to take into account hazards that have not been observed in the past.

From all this, I conclude that risk is, in principle, immeasurable. Like all other unmeasured quantities, we are each free to make our own guess as to its magnitude.

Part III

Estimation of Discount Rates in Canada

6

On Growth, Investment, Capital, and the Rate of Return

Arnold C. Harberger

This paper is aimed at introducing economic analysts and other interested parties to some interesting twists and turns that arise as one juxtaposes basic economic theory to real-world data. Readers will, I think, be quite surprised at the insights one gains from some very simple exercises. In addition, many may be led to appreciate aspects of a country's economic life of which they previously had little awareness. To give some focus to our story, we will concentrate on the idea that somehow, "hidden" in the standard national accounts of a country, lies the basis for measuring the contribution of investment to the growth process and also an overall "real" rate of return to reproducible capital in the country. In subsequent exercises, we will explore breaking down the capital stock of the country into segments, with different rates of return applying to each segment. In the process, we will explore how to build up a series of estimates of the "real" reproducible capital stock of a country, how to deal with land as an additional component of the total capital stock, how to allow for the special attributes of residential housing as a component of the capital stock and as a generator of a stream of real returns, how to handle the contributions of government investments in infrastructural items that yield little or no cash revenues, and finally, how to isolate the real rate of return to what might be called "ordinary business capital" apart from housing.

Expressing Gross Investment in Real Terms

Nearly all national accounts systems present time series on gross investment. Most of them include under this concept both private and public investment, and in this paper, we will assume that we are dealing with such a case. Non-economist readers should be aware that the focus of the national accounts is on the flow of goods and services being produced, consumed, or invested in a given period. Under this concept, a country cannot invest in land except by such actions as clearing, levelling, fencing, etc., and, of course, reclaiming land from rivers, lakes, or seas. Thus, the private purchase of a farm or residential lot is indeed an investment from the purchaser's point of view, but the national accounts view it as a disinvestment by the seller of same. These two entries cancel from the national accounts point of view. The same goes for the purchase and sale of a manufacturing plant, a truck, or any other pre-existing asset. The gross domestic investment that the national accounts measure consists of the goods and services that were produced in the country and used for domestic investment in the given period plus imported goods and services that likewise ended up being used for domestic investment in that same period. The sum of these two items is what the national accounts typically label gross investment.

To express investment in real terms, one needs to deflate the gross investment figure by some relevant price index. Most countries develop as part of their national accounting procedures an investment goods price index. For the purposes of the present paper, however, we want to use a more general index, the GDP deflator. The reason for this is that we are headed toward a direct measurement of the rate of return to capital. This consists of a ratio between the "return to capital" in the numerator and the "stock of capital" in the denominator. Obviously, one cannot take such a ratio and call it a rate of return if the numerator and denominator are measured in different units. Our procedure will end up measuring both numerator and denominator in units of "GDP baskets" of constant purchasing power (e.g., in terms of pesos of the year 2000 or some other base year). The "return to capital" in the numerator is obtained simply by summing the various sources of capital income (profits, interest, rents, etc.), usually in nominal pesos, then expressing this income as a fraction of nominal GDP, and then applying this fraction to the country's real GDP. In our numerical exercises, we will operate with alternative assumptions about the fraction of real GDP going to reproducible capital.

Arnold C. Harberger

Building a Capital Stock Time Series

The simplest method for building a capital stock on the basis of investment data uses what is called the *perpetual inventory approach*. This applies the following operation:

End of 2006 capital stock

equals

End of 2005 capital stock

plus

Gross investment during 2006

minus

Depreciation of existing stock during 2006

In symbols: $K_t = K_{t-1}(1-\delta) + I_{gt}$

where K_t is the capital stock at the end of period t, I_{gt} is gross investment during period t, and δ is the fraction of last year's capital stock that depreciates (in real terms) during period t. The formula provides a rolling evolution of the capital stock, moving from one year to the next by adding the next year's new investment and subtracting the real depreciation of the old capital stock during that same next year.

The question obviously arises, under this procedure: from where do we obtain an estimate of the initial capital stock (for some past year) from which to start this chain-link process? Here we will describe what is probably the simplest method for doing so. Alternative techniques are outlined in a companion paper.

Our simplest technique is based on a result that characterizes "growth equilibrium" under nearly all approaches to the analysis of economic growth. This result states that in growth equilibrium, an "equilibrium capital/output (K/Y) ratio" prevails, which in turn means that the capital stock series (K) and the real GDP (or other output) series grow at the same rate. To obtain an estimate of K_O (say K at the end of 1969) using the assumption of growth equilibrium, we assume that during 1970, both K and Y grew at the same rate. The increment to K is $\Delta K_{70} = I_{70} - \delta K_{69}$, or $(\Delta K_{70}/K_{69}) = (I_{70}/K_{69}) - \delta = \Delta Y_{70}/Y_{69}$. Since we have data on I_{70}, ΔY_{70}, and Y_{69}, and since our procedure uses an assumed value for δ, the above equation can be solved for K_{69}, which then can be used as the starting point for the chain-link, perpetual inventory method.[1]

We have yet to speak of the depreciation rate, δ. It would be nice if the national accounts would give us an accurate picture of the real depreciation occurring in an economy each year. But, in fact, the underlying data are distorted by several important factors.

a) In most countries, business accounts are kept in nominal terms with no attempt to convert them into real terms. Firms thus deduct as depreciation of each year a specified fraction of the nominal price paid for each asset. When inflation has intervened· between the year of purchase of the asset and the year for which depreciation is being calculated, this leads to a significant understatement of depreciation.

b) In many countries, governments permit the accelerated depreciation of assets for tax purposes. In these cases, tax depreciation often far exceeds true economic depreciation.

c) Independent of government policy, business firms typically have an incentive to exaggerate depreciation, as this gives them a bigger deduction for tax purposes.

For the above reasons, one can have little reliance on national accounts depreciation unless a very explicit effort has been made by the national accounts people themselves to do exercises of the type we are here examining. Hence, nearly all economists who engage in the exercise of building time series of the real capital stock make assumptions as to plausible rates of real depreciation. The best way to do this is to build separate capital stock series for buildings, machinery and equipment, vehicles, and inventories (plus other categories if and when the data exist and the categories seem relevant). However, to do this using direct data, one requires annual national accounts investment to be broken down into

---

[1] In my own applications, I have tried to use for I_{70} in the above formula an average like $(I_{69}+I_{70}+I_{71})/3$ and for $(\Delta Y_{70}/Y_{60})$ an average of $(\Delta Y_{69}/Y_{68})(\Delta Y_{70}/Y_{69})$ and $(\Delta Y_{71}/Y_{70})$. This helps guard against the chosen year being erratic in the sense of the real capital stock and real GDP growing at substantially different rates. In choosing the starting date for a given country, we also have tried to avoid "abnormal" periods (export booms, cyclical recessions, major inflationary bursts, etc.). Others would be well advised to adopt the same precautions.

Arnold C. Harberger

these component parts. In the absence of such a breakdown, and/or in studies in which a common methodology is being applied to many countries, the practice has been to make a sensible assumption as to the average rate of depreciation of the country's reproducible capital stock.

Here we will assume the rate of real depreciation on the entire stock of reproducible capital to be 4%. To justify this, we develop a "scenario analysis" showing the coherency and plausibility of the various components of the story.

First, we assume an economy in which real GDP is growing at the rate of 3% per year and in which real gross investment averages 20% of real GDP. This investment in turn is broken down as follows:

Investment in:
buildings $= 45\%$ of I_g, with a depreciation rate of 2%
machinery and equipment $= 30\%$ of I_g, with a depreciation rate of 8%
vehicles $= 22\%$ of I_g, with a depreciation rate of 12%
inventory investment $= 3\%$ of I_g, with a zero depreciation rate
(Standard national accounting practice considers inventory investment to represent the *net* increment to inventories. The depletion of old inventories has thus automatically been deducted in arriving at national accounts investment.)

Table 1 shows data for a typical year in such an economy. Gross investment is taken to be 100 in that year, so GDP is 500. What we do in the table is build equilibrium stocks of the different types of capital, following the "rule" that the equilibrium stock $K_{j,t-1}$ is equal to $I_{gjt}/(g+\delta_j)$. (I_{gjt} = gross investment of type j in year t; g = GDP growth rate.)

To these assumptions we add the allocation of annual investment – 45% to buildings, 30% to machinery and equipment, 22% to vehicles (row a). Three percent of I_g is allocated to inventory investment, but this figure is based not on total investment but on the growth of GDP. The assumption is that 20% of the increment to GDP is represented by inventory accumulation. This assumption in turn leads to an estimated total stock of inventory capital that is equal to 20% of one year's GDP (=100, in the units of the table). The assumed depreciation rates for the types of depreciable capital are shown in row b). Then the capital stocks of those three types are estimated by dividing the current gross investment of that type by (.03 + δ_j), as shown in row c). This assumes

Table 1: Scenario Analysis
Capital Stock and Depreciation Amounts
(by type of capital)

	Buildings	Machinery & Equipment	Vehicles
a) Investment in year t	$.45\ I_{gt}$ = 45	$.30\ I_{gt}$ = 30	$.22\ I_{gt}$ = 22
b) Depreciation Rate (δ_j)	.02	.08	.12
c) Capital Stock (= Investment/ $(.03+ \delta_j)$)	900	273	147
d) Depreciation Amount	18	21.84	17.64

Total Depreciation = 57.5

Inventory Investment = 20% of ΔY

$\Delta Y = .03Y = .03 \times 500 = 15$

Inventory Investment = $.2\Delta Y = 3.0$

If each ΔY leads to inventory investment of $.2\Delta Y$, then the total stock of inventory capital should be $.2Y$, or 100.

Total Reproducible Capital Stock = 900 + 273 + 147 + 100 = 1420

δ = Depreciation/Reproducible Capital Stock = 57.5/1420 ≈ 4%

that we are in growth equilibrium for each of these classifications of capital. The resulting capital stocks are shown in row d). Together with the estimate of 100 for inventory capital, they add up to a total capital stock of 1420. When we apply its appropriate depreciation rate to the capital stock of each type, we arrive at the depreciation amount shown in row d). These add up to 57.5, or almost exactly 4% of the estimated total capital stock of 1420.

This example is intended to give readers a sense of how this analysis is not just a blatant wave-of-the-hands assumption but rather a quite

Arnold C. Harberger

"textured" picture of the structure of a growing economy with capital stocks of different economic lives.

In point of fact, we will show later that our main conclusions would not differ much if the average depreciation rate were 3% or 5%. So readers should take from this exercise the reassurance of the seriousness of the framework and not worry about the precise figure of an average 4% annual depreciation rate.

Economic Growth and the Return to Capital

A standard breakdown of a country's growth rate is the following:

$$\frac{\Delta Y}{Y} = S_L \frac{\Delta L}{L} + S_K \frac{\Delta K}{K} + \frac{R}{Y}. \tag{1}$$

Here $(\Delta Y/Y)$ is the rate of growth of GDP, $(\Delta L/L)$ is the rate of growth of the employed labour force, $(\Delta K/K)$ is the rate of growth of the country's reproducible capital stock, and (R/Y) represents the amount of real cost reduction accomplished in the economy in the period in question, expressed as a function of the GDP. S_L and S_K are the shares of labour and capital in the GDP. One can see that the first two terms attribute to the increments of labour and capital, respectively, contributions measured by their respective shares in GDP.

The main objective of this section is to point out that the earnings of capital can be thought of as capital's gross-of-depreciation rate of return $(\rho + \delta)$ times K_{t-1}, the beginning of period capital stock; and the share of capital is therefore $(\rho + \delta) K_{t-1}/Y_t$. Taking the share of capital times $\Delta K_t/K_{t-1}$ gives us:

$$\frac{(\rho + \delta) K_{t-1}}{Y_t} \times \frac{\Delta K_t}{K_{t-1}} = (\rho + \delta) \times \frac{\Delta K_t}{Y_t} \tag{2}$$

that is,

$$\text{capital's contribution} = \frac{\text{net investment}}{\text{GDP}} \times \text{gross-of-depreciation}$$
$$\text{to growth in year } t \qquad\qquad\qquad\qquad \text{rate of return}$$

This is a much more insightful, much more intuitive, and much more readily communicable way of representing capital's contribution to the growth rate than the standard "share of capital" times "rate of net increase in the capital stock". Most business owners and business executives would balk at the standard definition, but all of them would quickly grasp the meaning (and the common sense) of measuring investment's contribution to growth as being equal to net investment times an appropriate rate of return. (That rate of return is measured gross of depreciation because we are estimating the effect of investment in GDP, and GDP itself is measured inclusive of depreciation.)

The specific point that I want to make in the present section is that as equation (2) tells us, the relevant rate of return is precisely the rate of return that generates capital's share, as measured in the traditional representation. That is to say, the whole return to reproducible capital is divided by the whole reproducible capital stock.

When we divide the GDP of a country into only two parts, we pretty much have to aggregate land along with reproducible capital. The easy way to deal with this is to separate "basic land" (call it A) from the rest of capital (what we call reproducible capital, including improvements to land, which are counted as investment in the national accounts). Doing this, we can reformulate the traditional approach as:

$$\frac{\Delta Y}{Y} = S_L \frac{\Delta L}{L} + S_K \frac{\Delta K}{K} + S_A \frac{\Delta A}{A} + \frac{R}{Y}. \tag{3}$$

Here ($\Delta A/A$) is equal to zero, but the term $\Delta A/A$ has meaning because attached to it is the share of GDP (S_A) that goes to the remuneration of the land factor. Here we will take S_A to be .04. When we make alternative assumptions about S_K and S_L, they will be .48 and .48 under one assumption and .40 and .56 under alternative assumptions.

Thus, reproducible capital's contribution to growth will be .0144 (=.48×.03) under the first set of assumptions and .012 (= .40×.03) and .0168 (= .56×.03) under the second and third sets.

Arnold C. Harberger

Rates of Return Are Implicit in the Mechanics of Growth

We have already introduced enough component parts to be able to show, quite simply, how a growth process implies (or perhaps better, has hidden within itself) a real rate of return to reproducible capital. Assume an economy that is growing at g percent per year, with reproducible capital receiving a fraction a of its GDP, and with gross investment accounting for the fraction s of GDP. If the depreciation rate is δ, then net investment ($=\Delta K$) is equal to gross investment minus depreciation.

$$\Delta Kt = sY_t - \delta K_{t-1}. \tag{4}$$

That is to say, new investment, sY_t, serves to cover the depreciation of the old capital stock plus the current increase in that stock.

$$sY_t = \delta K_{t-1} + \Delta K = \delta K_{t-1} + \frac{\Delta K}{K_{t-1}} \cdot K_{t-1} \tag{4'}$$

$$sY_t = (\delta + g)K_{t-1}. \tag{4''}$$

This last equation builds in the notion of growth equilibrium, with capital growing at the same rate (g) as output. This says that last period's capital stock is this year's gross investment divided by ($\delta + g$).

Here we can arrive directly at the gross-of-depreciation rate of return, ($\rho + \delta$):

$$(\rho + \delta) = \frac{return\ to\ reproducible\ capital}{stock\ of\ reproducible\ capital} = \frac{a}{s} \frac{Y_t}{Y_t / (\delta + g)} \tag{5}$$

$$(\rho + \delta) = a(\delta + g)/s \tag{5'}$$

$$\rho = [a(\delta + g)/s] - \delta. \tag{5''}$$

Table 2 elaborates on this result for a range of values of the key parameters. Our baseline case has GDP growth occurring at 3% per year, gross investment equal to 20% of GDP, reproducible capital receiving

Table 2: Rates of Return Implied by Growth Scenarios

Panel A: Varying Rates of Depreciation and Capital's Share in GDP

Share of Reproducible Capital in GDP	Rate of Depreciation		
	.03	.04	.05
	Net Rate of Return (ρ) under equilibrium growth		
.40	9%	10%	11%
.48	11.4%	12.8%	14.2%
.56	13.8%	15.6%	17.4%

Gross investment = .20 × GDP
Rate of GDP growth = .03

Panel B: Varying Rates of Depreciation and the Share of Gross Investment in GDP

Gross Investment ÷ GDP	Rate of Depreciation		
	.03	.04	.05
	Net Rate of Return (ρ) under equilibrium growth		
.15	16.2%	18.4%	20.6%
.20	11.4%	12.8%	14.2%
.25	8.5%	9.4%	10.4%

Rate of GDP growth = .03
Return to reproducible capital = .48 × GDP

Panel C: Varying Rates of Depreciation and the Rate of GDP Growth

Rate of GDP Growth, g	Rate of Depreciation		
	.03	.04	.05
	Net Rate of Return (ρ) under equilibrium growth		
.02	9.1%	10.4%	11.8%
.03	11.4%	12.8%	14.2%
.04	13.8%	15.8%	16.6%
.05	16.2%	17.6%	19.5%

Return to Reproducible capital = .48 × GDP
Gross Investment = .20 × GDP

a return equal to 48% of GDP, with a depreciation rate of 4% in such capital. This package of assumptions yields a gross-of-depreciation rate of return $(\rho+\delta)$ of 16.8% – not shown in the table – and a net rate of return – the object of our interest – of 12.8% (middle figure of Panel A).

Panel A explores how this "built-in" rate of return changes as one modifies the assumptions about the rate of depreciation and the share of reproducible capital. This panel reveals that the rate of return is modestly affected as the depreciation rate varies from 3 to 4 to 5% per year, becoming higher with higher depreciation rates. The effect of changing reproducible capital's share from .40 to .48 to .56 is somewhat more pronounced. It is interesting to note, however, that all but two of the calculated net rates of return in Panel A lie between 10% and 15.6%.

Panel B shows the sensitivity of the rate-of-return calculation to changes in the rate of gross investment, together with the rate of depreciation. Here the sensitivity to changes in the depreciation rate are still modest, but the rate responds quite strongly to changes in the rate of gross investment. It is pretty obvious that this should be so since the formula for generating the capital stock as a multiple of GDP shows that capital stock will be proportional to the share of investment in GDP. Note, however, that all but two of the net rates of return shown in Panel B lie between 9.4% and 18.4%.

Panel C of Table 2 shows how the results are modified if we change a) the rate of depreciation and b) the rate of GDP growth. Here the sensitivity appears to be quite strong to changes in g. This is to be expected. Note that the rate of investment is being held constant at 20% throughout this panel. A higher rate of growth coming from a given rate of investment is best explained by a higher rate of real cost reduction (increased total factor productivity). Such increased productivity is known to result in higher overall returns, typically to all factors of production. To conclude on Panel C, note that all but two of the rates of return reported there lie between 10.4% and 17.6%.

What If We Do Not Have Equilibrium Growth?

In this tumultuous world, some readers might be troubled by the idea of a set of calculations that are based on the convenient assumption of equilibrium growth – that is, of a situation in which the country's GDP and its stock of reproducible capital are growing at the same rate.

Fortunately, it is easy to correct for this situation. From equation (4), we know that

$$\frac{\Delta K_t}{K_{t-1}} = s\,\frac{Y_t}{K_{t-1}} - \delta. \tag{6}$$

Previously, we replaced $\Delta K_t/K_{t-1}$ by g (= the rate of growth of GDP), assuming that capital and output were growing at the same rate. Now we simply replace $\Delta K_t/K_{t-1}$ by $g + e$, which allows for the capital stock to be growing faster ($e > 0$) or slower ($e < 0$) than output.

In reality, it is quite plausible that capital will sometimes grow systematically faster than output, and sometimes slower, for a substantial period of time. For $e > 0$, we have the fact that in most low-income countries, the ratio of capital to output is lower than in most advanced countries. Thus, it is reasonable to believe that as a long-run tendency in the process of development, the rate of growth of capital might be a point or two higher than that of GDP. On the other hand, when a country is enjoying a spurt of growth as a result of very rapid real cost reduction (= TFP increase), without a big increase in the saving rate, we can expect output to be growing a point or two or three faster than GDP. Finally, we have cases like those of China and the other "Asian tigers" (Taiwan, Korea, Thailand, Malaysia). Here very rapid growth was accompanied by huge investment rates (reaching over 40% of GDP in China's case). Here it is almost certain that in spite of the high rates of GDP growth of these countries in their growth-boom periods, capital was almost certainly growing significantly faster than output.

Table 3 has the purpose of showing how rates of return respond when we have divergences between the rates of growth of capital and output.

In Panel A of Table 3, we examine the case of the ratio of capital to output gradually rising through the process of development. It seems reasonable that this would entail a higher than "normal" rate of gross investment, so Panel A allows for investment rates varying from 20 to 25 or 30%. Again, we find a significant concentration of calculated rates of return − all but two cases lie between 9.4% and 15.2%.

Tabe 3: Rates of Return When Capital Grows Faster or Slower Than Output

Panel A: Moderately Higher Investment Rates with "Normal" Growth (Long-Term Trend Case)

e = "excess" rate of growth of capital stock

Investment Rate (s)	.01	.02	.03
.20	12.8	15.2	17.6
.25	9.4	11.4	13.3
.30	8.8	10.4	12.0

Assumed: return to reproducible capital = .48 GDP
: rate of growth of output = 3%
: rate of depreciation = 4%

Based on the formula:
$$\rho = [a(g+e+\delta)/s] - \delta$$

Panel B: Spurts of Output Growth Driven by Productivity, with "Standard" Investment Rate

e = "excess" rate of growth of capital stock

Rate of GDP Growth (g)	0	-.01	-.02
.03	12.8%	10.4%	8.0%
.04	15.2%	12.8%	10.4%
.05	17.6%	15.2%	12.8%
.06	20.0%	17.6%	15.2%

Assumed: return to reproducible capital = .48 GDP
: investment rate = .20
: rate of depreciation = .04

Based on the formula:
$$\rho = [a(g+e+\delta)/s] - \delta$$

Table 3 (continued)

Table 3 (continued)

Panel C: High Growth Rates Together with High Investment Rates (Asian Tiger Case)

e = "excess" rate of growth of capital stock

Rate of GDP Growth	0	-.01	-.02
.06	9.7%	11.1%	12.5%
.08	12.5%	12.8%	15.2%
.10	15.2%	16.6%	17.9%

Assumed: return to reproducible capital = .48 GDP
: investment rate = .35
: rate of depreciation = .04

Based on the formula:
$$\rho = [a(g+e+\delta)/s] - \delta$$

Panel D: Very High Growth Rates Together with Very High Investment Rates (Chinese Case)

e = "excess" rate of growth of capital stock

Rate of GDP Growth	.02	.04	.06
.08	10.9%	13.1%	15.2%
.10	13.1%	15.2%	17.3%
.12	15.2%	17.3%	19.5%

Assumed: return to reproducible capital = .48 GDP
: investment rate = .45
: rate of depreciation = .04

In Panel B, we explore the case of rapid output growth largely propelled by real cost reduction (TFP improvement). In this case, output grows more rapidly than the capital stock ($e < 0$). Note that a declining capital stock (relative to output) implies a lower rate of return. Recall that our table deals with a given share of capital in the nation's GDP. If the capital stock is declining relative to output, that means that last period's capital stock is larger, relative to today's return to capital, than

Arnold C. Harberger

would be the case with a constant ratio of capital to output. Today's share of GDP going to capital is thus spread over a larger last-period capital stock, resulting in a lower rate of return. Note that in Panel B, we have all but two of the calculated rates of return lying between 10.4% and 17.6%.

Panel C tries to simulate the Asian tigers case – high growth rates together with a high rate of investment (equal to 35% of GDP). This has a surprisingly moderate effect on rates of return, with all but two of the cells in Panel C lying between 11.1% and 16.6%. I suspect that the Asian tigers' actual rate of return was higher than is shown here and that the reason for that was a return to capital accounting for more than 48% of GDP. But I do not want to exaggerate rates of return in the present paper – the results are high enough to be surprising, even when conservative assumptions are being made. Moreover, later explorations will result in even more surprising rates of return, again under quite conservative assumptions.

Panel D is designed to simulate the case of China, with its enormous ratio of investment to GDP. Under the assumption ($s = .45$), it seems reasonable to allow for capital's growth rate to exceed that of GDP by even more than we contemplate in Panel C. Thus, Panel D incorporates the possibility of capital growth rate being 4 or even 6 percentage points higher than that of GDP. Once again, we find a notable concentration of calculated rates of return. All but two of them lie between 13.1% and 17.3%.

Allowing for Infrastructure Investment

In this section, we explore the consequences of taking account of the fact that many public sector investments do not produce an income stream in the form of cash. This is not to say that they are not worthwhile; roads, bridges, the judicial system, the public administration – all have important roles to play in a functioning modern society. But their economic benefit lies in increasing the productivity of other factors of production, or adding to the utility of consumers, rather than generating a cash flow of their own.

So when we measure the profits, interest, and rents generated by an economy, these returns accrue to and reflect the marginal productivity of investments other than these "infrastructure" portions of the capital stock.[2]

It is obviously quite a task to separate out these non-revenue-generating investments from the others that do yield an income stream, but it should be feasible to reach a reasonable division in any given country. (The money-making public enterprises usually keep standard business accounts, publish annual reports, etc.) For our purposes in this section, we are seeking a rough idea of the likely order of magnitude of the share of infrastructure investment in a typical developing country's economy. To do this, I draw upon a study by Everhart and Sumlinski (2001), in which they present a breakdown of total investment into "private" and "public" categories for 63 developing countries. They show shares of public investment in GDP that range to over 20% and shares of public investment in total investment that range to over 50%. In more than half of the countries covered, public investment ranges between 5 and 10% of GDP and between 25 and 50% of total investment. Our decision was to consider the lower bounds of these ranges to represent the non-remunerative portion of public investment, the idea being that all countries have roads and schools and public buildings, and that the countries that go beyond this also have money-making public enterprises will reveal this in higher fractions of GDP and of total investment being devoted to public investment.

The end result of all of this is that in our "standard" example, where total investment is equal to 20% of GDP, we assign one quarter of this to "infrastructure". This enables us to calculate the average rate of return to reproducible capital in "remunerative" investment (both private and public) simply by dividing our previously calculated rate of return of 12.8% by .75. This reflects that the income we are counting in the

_____

[2]I am not happy with the term "infrastructure" in this connection but have found no easy substitute for it. What I am aiming at is to divide public investments into two big groups — those that really represent business investment, but with businesses in the public sector (like Chile's Codelco, Mexico's Pemex, plus many public sector electricity, gas, and water companies), on the one hand, and on the other hand those that yield absolutely no revenue (like the buildings that house public administration and free public schools) or very minor receipts (like national parks and museums that charge modest admission fees). The first group should be lumped together with private sector investments — they are the money-making part of the story. The second group should be separated out; and it is to this group that I am referring when I here use the term "infrastructure investments".

Arnold C. Harberger

numerator is in fact accruing to only 75% of our previously calculated capital stock.

Table 4 replicates two panels from Table 2, calculating the return to remunerative investments rather than the return to the total capital stock. It is easy to see that the "centre of gravity" of these estimates moves from the 10-15% range to the 15-20% range. But that is just the beginning. In the next section, we turn to the special case of investment in residential housing.

Table 4: Rates of Return to Remunerative Investments

Panel A: Varying Rates of Depreciation and Capital's Share in GDP

Share of Reproducible Capital in GDP	Rate of Depreciation		
	.03	.04	.05
	Net Rate of Return (ρ) under equilibrium growth		
.40	12%	13.3%	14.7%
.48	15.2%	17.1%	18.9%
.56	18.4%	20.8%	23.2%

Gross investment = .20 × GDP
Rate of GDP growth = .03

Panel B: Varying Rates of Depreciation and the Rate of GDP Growth

Share of Reproducible Rate of GDP Growth, g	Rate of Depreciation		
	.03	.04	.05
	Net Rate of Return (ρ) under equilibrium growth		
.02	12.1%	13.9%	15.7%
.03	15.2%	17.1%	18.9%
.04	18.4%	21.1%	22.1%
.05	21.6%	23.5%	26.0%

Return to Reproducible Capital = .48 × GDP
Gross Investment ÷ GDP = .20

Dealing with Investments in Residential Housing

There are several reasons why residential housing should be treated separately in an exercise like this. In the first place, a good share of such housing is owner-occupied; on this portion, the makers of a country's national accounts introduce an "imputed rent". Rarely does that rent imply a real rate of return (on housing investment) greater than 6% per annum. Secondly, rates of return implied by the ratio of rents to house values tend to be quite low. A long-time rule of thumb was that monthly rent should equal 1% of house value. This was often interpreted as covering 1-2% for taxes, 1-2% for maintenance, 1% for insurance, and 2-3% for depreciation, with 6% representing the net real rate of return. But today, one often finds free-market monthly rents in the range of 1/2% of the value of the dwelling. This can be rationalized by the owners expecting a good part of their return to come in the form of rising real values of their properties (negative depreciation = appreciation). But the national accounts do not measure this as part of the return to capital (profits, interest, rents). So in this case, the measured return turns out to be much less than 6%. Third, in most countries, the government engages in special housing projects for the poor and often also the not-so-poor. These units pay rents, but usually at a rate well below a standard market level, implying a real rate of return well below 6%.

The end of this story, for us, is that when we impute a 6% measured real rate of return to residential housing, we are probably erring on the upward side. From the point of view taken in this paper, this is a conservative assumption − if we imputed a 3 or 4% rate of real return to housing investment, we would end up with even higher implied rates of return to general business capital than the ones we are about to calculate.

To build a capital stock of residential housing, we take housing investment to equal 3% of GDP (typically a conservative assumption) and build its capital stock by the formula $K_h = .03Y/(g+\delta_h) = .03Y/(.03+.02) = .6Y$. A 6% net real return on this capital stock would yield net income equal to .036Y.

To obtain the implied net rate of return to non-infrastructure, non-housing capital, we go through the following steps:

i)   Total Stock of Reproducible Capital
   $= .2Y/(.03+.04)$ $= 2.857Y$

ii)   Total Stock of Remunerative Capital
   $= .75 \times 2.857Y$ $= 2.143Y$

iii)	Total Stock of Housing Capital	
	= .03Y/(.03+.02)	= .600Y
iv)	Total Stock of "Business Capital"	
	2.143Y - 600Y	= 1.543Y
v)	Total Return to All Capital	= .480Y
vi)	Total Depreciation on All Remunerated Capital	
	.04 × 2.143Y	= .086Y
vii)	Net Return to All Remunerated Capital	
	.480Y - .086Y	= .394Y
viii)	Net Return to Housing Capital	
	.06 × .600Y	= .036Y
ix)	Net Return to "Business Capital"	
	.394Y - .036Y	= .358Y
x)	Rate of Return in "Business Capital"	
	.358Y ÷ 1.543Y	= <u>23.2%</u>

We can reuse most of the above calculations if we stick to our "standard" assumption of a depreciation rate of 4% on the overall capital stock. *Changing the share of reproducible capital in GDP to .40, we have*:

v)	Total Return to All Capital	= .400Y
vi)	Total Depreciation on All Remunerated Capital	= .086Y
vii)	Net Return on All Remunerated Capital	= .314/Y
viii)	Net Return on Housing Capital	= .036Y
ix)	Net Return on "Business Capital"	= .278Y
x)	Rate of Return in "Business Capital"	
	.278Y ÷ 1.543Y	= <u>18.0%</u>

Now, *changing the share of reproducible capital to .56*, we have:

v)	Total Return to All Capital	= .560Y
vi)	Total Depreciation on All Remunerated Capital	= .086Y
vii)	Net Return on All Remunerated Capital	= .474Y
viii)	Net Return on Housing Capital	= .036Y
ix)	Net Return on "Business Capital"	= .438Y
x)	Rate of Return on "Business Capital"	
	.438Y ÷1.543Y	= <u>28.4%</u>

To explore the impact of changing GDP growth on the rate of return to "business capital", we have to go through all ten steps. To remain on the conservative side, we will do so under the assumption that the return to reproducible capital is 40% of GDP. In Table 2, this assumption, with a 4% overall depreciation rate, yields a rate of return to all reproducible capital equal to 10%. Our base case here is the one yielding an 18.0% return to "Business Capital". That is built on the assumptions of $\delta = .04$, $g = .03$, return to reproducible capital $= .40 \times$ GDP, investment $= .20 \times$ GDP (see the first case treated on the previous page).

Next, we maintain all of these assumptions but one, making the rate of growth, g, equal to .02. Now we have:

i)	Total Stock of Reproducible Capital	
	$= .2Y/(.02+.04)$	$= 3.333Y$
ii)	Total Stock of Remunerated Capital	
	$= .75 \times 3.333Y$	$= 2.500Y$
iii)	Total Stock of Housing Capital	
	$= .03Y/(.02+.02)$	$= .750Y$
iv)	Total Stock of "Business Capital"	$= 1.750Y$
v)	Total Return to All Capital	$= .400Y$
vi)	Total Depreciation on All Remunerated Capital	
	$.04 \times 2.500$	$= .100Y$
vii)	Net Return on All Remunerated Capital	$= .300Y$
viii)	Net Return to Housing Capital	
	$.06 \times .750Y$	$= .040Y$
ix)	Net Return on "Business Capital"	$= .260Y$
x)	Rate of Return on "Business Capital"	
	$= .260Y \div 1.750Y$	$= \underline{14.8\%}$

Now we *raise the GDP growth rate, g, to 4%*, and repeat the exercise:

i)	Total Stock of Reproducible Capital	
	$= .2Y/(.04+.04)$	$= 2.500Y$
ii)	Total Stock of Remunerated Capital	
	$= .75 \times 2.500Y$	$= 1.875Y$
iii)	Total Stock of Housing Capital	
	$= .03Y/(.04+.02)$	$= .500Y$
iv)	Total Stock of "Business Capital"	
	$1.875\%Y - .500Y$	$= 1.375Y$

v)	Total Return to All Capital	= .400Y
vi)	Total Depreciation on All Remunerated Capital	
	.04 × 1.875Y	= .75Y
vii)	Net Return on All Remunerated Capital	= .325Y
viii)	Net Return to Housing Capital	
	.06 × .500Y	= .030Y
ix)	Net Return on "Business Capital"	= .275Y
x)	Rate of Return on "Business Capital"	
	= .275Y/1.375Y	= <u>21.5%</u>

Needless to say, all these rates would be higher if we had assumed that the return to reproducible capital was .48Y or .56Y (the alternative assumptions we previously explored).

The conclusion to be drawn, which I believe to be inescapable, is that business capital, in most developing countries, receives a very substantial rate of return. This is a *fact* that, in my opinion, has not been fully "digested" by the Economics profession. Obviously, if it were easy for anybody (foreigner or local national, insider or outsider) to put down some capital and readily gain a real rate of return of 20% or more, we would see lots of money flowing into those opportunities, and the rate of return would be bid down.

Yet the rate of return *is there*. The national accounts do not exaggerate returns in capital (even implicitly). If anything, they understate them. So there is something of a mystery here to be delved into. Surely some of this measured return represents "monopoly profits", which are not properly part of the true return to capital but are hard to disentangle from ordinary profits. A further part of the high measured return to business capital surely represents "inframarginal investments" – that is, investments with individually high returns that are exploited in any given time period but that are not marginal investments. The image here is that there are probably some few investments each year that turn out to have real yields of 50, 40, and 30%. These yields contribute to a high average rate of return, but this does not mean that adding to the stock of investible funds would lead to any (or much) of that incremental money being invested in items of super-high yield (these opportunities being so attractive that they are exploited anyway, with or without extra funds being placed in the market). Still, there is evidence that at least in some developing countries, real yields on business capital in excess of 20% prevail year after year after year – suggesting at the very least either that important new "inframarginal" opportunities keep coming onto the scene year after year or, alternatively, that the inframarginal aspect is not a big part of the story and that a lot of business capital keeps earning very high real rates of return. Finally, there is the possibility that these high rates of return are really there but require a degree of local knowledge and "savvy" that is hard for outsiders to replicate. Perhaps outsiders do put up money, and it truly yields 20% or more, but foxy locals manage to cream off enough of this return (even quite legally), so that the investment no longer seems very attractive to foreigners.

The above are merely speculations on my part – they are one person's stabs at potential *answers* to the puzzle of how such high measured rates of return can exist and persist. They are not put forward as the *true answers*. My main purpose here is to call attention to the *facts* of the case and to the *puzzle* that those facts create for us and others to try to answer.

A final word about the facts. The numbers that I used in the examples in this paper delineate what I would consider a very reasonable range. It is hard to imagine a situation in which the real rate of depreciation on the total reproducible capital stock of a sizeable country were outside the range between .03 and .05. Likewise, in most countries, the ratio of gross investment to GDP actually *does* lie within the rage of .15 to .25.[3] Finally, it is hard to imagine a sizeable country in which the gross return to reproducible capital was less than 40% or more than 56% of its GDP. (Note that after depreciation, a gross return of 40% of GDP turns into a net return of less than a third of GDP and that a gross return of 48% of GDP turns into a net return of less than 40% of same.) Overall, the assumed "packages" of numbers seem to form a sort of cage that hems us in from all sides.

There is every reason for us and others to proceed down a more time- and resource-consuming route, of building up direct time series on the real capital stocks and real returns to capital of different classifications, for as many countries as we can. These are useful not only in order to generate more precise results for particular countries but also to reassure people of the reasonableness of the numerical assumptions made in studies like this one. But in the meantime, the exercises carried out in this paper present, I am sure, a broad picture quite similar to the one that will emerge from more careful study.

---

[3]In Everhart and Sumlinski's study (2001), the rate of gross investment to GDP lay between .15 and .25 for 37 out of 63 countries and between .12 and .30 for 53 of them.

Arnold C. Harberger

Dealing with R&D and Other "Hidden Investments"

A pharmaceutical company spends $100 million on research seeking a better treatment for diabetes; a restaurant opens a new campaign by blanketing its neighbourhood with advertising about the experience and honours of its new chef; an existing firm manages to disguise as an expense the costs of levelling and preparing the site for its new headquarters. From an economic point of view, all these costs represent investment − outlays in the current period aimed at generating or supporting an income stream that will flow over a number of future periods. Conceptually, they should *all* be capitalized, with the capital sum then being depreciated over the span of that future income stream. Legally, the first two are legitimately classed as expenses − the first because those expenses qualify as R&D, the second because advertising outlays are always expenses. Only in the third is it illegal to claim the outlays as a current expense.

But to estimate the true economic rate of return, one should really reclassify all three outlays as investment, and at the same time, augment the income of the firm by the same amount during the investment period. Many such operations occur in any national economy in a typical year, so when we are estimating rates of return, as in this presentation, we should be able to make adjustments so as to properly treat the outlays involved.

The needed adjustment entails three steps − first, to increase the GDP and the income received by capital by the amount of such outlays; second, to increase investment of the year by the same amount; and third, to depreciate that investment over time in an appropriate manner.

Assume that such expenses (of all kinds, legal and illegal) amount to 4% of a country's GDP in a typical year. To recalculate our base case, we therefore augment our GDP figure from Y^O to $1.04Y^O$, our investment figure from $.20Y^O$ to $.24Y^O$, and our income from capital figure from $.48Y^O$ to $.52Y^O$. (Note: Y^O should be thought of not as just the GDP of a given year but as a whole time series − in our case, growing at the rate of 3% per annum.)

Now we repeat our basic operations. The reproducible capital stock now becomes $.24Y^O/(g+\delta)$ − in this case, $.24Y^O/(.03+.04)$, and the return to reproducible capital becomes $.52Y^O(1.04)$. The gross rate of return is thus $.52Y^O(1.04)/[.24Y^O/(.03+.04)]$. This works out to a 15.8% rate of return, compared with a 16.8% rate in our base case −

$.48Y^O/[.20Y^O/(.03+.04)]$. The calculated net rate of return would be 11.8%, as compared with 12.8% in the base case.

It is likely, however, that these "new" types of investment depreciate more rapidly than the old, raising, say, the average rate of depreciation from .04 to .0425. This would change the calculated gross rate of return to $.52Y^O(1.04)/[.24Y^O/(.03+.0425)]$, which equals 16.34%. Its corresponding net rate of return is 16.34% minus 4.25%, or *12.09%*.

This exercise should be sufficient to dispel any doubts that making plausible adjustments for R&D and other "hidden investments" would change the order of magnitude of our results in any important way.

Reference

Everhart, S. and M.A. Sumlinski. 2001. *Trends in Private Investment in Developing Countries: Statistics for 1970-2000 and the Impact on Private Investment of Corruption and the Quality of Public Investments.* International Finance Corporation Discussion Paper No. 44. Washington, DC: The World Bank.

7

Risk-Adjusted Discount Rates for Public Sector Investments: With Illustrations for Transportation

Donald J.S. Brean and David F. Burgess

Introduction

In an earlier work, we estimated the social opportunity cost of capital (SOCC) in Canada to be 7.3%.[1] That value is a weighted average cost of capital drawn from three sources: Canadian savings (or deferred consumption), displaced private sector investment, and foreign borrowing. The SOCC is the primary reference for evaluating public sector investment in Canada. Since it is a discount rate that represents a broad average of social costs associated with an unspecified average investment, the SOCC implicitly incorporates a premium for the risk associated with a public sector investment of average risk.

A "riskless SOCC" ($SOCC_f$) can be derived from the general equation for SOCC. The parameter values that generate SOCC equal to 7.3% correspond to a $SOCC_f$ equal to 4.7%. From the social perspective,

---

[1]Brean *et al.* (2005). Our current estimate of the SOCC in Canada is based on the methodology applied by Jenkins (1977), which in turn drew substantially from Harberger (1973).

the risk premium for an investment of average risk is SOCC minus $SOCC_f$, or 2.6%.[2]

Private sector financial asset pricing, represented by the Capital Asset Pricing Model (CAPM), involves comparable concepts of average risky return, riskless return and a risk premium, the three market-based asset pricing parameters. The capital market puts a "price" on risk in the form of extra points of return required to compensate investors for the risk they bear.

Risk for private sector securities is measured by the variance of asset-specific returns. However, when less than perfectly correlated risky assets are held in a portfolio, the overall risk of the diversified portfolio equates to something less than the simple sum of the variances of the individual securities. The contribution of each individual asset to the risk of the portfolio is mitigated by its covariance with the other assets. The risk of individual securities that *cannot* be diversified away is referred to as "systematic" risk since it relates directly to the variance-generating process of the market as a whole, the "system". In the modern theory of financial asset pricing, only systematic risk is rewarded with additional points of return above the riskless return.

The return that private investors require for average risk and the return they earn on the riskless asset combine to generate a required average risky return that, with low inflationary expectations, is remarkably similar to our estimate of the SOCC. At the time of writing, the return on the riskless financial asset (Government of Canada 10+ year bonds) of 4.7% and an equity risk premium of 4.5% implies the required return on an equity-financed capital expenditure of average risk is 9.2%. The use of corporate debt for a typical 40% of the finance of a capital expenditure results in a weighted average cost of capital (WACC) that is similar to the real return of 7.3% proposed for the SOCC.

---

[2] Following Bailey and Jensen (1972), the risk-free SOCC in an open economy is $SOCC_f = r_f ((1-t_p)\partial S/\partial B - (1/(1-t_c))\partial I/\partial B + (1+1/ef)(1-tw) \partial F/\partial B)$, where r_f is the risk-free real interest rate, t_p is the personal tax rate, t_c is the corporate tax rate, tw is the withholding tax rate, ef is the elasticity of supply of foreign funding, and $\partial S/\partial B$, $\partial I/\partial B$, and $\partial F/\partial B$ are the proportions of incremental funding obtained from domestic saving, private investment, and net foreign saving, respectively. In Canada, a risk-free social opportunity cost rate of 4.7% equates to a risk-free real interest rate of 3.85%. A standard measure of the risk-free interest rate is the yield on real return bonds, which from 1990 to 2004 has varied from a low of 2.4% to a high of 4.9%.

Donald J.S. Brean and David F. Burgess

Although the SOCC framework and the CAPM represent different processes and generate their results in fundamentally different ways, the CAPM sheds light on the nature of empirical problems that arise in developing risk measures that can be applied in estimating an array of discount rates for risky public sector investments.

In the CAPM, the asset-specific (or risk-class) index of systematic risk is typically a regression coefficient in the regression of time-series data for ...

$$r_{i,t} - r_{f,t} = \alpha_i + \beta_i \left[r_{m,t} - r_{f,t} \right] + e_{i,t}$$

where $r_{i,t}$ = return on asset "i" in period t
$r_{f,t}$ = return on the risk-free asset (e.g., a Treasury Bill)
$r_{m,t}$ = return on the market index (e.g., the S&P/TSX)
$e_{i,t}$ = an error term; $E[e_{i,t}, e_{i,t-1}] = 0$

To compute the measure of systematic risk of asset "i":

$$\beta_i = \left[\sigma_i / \sigma_m \right] \rho_{i,m}$$

where σ_i = standard deviation of the return on asset "i"
σ_m = standard deviation of the return on the market index
$\rho_{i,m}$ = correlation coefficient between the return on asset "i" and the return on the market index

The average value of β_i is one that corresponds to the average amount of risk in the "system", i.e., the risk associated with the market portfolio. A value of β_i greater (less) than one corresponds to asset-specific risk that is proportionately greater (or less) than the risk of the market.

From a social perspective, one can similarly assume that risks are spread over a large number of individuals, and hence, the appropriate focus is on that component of risk that cannot be diversified away. As with the analysis of the risk of financial assets, the practical empirical issue for risky public sector investments is to devise a measure that reflects varying degrees of undiversifiable risk associated with specific assets in which the public has an ownership interest. That is the focus of this paper.

Socially Relevant Risk and Its Empirical Representation

An Illustrative Approach

An empirical measure of risk of public sector investment must satisfy two fundamental conditions:

- It must reflect risk from a *social* perspective.
- The measure of risk must be comparable across different categories of investment.

A public sector investment that bears average risk calls for an average risk premium applied to the social opportunity cost of the capital used in the project. On the other hand, a riskless public sector investment requires no premium for risk. In that case, the riskless social opportunity cost of capital is the relevant discount rate.

Inasmuch as average risk and zero risk represent relevant benchmarks, what defines "average"? Or "riskless"? A useful reference is gross domestic product (GDP), the most fundamental measure of economic performance. The variance of GDP is a basic measure of economic risk. The variance of GDP is axiomatically the *average* risk in the economy. Relevant measures of risk of specific public sector investments must be tied to the variance of GDP.

Specific public sector assets yield a social return based on their economic use. Roads, harbours, or airports, for example, provide economically important services. The risk of investment in such assets, from a public perspective, is that the road, the harbour, or the airport may fail to generate a socially justifiable level of use. The uncertainty of whether a specific asset will be fully used through its life is reflected in the volatility of use of that category of asset.

The empirical focus of risk is thus on the relation between the use of a specific asset and real overall economic activity. An estimate of the correlation of asset use to fluctuations in economic activity provides a measure of risk that satisfies the two criteria identified above.

There are various ways to measure the correlation between public sector asset use and total economic activity. The basic issues, however, can be illustrated by a simple regression of the form:

$$Lx_t = \beta_0 + \beta_1 Ly_t + u_t$$

where Lx_t is the logarithm of the measure of use of the public sector asset, Ly_t is the logarithm of real GDP, and u_t is the error term.

β_1 measures the impact of a change in Ly_t on Lx_t and may be interpreted as the sensitivity of asset use to variations in the total economic activity. In practical terms, the results suggest that if:

$\beta_1 = 1$ ➔ percentage change in y_t = percentage change in GDP
$\beta_1 > 1$ ➔ percentage change in y_t > percentage change in GDP
$\beta_1 < 1$ ➔ percentage change in y_t < percentage change in GDP

As an empirical measure of risk, β_1 has a number of desirable features. First, it is consistent through time and across assets. Second, it captures the social risk of assets regardless of whether ownership is public or private/commercial. Third, the measure is an index that readily indicates whether a specific asset has high, average, or low risk. Finally, and perhaps most important, the index of risk is directly applicable to known parameters – the SOCC and SOCC$_f$ – that enable computation of asset-specific, risk-adjusted SOCCs. The index is amenable to estimation with readily available data.

Useful reference values of β_1 are 0 and 1. An estimate of β_1 equal to zero indicates the absence of a statistical relation between the use of the specific asset – whose activity is measured by x_t – and real GDP. A potential explanation for β_1 equal to zero is that asset use (x_t) is stable in the face of varying real GDP. On the other hand, asset use (x_t) and real GDP may both vary but may do so independently, with a resulting zero estimate for β_1. Regardless, in terms of social risk in asset use, β_1 equal to zero indicates a riskless investment.

An estimate of β_1 equal to one indicates a statistical relation between the use of the specific asset and real GDP. When β_1 equals one, a given percentage change in GDP corresponds to a similar percentage change in x_t. If β_1 is greater than one, a given percentage change in real GDP, say quarter to quarter, is associated with an even greater percentage change in x_t. In other words, the ups and downs of activity x_t exceed the ups and downs of real GDP, where the latter is the reference for average risk.

While this representation of the risk of public sector investments has obvious similarity to the CAPM, there are important differences between social and private perspectives on risk.

The CAPM is concerned with private after-tax returns to equity capital. The CAPM is built on the reasonable assumptions – for market-traded financial assets – that the securities markets are informationally efficient, liquid, and readily accessible to a large number of informed investors. The CAPM risk measure is a company-specific "β_i" obtained by regressing a time series of returns on company "i" equity against the contemporaneous returns on a diversified market portfolio of equities. β_i captures risk as undiversifiable covariance between an individual stock's return and the market. The return on the market portfolio, of course, is an ever-present opportunity for a private sector investor in risky assets. Similar to our depiction of social risk, a CAPM β equal to one indicates "average" private sector risk. CAPM β_i greater (less) than one indicates more (or less) than average market risk.

In measuring the risk of public sector investment, the focus is on the risk that the investment may provide an unstable flow of services. The risk is not inherently financial. Instead, the socially relevant concern is for the likelihood that public sector resources are committed to a project that may turn out to have been wasted.

In the CAPM, the index of the "system", and hence the defining basis of systematic risk, is a broad equity market portfolio such as the S&P/TSX or the S&P 500. In the social risk framework, the index is real GDP, a macroeconomic accounting measure. The CAPM is a model of equilibrium prices of financial assets traded continuously in highly liquid markets. In the SOCC framework, risk-adjusted discount rates are not market-determined equilibrium values, except for the anchoring points of the risk-free SOCC and the SOCC with average risk.

Issues in Measuring Social Risk

A number of issues must be addressed in calculating risk-adjusted discount rates. First, we must identify the appropriate measure of asset-specific use, x_t, in the model. Second, the most appropriate way to estimate β_1 must be determined. Third, the process for translating the calculated risk measure into a risk-adjusted discount rate must be determined.

These issues are examined below. The next section looks at the third issue, which involves the computation of risk-adjusted discount rates from the beta estimated in the modelling exercise. Following this, we examine the issues involved in implementing a methodology to derive

Donald J.S. Brean and David F. Burgess

empirically sound measures of the systematic risk for different transport assets.

Computing Risk-Adjusted Discount Rates

With estimated activity-based measures of asset use defined relative to average risk, the measure can be incorporated into the SOCC framework as follows:[3]

$$r_i = SOCC_f + \beta_1 (SOCC - SOCC_f)$$

where r_i is the risk-adjusted discount rate, $SOCC$ is the average-risk-inclusive social opportunity cost of capital, and $SOCC_f$ is the risk-free social opportunity cost of capital.

The activity-based index of risk is the regression coefficient β_1 obtained in a model estimating the relation between asset use and fluctuations in real GDP. The value of β_1 for an asset with average risk is one. The value of β_1 for a riskless asset is zero. An estimate of β_1 used as a risk-adjustment index must be checked for statistical significance against both zero and one. A non-zero, non-one-point estimate should be used to compute a risk-adjusted discount rate only if the point estimate is statistically significantly different from both zero and one. If the estimate of β_1 is statistically different from zero but not from one, one should be used. If the estimate of β_1 is statistically different from one but not from zero, zero should be used.

Our estimate of the "average" SOCC is 7.3%. The corresponding risk-free SOCC is 4.7%. Considering a range of β_1 from 0 to 2, the risk-adjusted SOCC at each level of β_1 is given below.

---

[3]The social risk premium is $SOCC\text{-}SOCC_f$, so the risk-adjusted discount rate for the asset (project) is the risk-free discount rate plus the systematic risk of the asset (project) times the social risk premium. The relation of the social risk premium to the market risk premium is described in Bailey and Jensen (1972). The social risk premium is proportional to the market risk premium, with the proportionality factor being a weighted average of the distortions that drive a wedge between the rates of return on investment and saving and the risk-free market rate, and between the marginal cost of foreign funding and the risk-free market rate.

Table 1 sets out a mapping system that can be directly applied when an appropriate degree of confidence emerges from risk measurement calculations. Unfortunately, such confidence is often unwarranted. A more general approach is to divide assets into categories of low, medium, and high risk and to apply a SOCC appropriate to each category. When questions concerning the specifics of the risk adjustment calculations arise, analysts may be comfortable identifying whether an activity is high, low or medium risk. Based on how the risk-adjusted SOCC relates to the calculated beta, reasonable SOCC for different categories of transport assets are presented in Table 2.

The remainder of the paper illustrates the application of use-based measures of risk in determining risk-adjusted discount rates for investments in the Canadian transport sector.

Table 1: The Risk-Adjustment Index and Corresponding Asset-Specific Social Discount Rates

β_1	Asset-Specific SOCC
0.00	4.70
0.10	4.96
0.20	5.22
0.30	5.48
0.40	5.74
0.50	6.00
0.60	6.26
0.70	6.52
0.80	6.78
0.90	7.04
1.00	7.30
1.10	7.56
1.20	7.82
1.30	8.08
1.40	8.34
1.50	8.60
1.60	8.86
1.70	9.12
1.80	9.38
1.90	9.64
2.00	9.90

Table 2: SOCC by Risk Category

Risk	Risk-Adjusted SOCC
Low	6.0%
Average	7.3%
High	8.6%

Implementation Issues in Measuring Asset-Specific Risk

The Use Measure

In implementing a risk adjustment methodology, careful consideration must be given to the activity indicator, x_t, used in empirical analysis. Risk derives from the uncertainty of use. The risk of the social return from a specific investment is measured by the covariance of the *use* of the asset and the socially relevant measure of income, real GDP. For example, the socially relevant risk of a public sector investment in an airport is measured by the covariance of the use of the airport and real GDP. The focus then turns to the socially relevant and observable measure of use.

A number of proposed activity indicators are described in Table 3. Quarterly or monthly data are needed to estimate the risk coefficients. This limits the choice of activity indicators. The proposed indicators are based mainly on data that are (or should be) available monthly or quarterly, although, in some instances, numbers are published in raw form and need to be seasonally adjusted. For a number of assets, the most appropriate indicator is the corresponding industry quarterly, seasonally adjusted real output measure published by Statistics Canada. In some cases, such as rail transport, where the Statistics Canada numbers are not sufficiently disaggregated, the proposed output measures are similar to the component indices (i.e., for passenger and freight) that comprise the published Statistics Canada measure.

In a few cases, additional analysis is required to construct the appropriate output measure. For private trucking, information on the importance of own-activity trucking in different industries is needed to develop the base year weights for the proposed output measure. This

Table 3: Activity Indicators for Risk Analysis

Asset	Proposed Indicator
Aircraft	Real, quarterly, seasonally adjusted GDP for air transportation industry (#481).
Major airports, NAV Canada (Toronto, Vancouver, Montreal, Calgary, Edmonton, Ottawa, Winnipeg, Victoria)	Quarterly, seasonally adjusted landings and takeoffs, weighted by base year major airport average landing and takeoff fees.
Other airports	Quarterly, seasonally adjusted landings and takeoffs, weighted by base year "other airport" average landing and takeoff fees.
Freight rail – vehicles and track	Quarterly, seasonally adjusted tonne km for major commodities weighted by base year revenue per tonne km of each commodity.
Passenger rail assets	Quarterly, seasonally adjusted passenger km for short-, medium- and long-haul trips multiplied by a base year average revenue per passenger km for each trip category.
Domestic shipping fleet	Real, quarterly, seasonally adjusted GDP for water transport (#483) is reasonable (although ideally, ferries, which are part of industry 483, would be separated out).
Inland ports	Quarterly, seasonally adjusted domestic cargo by major commodity in tonnes multiplied by base year port revenue per cargo tonne for each commodity group.
Major international ports	Quarterly, seasonally adjusted international cargo in tonnes by major commodity multiplied by base year average port revenue per cargo tonne handled for each commodity group.
For-hire trucks	Real, quarterly, seasonally adjusted GDP for truck transportation (#484).

Table 3, continued

Private trucking fleet	Quarterly, seasonally adjusted data on constant dollar shipments of industries that are major users of private trucking weighted by base year data on private trucking costs of each industry. Base year data on importance of private trucking by industry should be available from input-out statistics.
Passenger vehicles	Quarterly, seasonally adjusted passenger vehicle km. Data on vehicle km are available from the Canada Vehicle Survey but cover a short period and are not seasonally adjusted. Data on monthly gasoline sales can be translated into a measure of passenger vehicle km using annual data on the percentage of gasoline consumed by passenger vehicles, passenger fleet composition, and average litres/100 km by vehicle type. (The annual data can be calculated from data made available for 1990 to 2002 on the NRCan Office of Energy Efficiency website.) Gasoline sales data need initially to be turned into a seasonally adjusted quarterly time series.
Roads, bridges	Quarterly, seasonally adjusted data on imputed passenger and freight vehicle toll revenues. Passenger vehicle km can be calculated as above. Using a similar procedure and available data on gasoline and diesel fuel sales, freight vehicle km can be calculated and translated into a seasonally adjusted, quarterly time series. A combined indicator of passenger and freight road usage can be calculated by weighting each series by a representative measure of the base year tolls charged by commercial operators.
Urban transit assets	Real, quarterly, seasonally adjusted GDP for urban transit system (#4851).
Interurban and rural buses	Real, quarterly, seasonally adjusted GDP for interurban and rural bus transportation (#4852).
Courier and messenger vehicles	Real, quarterly, seasonally adjusted GDP for courier and messenger services (#492).

information is available, but it would require a special analysis of the information in Statistics Canada's input-output database. In the case of roads, an index depicting the imputed real value of toll revenue would serve as a reasonable output measure. The required quarterly output index could be constructed using information on the tolls charged by a commercial operator, published monthly data on vehicle fuel sales, and available data on vehicle fuel use.[4]

With the exception of airports, our activity indicators are industry-based. In some cases, it may be useful to examine the risk profile of sub-components of an industry, although in such cases, data are difficult to assemble.

Model Specification

The illustrative model in the second section represents one way to test the sensitivity of transport activities to fluctuations in economic activity. In this section, we examine two alternative specifications.

Since we are interested in measuring the sensitivity of transport activities to fluctuations in economic activity, it is reasonable to consider a model based on growth rates. Growth rates measure short-run variations in the relevant variables and, therefore, represent fluctuations in activity.

The second specification is given by:

$$\Delta x_t = \beta_0 + \beta_1 \Delta y_t + u_t$$

where x_t again represents the activity measure and y_t is real GDP. However, both variables are now expressed in first-differences. The variables may be interpreted as growth rates since the variables are expressed in logarithmic form. The model provides a measure of β_1 that can be used to compute risk-adjusted SOCC rates, similar to the approach outlined in the third section.

The third model is represented by the following specification:

---

[4]Tolls are potentially an indicator of the services that roads provide to different types of transport vehicles – cars, small trucks, trucks with heavy axle weight. Their role would be to provide weights for distinguishing kilometres of road use by different types or classes of vehicles.

Donald J.S. Brean and David F. Burgess

$$Lx_t = \beta_0 + \beta_1(Ly_t - Ly_t^*) + u_t$$

where Lx_t and Ly_t are defined as in the first model, and u_t is the error term. Ly_t^* is the potential or maximum value of Ly_t, representing the long-run value of Ly_t. In other words, the focus of risk is represented by fluctuations of Ly_t with respect to its long-run value. This empirical specification isolates the cyclical component of GDP, which is of particular interest since the intention of the exercise is to measure the sensitivity of transport activities to the business cycle. The variable Ly_t^* is calculated using the filter proposed by Hodrick and Prescott (1997), a technique widely used in macroeconomics and macro-econometrics.[5]

Alternative specifications can be evaluated partly on the basis of the standard tests that are used to assess the adequacy and performance of regressions. In addition, a judgment is required as to how well particular specifications address the specific question that is being examined.

The three specifications are applied to transport data (which we describe in the next section) and evaluated using standard statistical tests. One obvious measure of the quality of the regression is the R^2, which measures the explanatory power of the independent variables. In addition, the performance of the residuals of each regression was examined in order to check for the presence of autocorrelation. Another issue that was evaluated was the normality of the estimated residuals of each regression. The empirical results for the third specification are presented in Table 4.

Overall, the first model and third model perform better than the second. The first and third specifications rate higher on standard statistical tests and yield results that are more robust and credible. The specifications were tested using regressions that involve not only different transport variables but also alternative independent variables – with total GDP being replaced by sectoral GDP for business goods, business services, and non-business goods and services sectors. In regressions using the first and third specification, the signs of the estimated coefficients are generally correct, and the estimates seem reasonable.

_____

[5]This technique for separating a time series into its cyclical and trend components is often employed in OECD business cycle studies. See, for example, OECD (2002).

Table 4: Transport Measure Used in Estimations

Transport Variable	Measurement Unit	Measurement Period
Air transport	Millions of $1992	1981:1 – 2001:2
Interurban & rural trans.	Millions of $1992	1981:1 – 2001:2
Railway	Millions of $1992	1981:1 – 2001:2
Urban transit systems	Millions of $1992	1981:1 – 2001:2
Water transport	Millions of $1992	1981:1 – 2001:2
For-hire trucking	Millions of $1997	1981:1 – 2004:4
Airports	Itinerant movements	1995:4 – 2004:4
Ocean shipping	Millions of tonnes	1990:1 – 1999:4
Passenger rail	Millions of rev. pass. kms	1981:1 – 1995:4
Passenger road/auto	Millions of kms	1993:1 – 2003:4

As noted above, models should be judged not only by their statistical qualities but also in terms of their explanatory power, given the particular issue in question. On this latter basis, there is reason to prefer the third specification. Since the objective of the exercise is to measure the sensitivity of transport activities to fluctuations in economic activity, it is desirable to have a model in which the independent variable has been adjusted to remove the trend component of the real GDP time series. Using the third specification and data that has been properly adjusted for seasonal and other structural changes, it is possible to focus on the correlation between transport activities and cyclical changes in economic activity.

Illustrative Calculations of Risk-Adjusted Discount Rates

In this section, we apply the proposed methodology involving the preferred model specification to develop illustrative calculations of risk-adjusted SOCC for a range of investments in assets in the Canadian transportation sector. These initial calculations are based on readily available monthly and quarterly transport data. With improvement in asset-use data, the estimates are likely to improve in accuracy and reliability.

For six of the ten transport activities examined, the data are the seasonally adjusted constant dollar industry output data published by

Donald J.S. Brean and David F. Burgess

Statistics Canada. For five of six industries (air, interurban and rural bus, urban transit, for-hire trucking, and water transport), this is consistent with the recommendations in Table 3. Published industry output measures were also used for rail. Although the Statistics Canada real output measure includes both freight and passenger rail, the domination of the freight segment suggests that the freight numbers best reflect rail activity. While current industry GDP series could be used for for-hire trucking, for the other five industries, a time series of the desired length is available only from a discontinued GDP series that ends in mid-2001.

For the remaining four transport sectors (airports, ocean shipping, passenger rail, and passenger vehicles), the dependent asset-use variable is based on available measures of output volume – itinerant movements, tonnes, kilometres, and revenue tonne kilometres. In the case of passenger vehicles, we develop the activity indicator identified in Table 4. Generally, however, these one-dimensional measures are inferior to multidimensional measures of industry output, such as industry GDP.[6] They will provide a misleading indicator of trends in industries that consist of a range of different activities that are changing in different ways. Changes in the main outputs of the air, passenger rail, and ocean shipping industries are likely correlated, so that the proposed volume measures reasonably represent industry activity. It would be wise to confirm this in subsequent research through the development of more sophisticated industry output measures.

Data Adjustments

To isolate the impact of cyclical fluctuations in economic activity, it is preferable to adjust for other factors influencing transport activity, including seasonal and structural changes as well as growth trends. Since these latter factors are not part of the systematic risk associated with transport investment, they should not be incorporated into the measurement of the beta. The model being applied will "filter out" the influence of growth trends, but additional adjustments may be needed to take account of the presence of seasonal and structural factors.

---

[6]As discussed above, constant-dollar industry GDP data are typically derived by aggregating an industry's sub-outputs using base year prices or value-added as weights.

Since the industry GDP data derived from Statistics Canada are seasonally adjusted, attention to seasonal factors is needed only for those transport activities measured using volume indicators. Figure 1 below illustrates the importance of seasonal factors for two such activities, passenger road and ocean transport. For all unadjusted data, seasonal components were captured in the regressions using centred dummy variables.

A number of transport industries have experienced significant structural changes over the period being examined. Sudden increases or decreases in activity have occurred as a result of policy changes or other developments unrelated to the business cycle. The significant structural changes experienced by the passenger rail and for-hire trucking sectors can be seen in Figure 2.

Structural changes were captured using dummy variables. Dummies were applied to adjust for outliers among the individual quarterly data and for periods characterized by structural change. Adjustments were applied to the trucking data for 1984:1, 1987:1, and the period 1990:1 to 2004:4; the urban transit data for 2001:2; the passenger rail data for 1990:1 to 1995:4; and the air transport data for 2003:2 and 2003:3.[7]

Figure 1: Passenger Road and Ocean Shipping Activity
(Data in Logarithms)

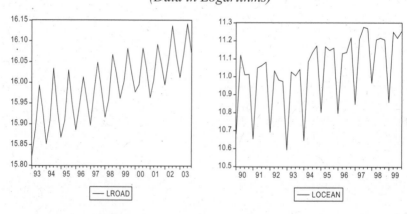

---

[7]Dummy variables to capture structural change over time intervals generally affect the intercept of the regression. In some cases, such as passenger rail, where the dummy variable was related to the explanatory variable, the purpose is to control for changes in the regression slope.

Figure 2: Passenger Rail and For-Hire Trucking Activity
(Data in Logarithms)

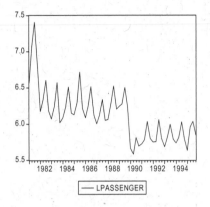

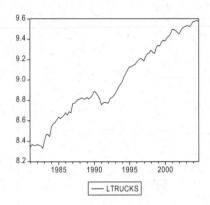

Results

Table 5 presents the results of activity-based risk estimates for a number of transport industries using the preferred model: $Lx_t = \beta_0 + \beta_1(Ly_t - Ly_t^*) + u_t$. The last four columns present standard statistical tests relating to "goodness of fit" and the performance of residuals. A p-value greater than 5.0% indicates that it is reasonable not to reject the corresponding null hypothesis. The regressions perform well, as indicated by their relatively high explanatory power and p-values for the three residual tests.

The second column provides the coefficient measuring the sensitivity of the transport activity to fluctuations in overall economic activity. The p-values corresponding to the null hypotheses that the true coefficient is equal to zero and unity are shown in the following two columns. A p-value less than or equal to 10% calls for rejection of the corresponding null hypothesis.

In the case of urban transit, water transport, and ocean shipping, the coefficients are statistically different from 0 but not from 1. This suggests that these activities fluctuate in pace with overall economic activity and that the corresponding assets – urban transit vehicles, Canadian ships, ocean ports – have an average degree of risk. The estimated coefficients for air transport, interurban and rural bus, rail

Table 5: Estimation Results

Type of transportation	Estimated β	p-value (t-stat $\beta=0$)	p-value (t-stat $\beta=1$)	$\overline{R}^2$	AR (1-4) (p-value)	JB (p-value)	ARCH (1) (p-value)
Air transport	3.137	0.000	0.003	0.887	2.460 (0.054)	4.831 (0.089)	3.534 (0.064)
Interurban/ rural bus	3.255	0.000	0.008	0.992	2.194 (0.078)	0.393 (0.822)	1.999 (0.161)
Railway	2.595	0.000	0.015	0.962	2.220 (0.075)	0.152 (0.927)	0.609 (0.437)
Urban transit systems	1.215	0.023	0.682	0.972	1.201 (0.318)	5.260 (0.072)	2.796 (0.099)
Water transport	1.587	0.050	0.465	0.769	0.601 (0.663)	3.989 (0.136)	0.293 (0.590)
Airports	0.453	0.706	0.648	0.958	0.213 (0.929)	0.546 (0.761)	1.256 (0.270)
Ocean shipping	2.709	0.064	0.235	0.954	0.652 (0.630)	0.069 (0.966)	0.033 (0.856)
Passenger rail	-0.615	0.512	0.090	0.938	0.673 (0.615)	0.133 (0.935)	0.964 (0.330)
Trucking	2.089	0.000	0.000	0.997	0.420 (0.793)	0.559 (0.756)	3.023 (0.085)
Passenger vehicles	0.167	0.430	0.000	0.965	1.165 (0.344)	1.702 (0.427)	0.670 (0.417)

transport, and for-hire trucking are well above one. For these industries, p-values are statistically different from both 0 and 1, and the results point to a relatively high degree of systematic risk. At the other extreme are passenger rail and passenger road (and vehicle), where the estimated coefficients are not significantly different from zero. For airports, neither of the alternative null hypotheses could be rejected, and it was not possible to derive a reasonable estimate for the coefficient. One might expect that the risk level for airports would approximate that for the air

Donald J.S. Brean and David F. Burgess

transport sector, but it is not possible to statistically confirm this without a larger airport data sample.

Results for rail and trucking accord with the *a priori* view that systematic risk tends to be relatively high for transport sectors involved in goods movement. Similarly, the results for passenger rail and autos are consistent with the view that these modes are much less sensitive to fluctuations in economic activity. Ocean shipping activity depends on economic conditions not only in Canada but also in offshore export markets, so it is reasonable to expect this sector to be less affected by the business cycle than rail and trucking. The relatively high risk for airline transport is also reasonable since business and leisure travellers, while unlikely to significantly alter their auto use in response to changing economic circumstances, can be expected to adjust the amount of their air travel.

In Table 6, the results are assigned to broad categories of risk-adjusted SOCC measures. Risk-adjusted SOCC should be 8.6% for transport assets in the four higher-risk sectors (air, freight rail, for-hire trucking, and interurban and rural bus), 7.3% for assets employed in the three sectors with average risk (urban transit, water transport, and ocean shipping), and 4.7% for assets associated with the two activities having below-average systematic risk (passenger rail transport and automobile travel).

Conclusion

This paper developed and illustrated a methodology for measuring the socially relevant risk of investments in Canadian transportation assets. Like the CAPM used in financial analysis, the methodology is directed at measuring systematic risk. The focus in the current exercise, however, is on social risk, which is quite different from the private sector financial risk that motivates the application of the CAPM. The proposed risk measure for transport assets is a sector-specific, activity-based index that focuses on the covariance of asset usage and real GDP. The index of risk is economically relevant, comparable across assets and independent of (public or private) ownership.

While different models can be adopted to measure risk, the preferred approach involves a filtering process to distinguish the cyclical from the trend components of GDP. This model is well suited to measuring the

Table 6: Risk-Adjusted SOCCs for Transport Activities

Industry	Assets	Estimated β	Risk Level	Risk-Adjusted SOCC (%)
Air transport	Aircraft	3.137	High	8.6
Interurban/ rural bus	Buses	3.255	High	8.6
Railway	Freight cars, track	2.595	High	8.6
Urban transit systems	Buses, subways	1.215	Average	7.3
Water transport	Ships, inland ports	1.587	Average	7.3
Airports	Terminals, runways	0.453	n.a.	n.a.
Ocean shipping	Ocean ports	2.709	Average	7.3
Passenger rail	Passenger rail cars	-0.615	Low	4.7
Trucking	For-hire trucks	2.089	High	8.6
Passenger Vehicles	Autos, SUVs	0.167	Low	4.7

sensitivity of transport activities to fluctuations in overall economic activity. Where necessary, adjustments should also be incorporated into the model for seasonal and other structural influences on transport activity. The model was applied using quarterly data that measure changes over time in the real output of a number of major transport industries. While the preference was for composite output indicators that take account of the sub-activities within different sectors, for lack of anything better, single-dimensional volume-based indicators were used as the dependent variable in some regressions.

The model generates reasonable results, which can be useful for classifying transport assets into risk categories with corresponding risk-adjusted social discount rates. The methodology for transforming risk

Donald J.S. Brean and David F. Burgess

coefficients derived from the model calculations into a measure of risk-adjusted social opportunity cost was initially suggested by Bailey and Jensen (1972). Based on the mapping system that results from applying this methodology, average social opportunity cost rates were developed for assets in "high", "low", and "average" risk categories.

The empirical illustrations indicate substantial variation in risk and the SOCC for investments in Canada's transportation sector. The illustrative calculations suggest that assets employed by the air, freight rail, for-hire trucking, and interurban bus industry tend to have above-average risk, while the assets involved in urban transit, water transport, and ocean shipping have average risk. The private automobile and assets involved in passenger rail transport belong in the low-risk category, according to the results of these initial calculations.

Discount rates for public sector investment are based on estimates of the SOCC. In this paper, our estimate of the social discount rate provides the benchmark estimate of the capital cost adjusted for systematic risk associated with transport assets. The question of whether to apply risk adjustments to the discount rate has generated significant discussion in the literature. With public as with private investment, if asset returns are influenced by the business cycle and correlated with national income, systematic risk ought to be taken into account explicitly through adjustment of the discount rate. To not do so is misleading. Risk is factored into the investment decisions of private sector firms, and to promote competitive neutrality, the opportunity cost of capital for public assets ought to incorporate a comparable risk adjustment.

To derive an updated baseline measure of social opportunity cost, estimates were made of the costs and relative importance of the different activities likely to be displaced by transport investment. The returns that could have been earned if resources had instead been directed to private sector investment were estimated using a "top down" productivity-based approach to calculate pre-tax returns on capital employed by the aggregate business sector. This methodology suggests that through the 1960s to the 1990s, returns to capital in the business sector have been remarkably stable, averaging just over 10%, or just over 11% when allowance is made for property tax payments. Residential investment, which accounts for about 20% of total investment, earned a somewhat lower return. When this is incorporated into the estimate, the average pre-tax return on private sector investment comes out to 10.3%. Alternative methodologies result in lower estimates, but the evidence suggests that real pre-tax returns on marginal investment are at least 8% or higher.

Public sector investment will displace consumption rather than private investment to the extent that interest rate increases resulting from this investment cause individuals to spend less and save more. The real after-tax return on incremental saving, which is a measure of the value individuals place on postponed consumption, is about 4%. Since the responsiveness of saving to higher interest rates tends to be quite low, displaced consumption has a much lower weight than displaced investment in calculations of the SOCC.

The other major source of funding for public sector investment is foreign borrowing. While Canada has access to well-integrated international capital markets, higher interest rates are needed to attract the additional foreign resources required to fund public sector investments. The responsiveness of foreign funding to interest rates was calculated using available evidence on "saving retention coefficients", which measure the impact of exogenous increases in national savings on investment. With information on savings retention coefficients and an understanding of the responsiveness of domestic saving and investment to interest rates, it is possible to indirectly come to an assessment of the relative importance of foreign funding as a source of the additional resources required for transport investment. Foreign borrowing costs less than displaced private sector investment and more than displaced private consumption; based on what foreign investors require to fund investment in Canada, the estimated real cost of this component of the social discount rate is 6%.

The SOCC was calculated for a range of saving retention coefficients and for real pre-tax private investment returns of between 8% and 10%. The resulting estimates of the SOCC range from 6.5% to 8.7%. Applying a reasonable mid-range savings retention coefficient and a 9% pre-tax return on investment, 50% of the resources required for additional transport investment come from displaced private investment, 10% from displaced private consumption, and 40% from foreign sources. The implied value of the SOCC is 7.3%.

To develop risk adjustments that could be applied to the SOCC, an approach was adopted that is similar to private sector techniques of risk measurement based on the traditional CAPM. The purpose of this approach is to understand the relation between the use of a specific asset and real GDP. By regressing activity levels against GDP, it can be determined whether the relevant assets have a high or low degree of systematic risk, and the SOCC should accordingly be adjusted upward or downward. There is a need to identify an appropriate output indicator (or indicators) for which suitable data is available, but the proposed methodology is economically relevant, independent of whether an asset is publicly or privately owned and relatively easily computed. Since the benchmark SOCC incorporates the average degree of risk in the economy, assets will have a SOCC above (below) the preferred rate of 7.3% only if they are subject to greater (lesser) than average risk. Given the margin of error that is necessarily associated with risk calculations, the appropriate focus is not on the specific risk estimate but the general finding of whether transport assets are being employed in an activity characterized by high, low, or average systematic risk.

Illustrative calculations of systematic risk were made for a number of transport industries using quarterly seasonally adjusted real output data as the activity indicator. Systematic risks were estimated using a model that allows the cyclical component of GDP to be separated from the trend component. Estimates could then be made of the sensitivity of various transport activities to fluctuations in real output. Based on these calculations and the proposed system for categorizing assets, there are some high-risk assets, such as freight rail and for-hire trucking, for which the proposed risk-adjusted SOCC should be 8.6%; and there are some relatively low-risk assets, such as the automobile, for which the adjusted SOCC should be 6.0%. The general implications of this analysis is that there are substantial differences in risk among transport assets that should be taken into account, and the proposed methodology provides a reasonable means for adjusting the proposed updated measure of SOCC to derive risk-adjusted rates that are appropriate for application in a full-cost accounting system.

References

Bailey, M.J. and M.C. Jensen. 1972. "Risk and the Discount Rate for Public Investment", in M.C. Jensen (ed.), *Studies in the Theory of Capital Markets.* New York: Praeger.

Brean, D., D.F. Burgess, R. Hirshhorn, and J. Schulman. 2005. *Treatment of Private and Public Charges for Capital in a Full Cost Accounting of Transportation*, for Transport Canada (Ottawa).

Harberger, A.C. 1973. "On Measuring the Social Opportunity Costs of Public Funds", in A.C. Harberger (ed.), *Project Evaluation: Collected Essays.* Chicago: Markham.

Hodrick, R.J. and E.C. Prescott. 1997. "Post-War U.S. Business Cycles: An Empirical Investigation", *Journal of Money, Credit and Banking* 29.

Jenkins, G.P. 1977. "Capital in Canada: Its Social and Private Performance 1965-1974", Discussion Paper No. 98, Economic Council of Canada.

Organisation for Economic Co-operation and Development (OECD). 2002. Chapter 5 ("Ongoing Changes in the Business Cycle"), *OECD Economic Outlook* No. 71, June.

Comment on "Risk-Adjusted Discount Rates for Public Sector Investments: With Illustrations for Transportation" by Donald J.S. Brean and David F. Burgess

Graham Glenday

The Brean and Burgess (B&B) paper presents an interesting approach to estimating the systematic risk premium that could be included in the social discount rate for various infrastructure sectors in Canada. The core of their approach is that they derive asset betas from the relationship between the usage of the asset type and cyclical fluctuations in gross domestic product (GDP). Based on time-series empirical estimates, they show that asset betas vary from zero for asset investments related to passenger car and rail usage; to one for asset investments related to urban mass transport, ocean shipping, and water transport; and to 1.5 for asset investments related to air transport, inter-urban and rural bus transport, rail freight, and trucking. B&B propose that these asset betas should be applied to a risk premium of 2.6%, which is included in the estimate of the social opportunity cost of capital (SOCC) of 7.3% for Canada following the methodology of Jenkins and Kuo (see chapter 8 in this volume). The beta-adjusted risk premium is then added to an estimate of the risk-free SOCC (SOCC$_f$) of 4.7%.

    This comment focuses on two key concerns with the B&B approach to risk-adjusting the SOCC. The first concerns the basic model of the SOCC that B&B use to adjust for risk. The second concerns the need to differentiate the appropriate use of risk adjustments for systematic risk in the costs of capital between (i) investment projects that are self-financing (or depend upon user-paid revenues to cover all financial costs), and (ii) those that are non-self-financing (or depend upon general government revenues to cover financial costs).

First, the B&B approach to estimate the risk-adjusted SOCC for investment in a particular type of asset, "i", is as follows:

$$r_i = SOCC_f + \beta_i \, (SOCC - SOCC_f)$$

where (a) following Bailey and Jensen (1972), $SOCC_f = r_f (1 + e)$, where r_f = risk-free cost of capital and e = weighted average externality relative to r_f depending upon the mix of sources of capital funds and the externality arising in each market segment[1], and (b) β_i is the asset beta for the type of asset.

The problem with this formulation is that B&B estimate the externality based on weighted average marginal effective tax rates for Canada and apply these to the risk-free interest rate. Based on an estimate of $r_f = 3.85$, they estimate $SOCC_f = 4.7\%$, which implies $e = 22\%$ of r_f, or alternatively, an externality per unit of capital of $e.r_f = 0.85\%$. This, in turn, implies a risk premium of 2.6% implicit in SOCC = 7.3% (or SOCC = 3.85%+0.85%+2.6% = 7.3%). Now, effective tax rates actually fall on the risk-inclusive returns on investments in the economy and not the risk-free interest rate. Taking the B&B estimate of $e = 22\%$ as accurate[2] and expressing it relative to the gross SOCC of 7.3% gives $e/(1+e) = 18\%$, and hence, an externality of 1.32% per unit of capital invested would be obtained. The implicit risk premium in the SOCC reduces to 2.1%.

---

[1] Based on Brean and Burgess, Chapter 7, footnote 2, $(1+e) = \{(1-t_p)\partial S/\partial B - (1/1-t_c)\partial I/\partial B + (1+1/e_f)(1-t_w)\partial F/\partial B\}$ where t_p is the personal tax rate; t_c is the corporate tax rate; t_w is the withholding tax rate; e_f is the elasticity of supply of foreign funding; and $\partial S/\partial B$, $\partial I/\partial B$, and $\partial F/\partial B$ are the partial effects of increased government borrowing on domestic savings, private investment, and net foreign funding, respectively.

[2] It is noted that a number of distortions are excluded from the B&B estimate. These appear to include property taxes and indirect taxes on invested capital. Therefore, the estimate of the weighted average externality is probably low.

Elsewhere in this volume, Glenday (chapter 4) presents an alternative formulation where r_i is estimated as the minimum competitive market supply price of capital to the investment (including systematic risk premiums borne by the financiers as appropriate to the capital market in which the investment resides) plus an economic externality arising from the use of capital from the market. In this approach, the economic externality is independent of the risk characteristics of the new investment, but depends on the distortions in the segments of the capital market from which the capital funds are sourced. The systematic risk premium is included in the supply price of capital and is the same one implicit in the required private cost of capital funds in the capital market for the type of investment.

The second concern is that the B&B approach does not address under what circumstances their "use-based" estimates of infrastructure asset betas can be used – for all or only some types of infrastructure investment project? Their approach is developed by analogy with the CAPM approach used for estimating risk premiums for market financial assets. The CAPM essentially recognizes that common factors such as cyclical economic fluctuations, market interest rates, and economic governance policies result in the returns to investors on the capital assets in a market experiencing significant covariance. This systematic element of returns on a financial asset is captured by the correlation between the return on the particular asset and the market return, where both are affected by the common factors. In all cases, the financiers are receiving the net returns on their share of the investment from the difference between the revenues captured by the investment project and the total financial costs of the project. These market investments can be referred to as *self-financing* in that the revenues have to cover the full current and capital costs of the project, including the costs of the debt and equity invested in the project. The common economic factors that affect these self-financing projects flow through to the bottom line of the project, resulting in the investors bearing the resulting fluctuations in returns. If these returns are correlated with the market returns, then to that extent the variability in the return cannot be diversified away, it is compensated by a systematic risk premium.

Aggregate economic fluctuations are generally taken as the major common factor that results in variations in the quantities sold in sectors. The quantity fluctuations, in turn, result in variations in net returns to the investment. The strength of the relationships of aggregate demand fluctuations to sales quantities and, in turn, to profitability varies across sectors, leading to different sector betas. The infrastructure analogy is that usage of infrastructure (roads, ports, railways, etc.) varies with aggregate demand in an analogous fashion to sales quantities. The analogy continues if the infrastructure is financed by user charges that ultimately cover all the costs. In such cases, the rate of return on the infrastructure investment is expected to show some degree of correlation with the capital market rate of return, and a systematic risk premium is expected. This analogy diverges from the CAPM story, however, if the infrastructure is *not self-financing*. In such cases, different groups experience the costs and benefits of the project investment. In the extreme, for public infrastructure, where all capital, operating, and maintenance costs fall on general government revenues, the costs ultimately fall on taxpayers. These costs can be expected to be weakly positively related to aggregate economic demand as operating and maintenance expenses would increase with added use. The taxpayer appears to be worse off from an infrastructure cost perspective as demand increases. The level of taxation and the use of tax revenues, however, do not have a necessary systematic relationship. First, a taxpayer does not know what incremental tax revenues are spent on, and second, in aggregate, public sector costs could decline or rise with aggregate demand, depending on the mix of public services. Even if a correlation can be found between demand and usage of a particular type of infrastructure and between usage and cost, it is, therefore, not clear that this results in an identifiable systematic risk on the taxpayer.

The benefits of an infrastructure project are concentrated on its users. The benefits vary with the use of the infrastructure demanded, and the use demanded is expected to fluctuate with cyclical GDP fluctuations. Where user charges finance the infrastructure, then these fluctuations in demand flow through to the bottom line return to the financiers. In the case of free public access to infrastructure, however, the added benefits (or user surpluses) are captured by the users. Ironically, with infrastructure with limited capacity, the normal positive relationship between demand growth and benefits turns around if the demand growth causes congestion which undermines the user benefits as demand grows. Expected economic growth and fluctuations that increase the expected periods of congestion effectively reduce the expected benefits of the users. The costs of such congestion risks should be captured by reducing the expected benefits of the users in the economic analysis of the infrastructure investment rather than costing this risk in the discount rate. By contrast, if user charges are in place, the project financiers benefit from increased demand, even with congestion, and more so if a congestion premium is added to the user charge. The users lose surplus in line with the level of user charges.

In summary, in the context of public private partnerships, such as for the creation and operation of infrastructure, it is recognized that the distribution of risks changes compared to fully publicly financed projects, depending upon the degree of cost coverage achieved through user charges. The inclusion of a sector-specific systematic risk premium in the cost of capital, such as estimated by B&B for infrastructure projects, needs to be proportional to the degree of coverage of the project costs by user charges. Where the project is fully publicly financed, then the systematic sector risk premium should be omitted from the cost of capital.

References

Bailey, M.J. and M.C. Jensen. 1972. "Risk and the Discount Rate for Public Investment", in M.C. Jensen (ed.), *Studies in the Theory of Capital Markets.* New York: Praeger.

Summary of Discussion

Finn Poschmann: What I'd like to do is to invite our presenters to make very short responses to the one or two things that they'd particularly like to respond to. And if we do it that way, we'll still have a chance for brief interaction and questions from the floor.

Donald Brean: First, with respect to Tony Deutsch's remarks, I don't think that Tony runs with Donald Rumsfeld, but his line, "Risk is the uncertainty of not knowing what we do not know" – has a certain ring to it. I appreciate what you were getting at. That's truly what risk is. You made that point, then, to impress upon us that what we see in history is not very useful for anticipating the future. I would take exception to that. I think that you perhaps quote Santayana: "If you don't learn the lessons of history, you're bound to repeat them."

There's a lot of information in movements of economic variables, whether they're securities prices or the types of returns that we tried to develop in our paper that *are* repeating. But there *are* limits. We do know that long-term capital management failed because of an extreme outlyer, which was not built within their models. Therefore, you go to a second stage of analysis of risk called stress testing, where you satisfy yourself that at least you are working within bounds of risk that you can be comfortable with, even though your model doesn't take full account of all of the things that you don't know.

Graham's comments were very interesting, especially as he pointed out the complexity of influences underlying the generation of correlations between usage, which is our indirect measure of benefits, and the index of the system, which is mainly real GDP. Well, yes, I certainly see that you have complex correlation-generating mechanisms, but some of the rather peculiar potential cases that Graham presents could be disheartening, especially the cases stemming from congestion in transportation infrastructure.

Now, I'll admit that our system does not entertain those considerations, but being a practical fellow, I wonder how important they are in, say, the context of Canada versus India. Also, Graham reminds us of the troublesome mismatch of benefits, which can be narrowly received, and costs, which could be widely distributed. Again, our framework does not take account of distributional effects. However, I would welcome the day, whenever it should arrive, when some workable framework for dealing with distributional concerns that cannot otherwise be addressed through lump-sum transfers becomes available.

Finn Poschmann: Thank you, Don. Are there further questions from the floor?

Lindsay Allison: I guess I'm condemned here because I'm both a lowly bureaucrat and a practitioner. I work on these deals. I'm sure everybody here understands the distinction, but I didn't necessarily see the distinction in the papers. It's that there are two decision points. The first is *when* you build the asset. Do you build a hospital? Do you build a light rail system? Or do you build one as opposed to the other? That's the first decision point. And how that's done is a lot more than just a simple minute in government.

But to me, the more interesting decision is the decision that once you've said, Yes, we're going to build this asset, the question is, Do you do an AFP – sorry, P3; we call them AFPs in Ontario – do you do a P3, or do you do it the traditional way? And there the social discount rate, I think, really plays a big part. Because you're applying that to the PSC, the public sector comparator. And that can sway one way or the other.

My questions are, and I apologize if these are naïve questions to either Mike or Donald. There are different kinds of AFPs. You've got DBFs, design-built finance, where they build it for you, and you're done after, let's say, three years. And then you get a design-built finance maintain, or DBFM, and that can go 30 years.

From a financial perspective, would you apply two different discount rates, one if the projects were DBFs, and another if projects were for DBFMs? Specifically why I'm asking is the time value of money inherent in whatever discount rate you choose. Does that fully encompass the risks associated? To my mind, there are two separate kinds of risks in there. Would you, in effect, to assess the PSC, be using two separate discount rates or just the one?

Donald Brean: Again, this is one where you'd want to just aggregate flows. When it comes to maintenance expenses, operational expenses, those have risks attached to them, and you'd do them in a cash-flow analysis.

Lindsay Allison: So you do a CF?

Donald Brean: I think there's another decision that you have not identified. You say that to build the hospital or the light rail system – that, you were implying, is largely a political decision. But then there's the question of how large. Once you talk about how large, then you're applying marginal analysis for both sides.

Lindsay Allison: No debate, no debate on that. Ten hospital beds in Toronto versus one up north or something like that. I've no debate about that. But my point is that to my mind, the PSC, the AFP or not AFP, that's really where the choice of discount rate is crucial. Take Mirabel, for example. Mirabel was not a decision that was going to be made based on whether they got 200 basis points one way or the other in the discount rate. It was a completely different set of factors. And that's all that I'm really saying.

Michael Spackman: A comment on Donald Brean's paper. This issue of correlation is something we looked at pretty thoroughly in the Treasury in the United Kingdom back in the 1980s. I did a lot of the work myself. It's very interesting to see figures. It's a very wide range of degree of correlation. The reason that we didn't go along with this – it's practically important in the Treasury, and I think it probably would be the same now – was simply the magnitude of the numbers.

The mean figure that you take is about 2.5%. That's less than the mean equity risk premium, which is about 4.5% on the figures that you're using, but even so 2.5% is still a big figure. Welfare economics has a very traditional way of looking at income-related impacts. You go back to your utility function and everything else – the formulas are all there – and you come out with a very low, something like a tenth of a percent. They're really very small figures.

There is a riposte to that: Oh well, but the equity-risk premium itself, if you apply that wealth economics approach to that, you get a very low figure. Are you saying that you should deny what the equity risk premium is saying? Well, I think not because it's very, very different. The kind of correlation everyone's talking about with a road, for example, whether it's a toll road or whether it's one the state paid for – they're fascinating comments from Graham Glenday. But either way, the actual co-variances with GDP are extremely small.

Also, frankly, these are figures that people aren't even particularly aware of at the time. They get a bit richer or poorer; it affects them. But in that very simple situation, you don't need to bother about any psychology or whatever, you can take these good old-fashioned wealth-economics formulas and apply them, and they'll give you, to my mind, a much lower number.

The equity market is very different. The equity market swings around like mad. You can put all your money in equities and lose half your savings for 10 years. This is really big stuff. I'm not at all surprised that when it comes to equity markets, people are actually averse. I think probably 2.5% or whatever is a more credible figure than the equity-risk premium. But it's entirely unsurprising that it's a lot bigger than the very conventional formula would apply.

But when it comes to the actual magnitude of the co-variances of GDP, you really are into much lower numbers where the traditional formulas do apply. That's the sort of debate that we had. I checked again about 10 years ago, and the numbers really are very low.

Finn Poschmann: There are a couple of comments I'd like to offer. This may reflect my entirely parochial view, but I would encourage people in future, in writing about P3s to have a clear view in mind of the context in which you're going to put it to use. So for me, this is the Canadian context – a small economy that is not capital-constrained, with projects that may or may not be large relative to the economy. That's going to colour some of these conversations. And if you're going to bring tax into the analysis, please examine your assumptions about incidence. If you're going to talk about taxes on capital, think through how much of that tax is in fact bearing on capital at the end of the day, because it may matter to the analysis.

The final thing I wanted to point to is: whether you're thinking of weighted average cost of capital or other project analysis, picture the marginal investor. For us, the marginal source of capital may well be tax-exempt institution domiciled resident in Canada or a foreign tax-exempt. That's probably going to add to it too.

Having abused my capacity as chair, I want to thank everyone very much, our presenters and our discussants. I think everyone did a terrific job.

8

The Economic Opportunity Cost of Capital for Canada: An Empirical Update

Glenn P. Jenkins and Chun-Yan Kuo

Alternative Approaches to Finding the Economic Net Present Value

Choosing the correct economic discount rate has been one of the most continuous issues in the field of cost-benefit analysis. This discount rate is used to calculate the economic net present value (NPV) of the resource cost and the benefits that accrue over time from an investment or policy initiative according to the NPV criterion. If the NPV of a project is positive, then from the perspective of a country, the project is worthwhile to implement. If it is negative, the project should not be undertaken. Because the size of the discount rate is so important in determining whether the economic NPV of a project or program is positive or negative, the choice of rate is often a controversial issue. The economic discount rate is similar to the concept of the private opportunity cost of capital used to discount the financial cash flows of an investment for the estimation of its financial NPV. The issues raised in the determination of

The authors are grateful to Helen Ma for research assistance. They also thank the participants of the Conference on Discount Rates for the Evaluation of Public Private Partnerships at Queen's University for valuable comments and suggestions. Nevertheless, responsibilities for any errors are solely the authors', and any opinions expressed herein are those of the authors alone.

the economic discount rate are, however, fundamental to our under-standing of how scarce resources are allocated within the economy.

People prefer to make payments later and receive benefits sooner. This is because they have a time preference for current consumption over future consumption. Similarly, there is an opportunity cost of the resources used in an activity, as they could have been invested elsewhere and produced a positive return that could be consumed later. This opportunity cost needs to be taken into consideration in the appraisal of any proposal that involves the creation of costs and benefits that occur in different time periods.

One approach to economic discounting is based on the fact that present consumption is valued differently than future consumption. Following this approach, all benefits and costs are first converted into quantities of consumption equivalents before being discounted. In this case, the discount rate is the rate of time preference at which individuals are willing to exchange consumption over time. To be analytically correct, all investment outlays must be multiplied by the shadow price of investment to convert them into units of consumption. Estimates of the shadow price of investment forgone are typically much larger than one and often in the range of two or three. After this is done, all the benefits and costs, now expressed in consumption units, can be discounted by the rate of time preference for consumption (see, e.g., Sjaastad and Wisecarver, 1977).

Another approach considers what society forgoes in terms of the pre-tax returns of displaced investment in the country. Using this approach, no account is made for time preference in terms of present versus future consumption. The discount rate is based purely on the opportunity cost of forgone investments.

An approach that captures the essential economic features of these two alternatives is to use a weighted average of the economic rate of return on private investment and the time preference rate for consumption (see, e.g., Sandmo and Dreze, 1971; Harberger, 1972). This opportunity cost of capital measures the economic value of funds forgone in all their alternative uses in the private sectors of the economy when resources are shifted into the public sector. It captures the repercussions not only of the forgone consumption but also of the forgone investment resulting from the expenditures being undertaken.[1]

---

[1] As has been shown elsewhere, the weighted average approach and the approach by the time preference for consumption are similar, but the latter can lead to incorrect results in a number of situations (see Burgess, 2006).

Glenn P. Jenkins and Chun-Yan Kuo

The social or economic discount rate is the threshold rate used to calculate the NPV of an investment project, a program, or a regulatory intervention to see whether the proposed expenditures are economically feasible. The magnitude of the economic opportunity cost of the resources used by any public or private sector investment is of utmost importance given its role as a guide in the selection of projects or programs, including the choice of their timing and scale.

The size of the discount rate has been an issue in Canada for many years. The debate has been primarily concerned with empirical measurement of the economic opportunity cost of funds, and even that discussion has been concerned with a relatively narrow range of values. The main purpose of this paper is to re-examine what is the appropriate economic discount rate for Canada.

Background

The weighted average concept has been used before in the measurement of the economic opportunity cost of capital for Canada (see, e.g., Jenkins, 1972, 1973; and Burgess, 1981). A 10% social opportunity cost of capital was first estimated using a detailed industrial data and macroeconomic environment over the period 1965-69 (Jenkins, 1973), and it was endorsed by the Treasury Board Secretariat (1976). Jenkins subsequently refined the estimates and extended the time period of the data based on the rates of return from investment in Canada from 1965 to 1974, but he reaffirmed his 10% estimate (Jenkins, 1977).

Using the data for the same time period, the magnitude of the discount rate for Canada was questioned by Burgess for a variety of theoretical and empirical reasons. He suggested that the social opportunity cost of capital for Canada should be lowered to a real rate of 7% because of a number of biases in the derivation of the 10% figure (Burgess, 1981). The main points of disagreement between Jenkins and Burgess lie in the use of different values for the parameters employed in the estimation of the economic opportunity cost of capital (EOCK) (Jenkins, 1981). In particular, the issues were related to (a) relative contribution of foreign funding and its social opportunity cost, (b) the interest elasticity of domestic saving and its social cost, and (c) the distortions associated with labour, foreign exchange, and subsidies in the Canadian economy. The difference between using a discount rate of 7%

and using a discount rate of 10% is not small and could easily lead to a different recommendation of whether to accept or reject a project when using the NPV criterion to measure the expected efficiency of the resources employed.

Subsequently, the social discount rate of 10% real was reviewed by Watson (1992), and it was again recommended for use in Canada by the Treasury Board Secretariat (1998). In 2004, the social or economic discount rate was re-estimated for Canada by Starzenski (2004), who found it to be a real rate of approximately 8%. Burgess (2005) also revisited his estimate of the social discount rate and proposed a rate of 7.3% using fairly aggregate economic data with alternative simulation scenarios.

With the exception of Starzenski, the above empirical estimates were largely based on the data over the period 1965 to 1974. The effects of inflation and changes in business taxes, and the structure of the Canadian economy since 1974, have not been fully taken into consideration. The estimation of the economic rates of return from investment that are derived from data for individual industries is a time-consuming process. An alternative approach is to use aggregate national income accounts data to estimate the pre-tax returns of domestic investment, one of the key parameters in the estimation of the social discount rate (e.g., Harberger, 1977; Kuo, Jenkins, and Mphahlele, 2003). For the other components of the discount rate, the most recent available data are incorporated into the estimation of the economic discount rate.

An Empirical Update

While Canada operates in a global capital market, the intensity by which it finances its capital formation from abroad will affect the cost it pays for such funds. In such an economy, when funds are raised in the capital markets, the cost of funds will tend to rise. Because of the higher financial cost, the funds obtained to finance a project are normally diverted from three alternative sources. First, funds that would have been invested in other investment activities have now been postponed or displaced by the expenditures required to undertake the project. The cost of these funds for society as a whole is the gross-of-income tax return that would have been earned on the alternative investments in the economy. Second, funds would come from different categories of domestic savers, who postpone their consumption in the expectation of earning a higher net of tax return now so that they can purchase additional consumption later. Third, some funds may be coming from abroad – that is, from foreign savers. The cost of these funds should be measured by the marginal cost of foreign capital inflows. This parameter is estimated by the direct cost of the incremental funds to the users of these funds plus any effects the additional foreign financing has on the future financing cost of other foreign capital already in Canada.

The social or economic discount rate will be measured as a weighted average of the economic costs of funds from these three sources: the rate of return on postponed or displaced investment, the social cost of newly stimulated domestic savings, and the marginal cost of additional foreign capital inflows. The weights are equal to the proportion of funds sourced from domestic private-sector investors, domestic private-sector savers, and foreign savers. They should be measured by the reaction of investors and savers to a change in market interest rates brought about by the increase in government borrowing. This can be written as:

$$EOCK = f_1\rho + f_2\gamma + f_3 (MC_f) \qquad (1)$$

where ρ stands for the gross-of-income tax return on domestic investments, γ for the social cost of newly stimulated domestic savings, and MC_f for the marginal cost of incremental capital inflows from abroad; f_1, f_2, and f_3 are the corresponding sourcing fractions associated with displaced investment, newly stimulated domestic savings, and newly stimulated capital inflows from abroad. Obviously, $f_1 + f_2 + f_3$ should equal one.

The weights can be expressed in terms of the elasticities of demand and supply, yielding the following:

$$EOCK = \frac{\varepsilon_r(S_r/S_t)*\gamma + \varepsilon_f(S_f/S_t)*MC_f - \eta(I_t/S_t)*\rho}{\varepsilon_r(S_r/S_t) + \varepsilon_f(S_f/S_t) - \eta(I_t/S_t)} \qquad (2)$$

where ε_r is the supply elasticity of domestic savings; ε_f is the supply elasticity of foreign funds; η is the elasticity of demand for domestic investment with respect to changes in the cost of funds; and S_t is the total private-sector savings available in the economy, of which S_r is the contribution to the total savings by residents, S_f is the total contribution of net foreign capital inflows, and I_t is the total private-sector investment.

We begin by estimating the economic cost of each alternative source of funds in equation (1). It will be expressed as a percentage of the respective stock of reproducible capital.

The Gross-of-Tax Return to Domestic Investment

In this study, the rate of return on domestic investment is calculated based on the country's national income accounts. This is a comprehensive account of the full range of economic activities in the country. It covers not only manufacturing and non-manufacturing sectors but also the imputed rents for owner-occupied houses.

The economic return of capital on domestic investment is the contribution of capital to the economy as a whole, which can be measured by the sum of the private net-of-tax returns on capital and all direct and indirect taxes generated by this capital. There are alternative ways of estimating this gross-of-tax return to a country's reproducible capital. Our approach is to sum all the returns to capital and then divide the total by the value of the stock of reproducible capital, including buildings, machinery, and equipment. The return on capital consists of the sum of interest, rent, and profit incomes that are recorded in the national accounts. However, some items, such as the surplus of unincorporated enterprises, do not separate out the return to capital explicitly. These are mainly small businesses and farm operations. Because the owners of the businesses and their family members are also workers and are often not formally paid with wages, the operating surplus of this sector includes the returns to both capital and labour. In this study, the labour content of this mixed income is assumed to be approximately 70% of the total. This is approximately labour's overall share of total value added for the economy.

Taxes include corporate income taxes, property taxes, as well as the share of sales and excise taxes attributed to the value added of reproducible capital. In the case of sales tax, if it is a consumption-type value-added tax, the tax is applied to the sales of goods and services at all stages of the production and distribution chain. At each stage, vendors are able to claim tax credits to recover the tax they paid on their business inputs, including capital goods such as machinery, equipment, and building. As a result, the value-added tax is not embodied in the value added of capital; it is effectively borne by labour. In 1991, Canada introduced a federal Goods and Services Tax (GST) at a rate of 7% to replace the manufacturer's sales tax.[2] At the same time, the Government of Quebec also replaced its retail sales tax by the same GST, at 8%. Later, on April 1, 1997, the provincial retail sales taxes in Nova Scotia, New Brunswick, and Newfoundland and Labrador were replaced and harmonized with the federal GST at a single rate of 15% on the same base of goods and services (The Governments of Canada, Nova Scotia, New Brunswick, Newfoundland and Labrador, 1997).

In addition, a considerable amount of federal and provincial excise taxes and duties have been imposed on alcoholic beverages, tobacco products, motor vehicle fuels, and so on. These taxes are mainly levied on consumer goods. Excise taxes on business inputs such as fuels are not creditable in the same way as is the GST paid on the purchase of inputs. The share of these excise taxes that are a component of the value added of capital needs to be estimated and included in the return to reproducible capital.

The value of the stock of reproducible capital excludes the value of land, so the income stream accruing to capital should also exclude the portion that is attributable to the unimproved land. This is significant only in the cases of agriculture and housing. All improvements to land, however, such as clearing; levelling; and installation of infrastructure for utilities, fencing, irrigation, and drainage should be considered part of reproducible capital. Thus, the share of unimproved land in the total capital stock is quite small. The precise data on the contribution of land are not readily available. From the analysis of farm budgets, it is estimated that for Canada, approximately 25% of the total value added of the agricultural sector could be attributed to land. In the case of the housing sector, information is not available on the value of land embodied in this sector, nor is the land component of the value added available for the sector. In the estimates of the total return to capital in the economy, the value of net imputed rent on owner-occupied houses is included.[3] The value of imputed rent, however, excludes the contribution

---

[2]Department of Finance Canada (1989). The current government has now lowered the GST rate to 5%.

[3]It should be noted that the data obtained from Statistics Canada is the value of gross imputed rent on owner-occupied houses. The value is reduced by the amount of depreciation, which is estimated by the fraction of owner-occupied imputed rent in total imputed rent (including paid rent) times the residential stock in the previous year and the depreciation rate (i.e., 2%).

of land to the value added of the housing sector. By excluding from the income to capital the contribution of land in residential housing, we are able to derive the rate of return to reproducible capital alone.

To calculate the rate of return on reproducible private-sector capital, we use the values for the year-end residential and non-residential capital stock estimated by Statistics Canada. These values are derived by breaking down investment into its components, such as buildings, machinery, and equipment. Different depreciation rates are applied yearly to the cumulated value of the stock of the capital for each of these categories, while the value of the stock is augmented by the value of new gross investment made each year. The time path of capital stock, appropriate depreciation rates, and new investment by categories are estimated for individual sectors to arrive at the year-end values for the net capital stock.[4] Given the year-end net capital stocks, we can calculate the mid-year fixed capital stocks. We include in the stock of reproducible capital the value of the investment made by Canadian public-sector enterprises that operate as business firms. However, we exclude the capital used in the general public administration from the capital base since this part of the public sector involves activities such as public security, national defence, and public administration, for which no valuation is made in the national accounts for the services they produce. Investment in these types of operations would generally not be affected by government borrowing in the capital markets. The figures are deflated by the GDP deflator and expressed in 1997 prices.

The detailed computations for the estimation of the gross-of-tax rate of return on domestic investments are presented in Table 1 (see page 282). For the past 40 years, the average real rate of return on investment (ρ) in Canada has been about 12.29% in 1966-75, 12.57% in 1976-85, 10.86% in 1986-95, and 11.28% in 1996-2005. The rate of return ranges from 10.00 to 14.00% over these years, with the exception of the recession years of 1991 and 1993. For the purpose of this analysis, we use 11.0% as the value of the economic rate of return on domestic investment. This estimate, however, contains some element of risk in the rate of return to the forgone domestic investment either displaced or postponed (see, for example, Glenday, this volume). To estimate and remove the risk component, we will have to measure the rate of return to

---

[4]See, e.g., Huang (2004). It may be noted that changes in inventories are not included as part of the total net capital stock in this study.

newly stimulated domestic savings and compare it with the return on risk-free financial instruments; this will be dealt with in the next section.

The Cost of Newly Stimulated Domestic Savings

When new project funds are raised in a country's capital market, the result is an increase in the cost of funds, which in turn stimulates additional private-sector savings. This additional savings comes at the expense of postponed consumption, which has an average opportunity cost equal to the return obtained from the additional savings, net of all taxes and financial intermediation costs.

The opportunity cost of the newly stimulated domestic savings can therefore be measured by the gross-of-tax return to reproducible capital minus the amount of corporate income taxes paid directly by business entities and minus the property taxes paid by these entities and homeowners. It is further reduced by the personal income taxes that are paid on the income generated from reproducible capital. This net-of-tax income received by individual owners of capital is further reduced by the costs of financial intermediations provided by banks and other deposit-taking institutions. These intermediation costs are one of the components that create a gap between the gross-of-tax return to investment and the net-of-tax return to savings. The final result is the net return on domestic savings. It also reflects the rate of time preference of individuals for consumption forgone.

Our empirical estimation of this parameter starts with the gross-of-tax return to reproducible capital generated in the previous section. As is shown in Table 2 (see page 285), the gross-of-tax return is reduced by the amounts of corporate income taxes and the property taxes paid by corporations and homeowners to arrive at the net-of-capital tax return to reproducible capital. The estimate is further reduced by the amount of the personal income tax on these capital incomes as well as intermediation services charged by financial institutions in order to derive the net return to domestic savings.

It should be noted that we estimate the costs of basic financial intermediation services, such as lending and deposit-taking provided by banks, trust companies, credit unions, and other deposit-taking institutions, by deducting the total payments to labour as part of the general deduction for the value added of labour and deducting the value of gross profits for the sector. The depreciation component of the gross value added of the financial sector has already been deducted in the calculation of net after-tax profits; hence, only the net profits of the financial sector associated with intermediation services need to be deducted. The proportion of non-intermediation services and even intermediation services in banks and other deposit-taking institutions that are charged for directly through fees has increased over time. For the purpose of this exercise, the financial intermediation services are assumed to account for 50% of the total net-of-tax profits in deposit-taking institutions.

To estimate the net return to newly domestic savers, one has to further subtract personal income taxes on capital income. Because of lack of data on taxes paid by savers exclusively on their capital income, we are making an estimation based on the assumption that the effective rate of income taxes on the income from capital is the same as the rate of income taxes on wages and salaries. This assumption might bias downward the amount of taxes paid on the income from capital as investors tend to be relatively wealthy and are likely to be at a higher marginal rate of personal income tax than are wage earners. With these assumptions, an estimate of the annual amount of the personal income tax on capital is made.

The rate of time preference for consumption is then estimated by dividing the estimated net return income accruing to domestic savings by the stock of reproducible capital. This is presented in the last column of Table 2. Over the past 40 years, the economic cost of newly stimulated domestic savings for Canada would be on average 7.00% in 1966-75, 7.79% in 1976-85, 6.37% in 1986-95, and 6.53% in 1996-2005. For the purpose of this analysis, we use 6.50% as the rate of return to newly stimulated domestic savings. The estimate was derived beginning from ex-post value of return to gross-of-tax income to capital net of direct and indirect taxes and financial intermediation services. This implies that the value contains the risk premium over the study period. The question is what the magnitude of the risk premium is in order to estimate the rate of time preference.

Government of Canada bonds are conceivably a risk-free financial instrument. The average yield of Government of Canada marketable bonds with maturity more than 10 years was about 5.78% issued in 2001, 5.66% in 2002, 5.28% in 2003, 5.08% in 2004, and 4.39% in 2005.[5] For this study, we assume the average yield of long-term bonds will remain around 5.25% with an inflation rate at 2%. Suppose the yield is subject to

---

[5]Statistics Canada, CANSIM Vector V122487.

the personal income tax rate at 25% in the base case: then the real rate of return to risk-free bonds would be approximately 1.90%. Let us assume that the average risk is around mid-point between the previous estimate of 6.5% and the risk-free rate of 1.9%; that is, 2.3%.[6] For the purpose of this study, we assume that a risk premium of 2% is contained in the previous estimates of the rate of return to domestic investment and newly stimulated domestic savings. In other words, we will use 9% and 4.5% as the values of ρ and γ, respectively, in the estimation of the EOCK.

Marginal Economic Cost of Foreign Financing

The last component of the EOCK from raising funds through the capital market is the marginal economic cost of newly stimulated capital inflows from abroad. Foreign capital inflows reflect an inflow of savings from foreigners that augments the resources available for investment. When the demand for investible funds is increased, the market interest rates increase, and as a consequence, funds are attracted to the market. In the case of foreign borrowing, an additional cost is created. As the quantity of foreign obligations increases relative to the country's capacity to service these foreign obligations, one would expect the return demanded by foreign investors to rise. For the country as whole, the cost of foreign borrowing is not just the cost of servicing the additional unit of foreign funds, but it is also the extra financial burden of servicing all other foreign financing where the cost of this financing is responsive to the market interest rate. As a consequence, the marginal cost of additional foreign borrowing increases as the proportion of the country's capital stock that is financed from foreign sources increases.

The marginal economic cost of foreign borrowing (MC_f) can be expressed as follows:

$$MC_f = i_f \times (1-t_w) \times \{1+\phi \times (1/\varepsilon_s^f)\} \tag{3}$$

---

[6]Because individual investors have different risk preferences, the marginal cost of risk that determines asset yields will overstate the average cost of risk in the market. If risk premiums demanded by individuals are linearly distributed, the average cost of risk will be approximately half of the differential between the returns observed in the market and the riskless rate of return.

where i_f is the real interest rate on foreign borrowing by the project, t_w is the rate of withholding taxes charged on interest payments made abroad, ϕ is the ratio of [the total foreign financing whose interest rate is flexible and will respond to additional foreign borrowing] to [the total amount of foreign borrowing and foreign direct investment], and ε_s^f is the supply elasticity of foreign funds to a country with respect to the interest rate the country pays on its incremental foreign capital flows.

The Canadian capital markets are highly integrated with the rest of the world, especially with the United States. The real rate of return on total US direct investment net of any withholding tax that is either repatriated to the United States or reinvested in Canada was estimated to average 6.11% from 1964 to 1973 (Jenkins, 1977). The cost of US foreign investment in Canada was subsequently re-estimated by Evans and Jenkins (1980) over the period 1951–1978. They found that the net income received and accrued by the US owners of direct investment in Canada ranged from 5.75% to 6.03%. No further update has been made in recent years. For the purpose of this analysis, 6% will be assumed for the average rate of return for non-resident owners of investment in Canada.

It is also reasonable to assume that about 30% of foreign investment in Canada is represented by variable-interest rate loans, and thus ϕ is taken as .3. The supply curve of funds facing a country would generally be upward sloping. If we assume an elasticity of supply of 3.0, the marginal cost of foreign capital inflow would be about 6.60%.[7] As our estimate of the marginal cost of foreign financing includes only the cost of servicing Canada's direct investment, both debt and equity, and not the portfolio investment in Canada that might cost less, our estimated cost of foreign financing might be biased upward. To adjust for this bias, we assume the marginal cost of all foreign financing in Canada to be a real rate of approximately 6%.

Measurement of the EOCK

As was mentioned earlier, the EOCK is estimated as a weighted average of the gross-of-tax rate of return on domestic investment, the cost of

---

[7]The elasticity of supply of foreign funds investment is measured with respect to changes in the stock of foreign investment for changes in the return to foreign investment.

newly stimulated domestic savings, and the marginal cost of newly induced foreign capital inflows, as shown in equation (2). The marginal cost for each of the three components was estimated in the previous sub-sections. The weights associated with each source of funding at the margin depends upon the average contributions made from each source and their responses to the change in interest rate as a result of borrowing in the capital market.

The annual gross fixed investments made by private corporations, public corporations and general public administration services are shown in Table 3 (see page 286). Over the past 40 years, the contribution by the general public administration services has accounted for an average of 21.73% of national gross investment. This share, however, has declined to an average of 19.74% over the past 20 years and to 17.56% over the past 10 years. This is consistent with the cumulated reproducible capital used to calculate the rate of return on domestic investment and the cost of newly stimulated domestic savings.

Over the years, private-sector investment in Canada has been financed by private-sector savings. The situation has been quite different for the public sector. The Government of Canada was in deficit in the 1980s, and for a period, the deficit was as high as one-third of the national budget. The fiscal situation later improved, and in recent years, the federal government has been running a surplus. As of January 31, 2007, the federal debt was approximately $526,697 million, which accounts for almost 35% of GDP. If the debt is expressed as the percentage of the current private- and public-sector reproducible capital, it would be about 11.7%.[8] In other words, investment by the general public administration has been financed in part by private-sector savings. For the purpose of this analysis, the ratio of the private-sector investments to the private-sector savings of residents and non-residents (I_t/S_t) is set at 0.9 in the base case. Taking into account the debt held by provincial and municipal governments, this ratio could be slightly lower.

During the period 1947 to 1973, on average, approximately 20% of gross fixed capital formation in Canada was financed by foreign capital inflows. With the introduction of NAFTA in 1990 and the further integration of Canadian capital markets with those of the rest of the world, one would expect a higher proportion of gross capital formation

---

[8]This is calculated by the ratio of the federal debt, $527 billion, to the total national reproducible capital, $4,500 billion, expressed in 2007 prices. See Table 1 (on pages 282–284).

being financed by foreign savings.[9] For this analysis, we assume the percentage (S_f/S_t) to have increased to 25%. The remainder (S_r/S_t) will be financed by domestic savings.

Following equation (2), to estimate the weights assigned to each source of funding, we need to specify the elasticity of supply of each source with respect to the real cost of funds. The initial estimation is carried out using a value for the demand elasticity for domestic investment of -1.0, a supply elasticity of newly stimulated domestic savings of 0.4, and a supply elasticity of foreign savings of 3.0 (see, e.g., Boskin, 1978; Jenkins and Mescher, 1981; Leipziger, 1974). With these assumptions, the proportions of funds obtained from these three sources are 15.38% from domestic savings, 38.46% from foreign capital, and 46.16% from displaced or postponed domestic investment. Substituting these data into equation (2), one obtains a base-case estimation of the EOCK for Canada of 7.15%.

Sensitivity Analysis

The above empirical estimates depend upon the value of several key parameters, such as the rate of return on domestic investment (ρ), the supply elasticity of foreign capital inflow (ε_f), the ratio of the private-sector investments to the private-sector savings of residents and non-residents (I_t/S_t), time preference for consumption (γ), and risk premium embodied in the estimated rates of return on domestic investment and domestic savings. In the sensitivity analysis, we assess the impact of changes in the value of these key parameters on our estimate of the EOCK for Canada.

The Rate of Return on Domestic Investment

If the average rate of return on domestic investment is a 0.5-percentage point lower than the base case, it would imply a value of 8.5% instead of

---

[9]In fact, more than 1.3 million corporations currently exist in Canada; of these, about 8,000 are foreign-controlled and account for 21.9% of the assets for the country as a whole.

9.0%. With this value, the EOCK for Canada is about 6.92%, 0.23 of one percentage point lower than the base case.

The Supply Elasticity of Foreign Capital

We have assumed a value of 3.0 in the base case for the supply elasticity of the stock of foreign savings to Canada. Suppose the elasticity of foreign capital is as high as 6.0 instead of the 3.0; then the share of financing from foreign funds to investment projects will be much larger. The sourcing of funds would become 11.11% from domestic savings, 55.56% from foreign capital, and 33.33% from displaced or postponed domestic investment. As a result, the EOCK decreases to 6.83%, or 0.32 of one percentage point lower than the estimate for the base case.

The Ratio of the Private-Sector Investments to the Private-Sector Savings

As was discussed earlier, the 90% ratio for the private-sector investments to the private-sector savings was based on the federal debt alone. If the debt for the provincial and municipal governments is also taken into account, the 90% share could go down to 80%. Let us assume that the ratio of I_t/S_t is 80%. The proportions of funds diverted to finance the investment project would become 16.22% from newly stimulated domestic savings, 40.54% from foreign savings, and 43.24% from displaced or postponed domestic investment. As a consequence, the EOCK would decrease to 7.05%.

As the federal and several provincial governments in recent years have had budget surpluses, we may assume that the ratio of I_t/S_t would be equal to unity. In this scenario, the sourcing of funds directed from the private sectors to government borrowing would be 14.63% from domestic savings, 36.59% from foreign capital inflow, and 48.78% from displaced or postponed domestic investment. This suggests that the EOCK would rise to 7.24%, approximately 0.09 of one percentage point higher than the base case.

Time Preference for Consumption

The time preference for consumption is measured by the cost of newly stimulated domestic savings. The 4.5% estimate was based on the average rate over the past 25 years. As a matter of fact, it has been declining over years. In the past 15 years, it was averaged at 4.3%. Suppose it is 4.0% instead of the 4.5% assumed for the base case: the EOCK would then become 7.07%, about 0.08 of one percentage point lower than the base case.

Risk Premium

The 2.0-percentage point estimate of the risk premium is influenced by the assumption of the marginal personal income tax rate applied to yields on government bonds received by newly stimulated domestic savers. Suppose the marginal income tax rate for these savers is 35% instead of 25%; then the after-tax real rate of return on the government bonds would be 1.38%. Thus, the risk premium contained in the estimates of the rate of return to domestic investment and newly stimulated domestic savings would be about 2.56%. For this analysis, it is assumed at 2.5%. As a consequence, the rate of return to domestic investment and savings after removing the risk premium would become 8.5% and 4.0%, respectively. The EOCK would then decrease to 6.85%.

From the above sensitivity analyses, we find that the EOCK ranges from 6.83% to 7.24%. We can conclude that a conservative estimate of the EOCK for Canada would be a real rate of 7.00%.

Concluding Remarks

The economic or social discount rate is a key parameter used for investment decision-making. The value of this variable has been controversial and debated for years. The issue is even more critical when applied to social sector projects and programs such as health, education, the environment, and regulations.

This paper has reviewed some theoretical issues and described a practical framework for the estimation of the economic cost of capital for Canada. It is in the framework of a small open economy in both commodity and capital markets. When funds are raised in the capital markets for use in an investment project, these funds are obtained from three sources: displacement or postponement of private domestic investment, newly stimulated domestic savings, and newly stimulated inflows of capital from abroad. Employing this framework, we estimate that the real EOCK would be approximately 7.15% in the base case.

We have performed a sensitivity analysis by allowing the key parameters that have an impact on the measurement of the economic discount rate. These parameters include the rate of return on domestic investment, the supply elasticity of foreign capital inflows, the ratio of total private investment to total private savings, the time preference for consumption, and the risk premium contained in the rates of return on domestic investment and domestic savings. The results suggest that the discount rate can range from 6.83% to 7.24% real. As a consequence, we conclude that for Canada, a 7% real rate is an appropriate discount rate to use when calculating the economic NPV of the flows of economic benefits and costs over time.

Table 1: Return to Domestic Investment, 1965-2005

Year	Corporation Profits before Income Taxes	Public Enterprise Profits before Income Taxes	Interest and Other Investment Income	Accrued Net Income of Farming	Net Income of Non-Farming	Net Imputed Rent	Real Property Taxes	Gross-of-Tax Income to Capital without Having Indirect Taxes
				(millions of dollars)				
1965	6,543	453	1,917	1,450	4,185	2,802	2,024	15,321
1966	7,031	424	2,130	2,000	4,391	3,034	2,250	16,636
1967	7,211	486	2,360	1,272	4,671	3,363	2,478	17,586
1968	8,079	514	2,796	1,367	5,112	3,765	2,771	19,767
1969	8,579	673	3,158	1,503	5,505	4,177	3,074	21,650
1970	8,089	771	3,493	1,342	5,721	4,669	3,315	22,355
1971	9,092	786	3,959	1,442	6,116	5,107	3,537	24,640
1972	11,237	857	4,700	1,349	6,529	5,468	3,839	28,363
1973	15,939	949	5,845	2,828	7,076	5,891	4,129	35,512
1974	20,738	1,241	8,594	3,593	7,331	6,481	4,600	44,662
1975	20,220	1,153	10,407	3,731	8,149	7,549	5,314	47,927
1976	21,009	1,658	12,961	3,111	9,077	9,176	6,366	54,593
1977	21,922	2,148	15,489	2,420	10,139	11,146	7,253	61,545
1978	26,409	2,694	18,877	3,015	11,573	13,029	7,937	73,097
1979	34,927	3,895	23,185	3,103	12,744	14,582	8,260	89,370
1980	38,382	4,334	27,256	3,167	13,585	16,544	9,436	100,741
1981	35,831	4,954	33,277	2,823	14,680	19,075	10,706	108,883
1982	26,697	2,509	37,991	2,191	16,984	21,657	11,500	105,942
1983	36,730	4,432	37,062	1,827	20,901	24,352	12,232	121,490
1984	45,686	4,936	39,618	2,099	23,473	26,437	13,050	137,241
1985	49,728	4,937	40,763	2,839	25,904	28,610	13,897	146,345
1986	45,217	4,564	39,481	3,825	28,574	31,237	15,024	144,956
1987	57,888	5,126	38,841	1,985	30,761	33,787	16,286	161,603
1988	64,891	6,829	42,188	3,283	33,113	36,928	17,675	179,184
1989	59,661	7,246	48,013	1,986	34,856	40,953	19,534	186,310
1990	44,936	6,460	54,874	2,053	35,544	44,375	21,304	183,074
1991	32,920	5,179	54,486	1,853	37,022	47,683	22,974	174,766
1992	32,648	5,993	52,742	1,727	39,406	50,717	24,604	178,914
1993	41,102	4,694	52,381	2,017	42,068	53,047	25,512	189,810
1994	65,464	5,827	52,000	1,255	44,931	56,249	25,469	218,770
1995	76,270	6,709	50,981	2,702	46,363	58,545	25,737	232,759
1996	80,335	6,143	50,477	3,825	49,278	60,581	26,322	239,502
1997	87,932	6,653	48,881	1,663	54,663	62,619	27,125	249,983
1998	86,132	7,080	47,134	1,724	57,936	64,906	28,795	251,815
1999	110,769	8,401	47,249	1,819	61,466	66,981	29,809	282,058
2000	135,978	11,329	55,302	1,243	64,944	69,680	29,898	321,950
2001	127,073	10,787	52,579	1,675	68,857	72,515	30,721	314,709
2002	135,229	11,661	46,693	1,101	74,292	76,014	31,461	323,594
2003	144,821	12,290	49,679	1,373	77,014	79,110	33,557	342,870
2004	171,323	12,508	54,084	3,256	80,828	82,465	35,442	380,803
2005	189,455	14,481	60,403	1,706	84,500	85,493	37,106	412,671

Glenn P. Jenkins and Chun-Yan Kuo

Year	Gross-of-Tax Income to Capital without Having Indirect Taxes	Labour Income of Incorporated	Total Labour Income Including Unincorporated Businesses	Federal Manu-facturer's Sales Tax	Federal Goods and Services Tax	Federal Excise Taxes	Provincial Retail Sales Tax	Provincial Goods and Services Tax	Provincial Excise Taxes	Gross-of-Tax Income to Capital Taking into Account Indirect Taxes
					(millions of dollars)					
1965	15,321	29,630	33,575	1,343		2,560	818		1,030	17,123
1966	16,636	33,507	37,981	1,468		2,788	1,000		1,168	18,593
1967	17,586	37,065	41,225	1,580		2,923	1,252		1,251	19,681
1968	19,767	40,297	44,832	1,580		2,997	1,414		1,463	22,047
1969	21,650	45,065	49,971	1,712		3,182	1,678		1,625	24,128
1970	22,355	48,851	53,795	1,696		3,214	1,832		1,794	24,861
1971	24,640	53,556	58,847	1,912		3,533	1,989		1,933	27,405
1972	28,363	60,108	65,623	2,246		3,970	2,320		2,177	31,596
1973	35,512	69,243	76,176	2,496		4,510	2,894		2,400	39,423
1974	44,662	82,571	90,218	2,962		6,699	3,603		2,598	49,914
1975	47,927	96,305	104,621	2,971		6,042	3,655		2,784	52,782
1976	54,593	111,413	119,945	3,911		6,503	4,661		3,152	60,294
1977	61,545	123,390	132,181	4,284		6,718	5,034		3,523	67,758
1978	73,097	134,216	144,428	4,766		6,984	4,773		3,700	79,892
1979	89,370	150,946	162,039	4,593		7,136	5,812		3,971	97,017
1980	100,741	170,643	182,369	5,173		8,007	6,366		4,410	109,265
1981	108,883	196,716	208,968	6,279		10,276	7,270		5,288	118,856
1982	105,942	210,083	223,506	5,926		10,118	7,844		6,481	115,708
1983	121,490	220,283	236,193	6,491		10,022	9,166		7,111	132,627
1984	137,241	237,248	255,148	7,434		10,867	10,454		7,613	149,961
1985	146,345	255,825	275,945	9,096		12,736	11,816		8,195	160,846
1986	144,956	272,755	295,434	11,841		16,128	13,198		8,853	161,420
1987	161,603	296,442	319,364	12,726		18,508	14,548		9,460	180,164
1988	179,184	325,250	350,727	14,329		20,303	16,925		10,277	200,092
1989	186,310	350,743	376,532	16,253		23,188	18,468		10,930	209,097
1990	183,074	368,891	395,209	14,288		21,577	18,668		11,383	203,942
1991	174,766	379,092	406,305		17,379	25,295	14,412	4,280	11,653	190,213
1992	178,914	387,788	416,581		17,786	25,655	13,066	5,519	12,671	194,355
1993	189,810	394,816	425,676		18,153	26,346	13,386	5,488	13,383	206,191
1994	218,770	404,918	437,248		19,058	25,434	15,347	5,099	13,928	237,015
1995	232,759	418,825	453,171		19,650	26,810	16,357	4,964	14,673	252,386
1996	239,502	428,792	465,964		20,613	28,022	16,008	5,137	15,343	259,659
1997	249,983	453,073	492,501		22,559	30,566	15,921	6,113	16,528	271,199
1998	251,815	474,335	516,097		23,159	31,443	17,481	6,100	17,678	273,656
1999	282,058	502,726	547,026		25,053	33,339	18,477	7,065	18,817	306,087
2000	321,950	545,204	591,535		27,090	35,369	19,994	7,388	19,389	348,295
2001	314,709	570,008	619,380		27,915	36,487	20,108	8,092	20,482	340,677
2002	323,594	593,307	646,082		30,072	39,417	21,014	8,284	22,244	351,183
2003	342,870	621,003	675,874		31,564	41,247	21,498	9,044	23,355	371,848
2004	380,803	651,888	710,747		32,989	42,594	21,999	9,795	24,613	411,924
2005	412,671	688,150	748,494		34,819	44,541	23,234	10,186	25,519	445,828

Table 1: Return to Domestic Investment, 1965–2005 (cont'd)

Year	Gross-of-Tax Income to Capital Taking into Account Indirect Taxes	GDP Deflator [1997=100]	Real Gross-of-Tax Income to Capital Taking into Account Indirect Taxes [$1997]	Year-End Real Non-Residential Capital Stock [$1997]	Year-End Fixed Residential Capital Stock [$1997]	Year-End Capital Stock for Public Administration [$1997]	Year-End Real Capital Stock Net of Public Administration [$1997]	Mid-Year Real Capital Stock Net of Public Administration [$1997]	Real Rate of Return to Capital (%)	10-Year Average Return to Capital (%)
				(millions of dollars)						
1965	17,123	18.51	92,508	666,687	219,181	150,265	735,604	367,802	12.58	
1966	18,593	19.42	95,740	705,683	228,048	157,582	776,149	755,876	12.34	
1967	19,681	20.29	96,998	742,946	237,091	164,821	815,216	795,682	11.90	
1968	22,047	21.13	104,342	777,811	248,029	171,807	854,033	834,624	12.22	
1969	24,128	22.16	108,881	812,671	261,240	179,098	894,813	874,423	12.17	
1970	24,861	23.13	107,485	849,038	272,873	186,137	935,774	915,293	11.49	
1971	27,405	24.25	113,009	886,412	287,027	194,296	979,143	957,459	11.54	
1972	31,596	25.68	123,039	923,433	302,687	202,957	1,023,163	1,001,153	12.03	
1973	39,423	28.17	139,946	963,977	319,469	211,312	1,072,133	1,047,648	13.05	
1974	49,914	32.45	153,818	1,007,225	336,658	219,596	1,124,286	1,098,210	13.68	
1975	52,782	35.92	146,942	1,053,439	352,712	228,175	1,177,976	1,151,131	12.47	12.29
1976	60,294	39.33	153,303	1,097,450	373,359	236,030	1,234,778	1,206,377	12.42	
1977	67,758	42.01	161,291	1,141,524	393,622	243,996	1,291,150	1,262,964	12.49	
1978	79,892	44.78	178,410	1,185,390	413,377	251,526	1,347,241	1,319,195	13.24	
1979	97,017	49.25	196,989	1,235,370	432,013	258,506	1,408,877	1,378,059	13.98	
1980	109,265	54.21	201,559	1,292,781	447,951	265,154	1,475,579	1,442,228	13.66	
1981	118,856	60.05	197,928	1,360,731	465,828	272,848	1,553,712	1,514,645	12.74	
1982	115,708	65.15	177,603	1,416,399	479,168	280,298	1,615,270	1,584,491	11.00	
1983	132,627	68.69	193,081	1,462,207	496,571	287,128	1,671,650	1,643,460	11.55	
1984	149,961	70.94	211,392	1,506,562	513,844	294,507	1,725,899	1,698,774	12.25	
1985	160,846	73.14	219,916	1,553,298	533,011	302,708	1,783,601	1,754,750	12.33	12.57
1986	161,420	75.36	214,198	1,596,208	556,010	310,079	1,842,139	1,812,870	11.63	
1987	180,164	78.83	228,548	1,641,104	584,993	317,547	1,908,550	1,875,345	11.97	
1988	200,092	82.37	242,919	1,695,129	613,798	324,878	1,984,048	1,946,299	12.24	
1989	209,097	86.11	242,826	1,751,518	643,943	332,894	2,062,567	2,023,308	11.77	
1990	203,942	88.84	229,561	1,803,230	670,134	341,025	2,132,338	2,097,453	10.77	
1991	190,213	91.47	207,951	1,847,236	689,164	348,658	2,187,742	2,160,040	9.51	
1992	194,355	92.67	209,728	1,881,169	710,009	356,018	2,235,160	2,211,451	9.38	
1993	206,191	94.01	219,328	1,911,096	728,756	362,573	2,277,279	2,256,219	9.63	
1994	237,015	95.09	249,253	1,947,075	748,568	369,714	2,325,930	2,301,604	10.72	
1995	252,386	97.24	259,549	1,984,251	762,479	376,870	2,369,860	2,347,895	10.95	10.86
1996	259,659	98.81	262,786	2,023,949	778,243	383,010	2,419,182	2,394,521	10.86	
1997	271,199	100	271,199	2,079,298	797,597	387,625	2,489,270	2,454,226	10.89	
1998	273,656	99.57	274,838	2,138,742	815,622	391,608	2,562,756	2,526,013	10.72	
1999	306,087	101.31	302,130	2,206,295	834,389	395,686	2,644,997	2,603,877	11.42	
2000	348,295	105.5	330,138	2,277,928	855,171	400,859	2,732,239	2,688,618	12.08	
2001	340,677	106.68	319,345	2,348,605	879,571	407,521	2,820,655	2,776,447	11.32	
2002	351,183	107.82	325,713	2,411,844	909,666	414,620	2,906,889	2,863,772	11.20	
2003	371,848	111.45	333,645	2,482,241	942,421	421,624	3,003,039	2,954,964	11.11	
2004	411,924	114.77	358,913	2,559,240	978,687	428,817	3,109,111	3,056,075	11.54	
2005	445,828	118.46	376,353	2,646,432	1,015,902	436,909	3,225,425	3,167,268	11.67	11.28

Glenn P. Jenkins and Chun-Yan Kuo

Table 2: Return to Domestic Savings, 1965–2005

Year	Gross-of-Tax Income to Capital with No Indirect Taxes	Corporate Income Tax	Real Property Taxes	Total Personal Income Taxes	Total Labour Income Including Unincorporated Businesses	Personal Income Taxes Paid on Capital Income	Profits after Taxes for Deposit-Taking Institutions	Return to Domestic Savings	GDP Deflator [1997=100]	Mid-Year Real Capital Stock Net of Public Administration [$ 1997]	Real Return to Domestic Savings	10-Year Av. Real Return to Savings
	(millions of dollars)										(%)	(%)
1965	15,321	2,197	2,024	3,563	33,575	1,001	-166	10,016	18.51	717,574	7.54	
1966	16,636	2,355	2,250	4,114	37,981	1,124	186	10,814	19.42	755,876	7.37	
1967	17,586	2,396	2,478	5,106	41,225	1,375	210	11,232	20.29	795,682	6.96	
1968	19,767	2,852	2,771	6,145	44,832	1,683	250	12,335	21.13	834,624	6.99	
1969	21,650	3,221	3,074	7,697	49,971	2,074	303	13,130	22.16	874,423	6.78	
1970	22,355	3,070	3,315	9,069	53,795	2,393	334	13,410	23.13	915,293	6.33	
1971	24,640	3,346	3,537	10,417	58,847	2,768	374	14,802	24.25	957,459	6.38	
1972	28,363	3,920	3,839	11,611	65,623	3,151	426	17,240	25.68	1,001,153	6.71	
1973	35,512	5,079	4,129	13,618	76,176	3,887	540	22,146	28.17	1,047,648	7.50	
1974	44,662	7,051	4,600	16,602	90,218	4,885	438	27,907	32.45	1,098,210	7.83	
1975	47,927	7,494	5,314	18,538	104,621	5,167	835	29,534	35.92	1,151,131	7.14	7.00
1976	54,593	7,128	6,366	21,400	119,945	6,067	940	34,562	39.33	1,206,377	7.28	
1977	61,545	7,238	7,253	23,811	132,181	6,934	1,169	39,535	42.01	1,262,964	7.45	
1978	73,097	8,188	7,937	24,728	144,428	7,667	1,220	48,694	44.78	1,319,195	8.24	
1979	89,370	10,038	8,260	27,774	162,039	9,129	995	61,446	49.25	1,378,059	9.05	
1980	100,741	12,078	9,436	32,139	182,369	10,514	1,399	68,013	54.21	1,442,228	8.70	
1981	108,883	12,796	10,706	38,565	208,968	12,147	2,188	72,139	60.05	1,514,645	7.93	
1982	105,942	11,755	11,500	43,098	223,506	12,777	2,108	68,856	65.15	1,584,491	6.67	
1983	121,490	12,320	12,232	45,667	236,193	14,435	2,347	81,329	68.69	1,643,460	7.20	
1984	137,241	14,984	13,050	48,721	255,148	15,783	2,292	92,279	70.94	1,698,774	7.66	
1985	146,345	15,563	13,897	53,262	275,945	17,126	2,476	98,521	73.14	1,754,750	7.68	7.79
1986	144,956	14,573	15,024	61,618	295,434	18,867	2,107	95,438	75.36	1,812,870	6.99	
1987	161,603	16,990	16,286	69,288	319,364	21,596	702	106,380	78.83	1,875,345	7.20	
1988	179,184	17,586	17,675	77,568	350,727	24,467	3,691	117,611	82.37	1,946,299	7.34	
1989	186,310	18,566	19,534	83,222	376,532	25,649	3,500	120,812	86.11	2,023,308	6.93	
1990	183,074	16,834	21,304	96,171	395,209	28,475	4,806	114,058	88.84	2,097,453	6.12	
1991	174,766	15,015	22,974	97,154	406,305	27,419	4,828	106,944	91.47	2,160,040	5.41	
1992	178,914	14,517	24,604	97,283	416,581	27,528	3,068	110,731	92.67	2,211,451	5.40	
1993	189,810	16,263	25,512	96,379	425,676	27,913	5,264	117,490	94.01	2,256,219	5.54	
1994	218,770	19,342	25,469	100,311	437,248	31,421	5,484	139,797	95.09	2,301,604	6.39	
1995	232,759	22,138	25,737	106,190	453,171	33,694	9,289	146,545	97.24	2,347,895	6.42	6.37
1996	239,502	26,239	26,322	113,608	465,964	35,671	9,494	146,523	98.81	2,394,521	6.19	
1997	249,983	32,250	27,125	120,790	492,501	37,030	11,325	147,915	100	2,454,226	6.03	
1998	251,815	30,800	28,795	128,935	516,097	38,660	8,447	149,337	99.57	2,526,013	5.94	
1999	282,058	39,410	29,809	134,197	547,026	41,236	9,960	166,623	101.31	2,603,877	6.32	
2000	321,950	48,175	29,898	143,951	591,535	45,545	11,303	192,681	105.5	2,688,618	6.79	
2001	314,709	36,352	30,721	145,926	619,380	45,247	10,277	197,251	106.68	2,776,447	6.66	
2002	323,594	35,746	31,461	138,655	646,082	42,735	11,650	207,827	107.82	2,863,772	6.73	
2003	342,870	39,158	33,557	139,301	675,874	43,189	14,022	219,955	111.45	2,954,964	6.68	
2004	380,803	44,132	35,442	150,813	710,747	48,476	16,687	244,410	114.77	3,056,075	6.97	
2005	412,671	48,514	37,106	165,983	748,494	54,324	17,306	264,074	118.46	3,167,268	7.04	6.53

Table 3: Gross Fixed Investment, 1965–2005

Year	The Amount of Investment				Percentage Distribution			
	Private Corporations	Public Corporations	Government Public Administrations	Grand Total	Private Corporations	Public Corporations	Government Public Administrations	Grand Total
	(millions of dollars)				(%)			
1965	6,352	1,640	2,804	10,796	58.84	15.19	25.97	100.00
1966	7,464	1,877	3,289	12,630	59.10	14.86	26.04	100.00
1967	6,423	1,997	3,457	11,877	54.08	16.81	29.11	100.00
1968	6,557	1,881	3,627	12,065	54.35	15.59	30.06	100.00
1969	8,106	1,977	3,553	13,636	59.45	14.50	26.06	100.00
1970	8,316	2,186	3,625	14,127	58.87	15.47	25.66	100.00
1971	9,034	2,304	4,292	15,630	57.80	14.74	27.46	100.00
1972	10,234	2,386	4,472	17,092	59.88	13.96	26.16	100.00
1973	12,532	3,419	4,454	20,405	61.42	16.76	21.83	100.00
1974	16,814	4,289	5,967	27,070	62.11	15.84	22.04	100.00
1975	15,341	6,475	7,035	28,851	53.17	22.44	24.38	100.00
1976	17,354	7,057	6,904	31,315	55.42	22.54	22.05	100.00
1977	17,414	8,499	7,925	33,838	51.46	25.12	23.42	100.00
1978	19,050	8,852	7,905	35,807	53.20	24.72	22.08	100.00
1979	28,424	9,180	8,406	46,010	61.78	19.95	18.27	100.00
1980	31,777	8,377	9,487	49,641	64.01	16.88	19.11	100.00
1981	40,694	11,507	10,987	63,188	64.40	18.21	17.39	100.00
1982	25,171	13,436	12,510	51,117	49.24	26.28	24.47	100.00
1983	30,022	12,797	12,269	55,088	54.50	23.23	22.27	100.00
1984	38,831	12,264	13,173	64,268	60.42	19.08	20.50	100.00
1985	44,024	11,500	15,470	70,994	62.01	16.20	21.79	100.00
1986	47,596	9,448	15,031	72,075	66.04	13.11	20.85	100.00
1987	56,700	8,696	15,534	80,930	70.06	10.75	19.19	100.00
1988	63,984	11,056	16,634	91,674	69.80	12.06	18.14	100.00
1989	68,776	11,862	18,989	99,627	69.03	11.91	19.06	100.00
1990	57,256	12,966	20,748	90,970	62.94	14.25	22.81	100.00
1991	49,164	13,639	21,047	83,850	58.63	16.27	25.10	100.00
1992	46,531	11,191	20,656	78,378	59.37	14.28	26.35	100.00
1993	51,671	9,542	19,887	81,100	63.71	11.77	24.52	100.00
1994	64,505	8,123	21,251	93,879	68.71	8.65	22.64	100.00
1995	74,645	9,117	21,661	105,423	70.81	8.65	20.55	100.00
1996	73,887	9,069	19,368	102,324	72.21	8.86	18.93	100.00
1997	100,411	7,376	20,317	128,104	78.38	5.76	15.86	100.00
1998	104,432	7,487	20,188	132,107	79.05	5.67	15.28	100.00
1999	113,938	6,937	20,133	141,008	80.80	4.92	14.28	100.00
2000	124,911	6,892	24,710	156,513	79.81	4.40	15.79	100.00
2001	109,581	7,967	27,448	144,996	75.58	5.49	18.93	100.00
2002	107,126	8,196	28,544	143,866	74.46	5.70	19.84	100.00
2003	114,078	9,350	30,100	153,528	74.30	6.09	19.61	100.00
2004	126,471	9,354	31,574	167,399	75.55	5.59	18.86	100.00
2005	140,884	12,513	34,264	187,661	75.07	6.67	18.26	100.00

Glenn P. Jenkins and Chun-Yan Kuo

References

Boskin, M.J. 1978. "Taxation, Saving, and the Rate of Interest", *Journal of Political Economy* 86(2), S3-27.

Burgess, D.F. 1981. "The Social Discount Rate for Canada: Theory and Evidence", *Canadian Public Policy* 7(3), 383-394.

_____. 2005. "An Update Estimate of the Social Opportunity Cost of Capital for Canada", University of Western Ontario (March).

_____. 2006. "Removing Some Dissonance from the Social Discount Rate Debate", University of Western Ontario (June).

Department of Finance Canada. 1989. *Goods and Services Tax – Technical Paper* (August).

Evans, J.C. and G.P. Jenkins. 1980. "The Cost of U.S. Direct Foreign Investment", Harvard Institute for International Development, Development Discussion Paper No. 104 (November).

Harberger, A.C. 1972. "On Measuring the Social Opportunity Cost of Public Funds", *Project Evaluation: Selected Papers*. Chicago: University of Chicago Press.

_____. 1977. "Private and Social Rates of Return to Capital in Uruguay", *Economic Development and Cultural Change* (April).

Huang, K.H. 2004. "The Method of the Quarterly Capital Stock Estimation and User Cost of Capital", paper prepared for Investment and Capital Division, Statistics Canada (December).

Jenkins, G.P. 1972. "Analysis of Rates of Return from Capital in Canada", unpublished Ph.D. dissertation, University of Chicago.

_____. 1973. "The Measurement of Rates of Return and Taxation from Private Capital in Canada", in W.A. Niskanen *et al.* (eds.), *Benefit-Cost and Policy Analysis*. Chicago: Aldine.

_____. 1977. *Capital in Canada: Its Social and Private Performance 1965-1974*, Economic Council of Canada, Discussion Paper No. 98 (October).

_____. 1981. "The Public-Sector Discount Rate for Canada: Some Further Observations", *Canadian Public Policy*.

Jenkins, G.P. and M. Mescher. 1981. "Government Borrowing and the Response of Consumer Credit in Canada", paper prepared for Department of Regional Economic Expansion.

Kuo, C.-Y., G.P. Jenkins, and M.B. Mphahlele. 2003. "The Economic Opportunity Cost of Capital in South Africa", *The South African Journal of Economics* 71(3) (September).

Leipziger, D.M. 1974. "Capital Movements and Economy: Canada under a Flexible Rate", *Canadian Journal of Economics* (February).

Sandmo, A. and J.H. Dreze. 1971. "Discount Rates for Public Investment in Closed and Open Economies", *Economica*, XXXVIII(152) (November).

Sjaastad, L.A. and D.L. Wisecarver. 1977. "The Social Cost of Public Finance", *Journal of Political Economy* 85(3) (May), 513-547.

Starzenski, N.A. 2004. "The Social Discount Rate in Canada: A Comprehensive Update", a M.A. thesis submitted to Queen's University (November).

The Governments of Canada, Nova Scotia, New Brunswick, Newfoundland and Labrador. 1997. *Harmonized Sales Tax*. Technical Paper. Ottawa: Department of Finance.

Treasury Board Secretariat. 1976. *Benefit Cost Analysis Guide*. Ottawa: Minister of Supply and Services Canada.

_____. 1998. *Benefit Cost Analysis Guide* (July).

Watson, K. 1992. "The Social Discount Rate", *Canadian Journal of Program Evaluation* 7(1).

Glenn P. Jenkins and Chun-Yan Kuo

Comment on "The Economic Opportunity Cost of Capital for Canada: An Empirical Update" by Glenn P. Jenkins and Chun-Yan Kuo

David F. Burgess

Jenkins and Kuo have performed a very useful exercise in updating their estimate of the economic opportunity cost of capital (EOCK) for Canada. Unlike previous work, the calculation is performed at the level of the economy as a whole. My comments are directed primarily at empirical issues.

The EOCK is a weighted average of the economic cost of forgone investment and consumption and the economic cost of incremental foreign funding, with the weights representing the proportions of funding drawn from each source. I will first comment on the estimation of the rates of return and then present what I believe to be a more reliable method for estimating the weights. I conclude by deriving estimates of the economic opportunity cost of capital based upon the same rates of return calculated by Jenkins and Kuo, but using the new procedure for estimating the weights.

Estimating Rates of Return

It is assumed that the economic cost of displaced private investment is well approximated by the pre-tax rate of return to capital in place. The latter is measured by adding up all the income attributable to capital and dividing by the replacement cost of capital. This is an accounting rate of return, not a financial rate of return, since capital is measured at replacement cost rather than at market prices. It is also important to recognize the conditions that must hold for the rate of return on an increment to the capital stock to be equal to the rate of return on the stock of capital currently in place. Capital must be homogeneous, and there must be perfectly competitive product and factor markets, with constant returns to scale in production.

Some critics have argued that the pre-tax rate of return to capital will overstate the rate of return on the marginal investment because the best investment opportunities will be undertaken first. However, one could just as easily argue that the marginal investment will be directed to the most attractive opportunity available, thus avoiding low-return sectors or investments that are included in the pre-tax rate of return to capital. Thus, I see no bias either way on this account.

It is true that if firms have monopoly power, labour will earn less than its marginal product, so capital, which captures the residual, will earn more than its marginal product. But this conclusion is valid only if production exhibits constant returns to scale. If firms produce imperfectly substitutable goods under increasing returns to scale and there is free entry, price will equal average cost, and labour will earn its marginal product, but capital will earn less than its marginal product.

There are several distinct types of capital, so capital is not homogeneous. Jenkins and Kuo argue that only reproducible capital should be included in the calculation, and they attempt to exclude the rents from unimproved land. However, it is hard to do this reliably, and for this reason, it may be preferable not to attempt to eliminate land as a component of the capital stock but to assume that asset holders will behave to equalize after-tax rates of return on land and other forms of capital. Also, only buildings and equipment are considered as components of reproducible capital, not inventories. There is some evidence from productivity studies that including land and inventories along with buildings and equipment lowers the measured rate of return to capital by a percentage point or more in the Canadian case (see Diewert and Lawrence, 2000).

Jenkins and Kuo calculate that the pre-tax rate of return to reproducible capital has averaged 11% over the 40-year period from 1965 to 2005. This return has been remarkably stable (though much of the stability is attributable to capital being measured at replacement cost). Equally important, it exhibits no downward or upward trend despite significant changes in the tax treatment of income from capital over the period. They assume that 11% is a reasonable estimate of the rate of return that Canada as a whole can expect to forgo when a dollar of private investment is displaced.

They then subtract corporate, property, and personal income taxes plus an estimate of financial intermediation costs to arrive at the net of tax rate of return earned on saving and conclude that the average annual rate of return is approximately 6.5%. This rate of return is higher than one might perhaps expect. However, about one third of the capital stock represents residential structures, and the after-tax rate of return on this component (gross imputed rents minus property taxes divided by the replacement cost of residential capital) is significantly higher than the after-tax rate of return on the other components. In addition, it is important to recognize that 6.5% is an average rate of return, whereas what we are after is the rate of return on an incremental dollar of saving. If marginal tax rates are above average tax rates, the 6.5% figure will be an overstatement.

Since Canada is an open economy, we need to estimate the marginal cost of an incremental dollar of funding from abroad. Jenkins and Kuo rely on a study undertaken in the late 1970s, which concluded that the rate of return paid to foreign investors in Canada was approximately equal to 6% of the replacement cost of the capital being financed. This rate of return deducts corporate, property, and withholding taxes, and other fees, from the pre-tax rate of return, but not personal income taxes or financial intermediation costs. Since non-residential capital bears the burden of corporate, property, and personal income taxes plus financial intermediation costs, one would expect its after-tax rate of return to be somewhat lower than the 6% rate of return paid to foreign investors.

If the required rate of return on foreign investment is an increasing function of the amount of foreign investment, the 6% rate of return will understate the economic cost of an incremental dollar of foreign funding. However, no adjustment is made for any divergence between the average and the marginal cost, which would be appropriate if the withholding tax on foreign investment income corrected the gap between the marginal and average cost.

There is one further point to be made with respect to the rates of return. Part of private investment displaced represents foreign direct investment (FDI). The economic cost to Canada of FDI forgone is just the taxes that FDI pays to the host government. Therefore, the pre-tax rate of return on private investment displaced in Canada will overstate its true economic cost to Canada. However, if the after-tax rate of return on

FDI is approximately equal to the marginal cost of incremental foreign funding, the approach taken by Jenkins and Kuo is on firm ground. But it does require that the response of net foreign funding to the rate of return must represent the difference between an increase in portfolio capital inflows and a decrease in FDI.

Estimating Weights

In measuring the EOCK, it is crucial to have reliable estimates of the proportions of funding that will be drawn from each source: displaced private investment, postponed consumption, and net exports. Jenkins and Kuo apply the usual formula, where the weights are expressed as functions of the proportions of investment to total saving, resident saving to total saving, foreign saving to total saving, and the elasticities of investment, resident saving, and foreign saving to the rate of return. For their base case calculation, they assume that 90% of total saving finances private capital formation and 10% finances public capital formation, with foreign saving comprising 25% of total saving. But these proportions ignore the amount of saving by Canadian residents that is invested abroad. Canada's international assets are currently approximately equal to its international liabilities.[1] The appropriate concept is the net contribution of the foreign sector to capital formation in Canada, and this is approximately zero. Thus, for the base case calculation, I would assume that the foreign sector makes no net contribution to the total pool of saving available to finance capital formation in Canada.

The usual method for deriving the weights is to multiply the proportions by their respective elasticities. Jenkins and Kuo assume that the elasticity of private investment to the cost of capital $\eta = -1.0$ and the (compensated) elasticity of supply of resident saving with respect to the after tax rate of return is $e = 0.4$. I have no problem with these values: they are consistent with other well-known studies. However, in light of recent work on the determinants of saving, a value of $e = 0.2$ might be a

---

[1]Canada's International Investment Position, Statistics Canada – Catalogue No. 67-202-X.

David F. Burgess

better consensus value of the responsiveness of saving to the rate of return. [2]

I have a major concern about the reliability of any estimate of the elasticity of supply of net foreign funding to the rate of return. Jenkins and Kuo assume a value of 3.0 for this parameter. Many would regard this as much too low in light of the fact that Canada is well integrated into the international capital market and international flows of financial capital are highly responsive to interest rate differentials. However, as pointed out earlier, the response in net foreign funding to an increase in the rate of return consists of both positive and negative elements: some FDI is displaced, and some portfolio capital is induced. What we are after is the net impact of these two countervailing effects. Unfortunately, what we know about this key parameter is so imprecise and unreliable that any derivation of the EOCK that is contingent upon it is suspect.

I would like to present an alternative approach to estimating the weights that enter into the EOCK formula – an approach that does not rely upon a point estimate of the elasticity of supply of foreign funding. The approach draws on research inspired by the Feldstein-Horioka puzzle (see Feldstein and Horoika, 1980). When these authors ran regressions of national investment rates on national saving rates for OECD countries, they estimated a "saving retention coefficient" in the order of .7-.9. They interpreted this as implying that 70% to 90% of an increment in saving translates into increased investment within the country rather than flowing abroad to finance investment and consumption elsewhere. More recent studies obtain estimates somewhat lower – in the range of .3-.7 (see Helliwell, 1998).

Estimates of the saving retention coefficient can be used along with estimates of the responsiveness of investment and saving to the rate of return to infer the proportions of funding that are drawn from each source and the implied economic opportunity cost of capital.

Let us start with the condition for equilibrium in the capital market. National saving, S, plus net foreign funding, F, must equal private

---

[2] The general consensus is that it is not possible to provide precise estimates of the compensated interest elasticity of saving with any confidence. Nevertheless, the models that likely describe the behaviour of the people who account for most of aggregate saving imply positive elasticities. For life cycle consumers, the compensated interest elasticity of saving must be positive if the elasticity of substitution between present and future consumption is greater than zero. For a comprehensive survey of the issues, see Elmendorf (1996).

investment, I, plus exogenous funding for the project in question.[3] Each of these components depends upon the rate of return, r, plus other unspecified factors. Capital market equilibrium can then be written as:

$$S(r) + F(r) = I(r) + B \qquad (1)$$

An increase in demand for funding for a project will drive up the rate of return and thereby affect S, F, and I. The social discount rate (EOCK) can then be written as:

$$EOCK = r\,(dS/dB) + MCf\,(dF/dB) - \rho\,(dI/dB) \qquad (2)$$

where $MCf = r^*(1+1/e^f)$ is the marginal cost of foreign funding, r^* is the average cost, and e^f is the elasticity of supply of foreign funding with respect to the rate of return.

Capital market equilibrium requires that:

$$dS/dB + dF/dB - dI/dB = 1 \qquad (3)$$

The saving retention coefficient (SRC) measures the proportion of a change in national saving that ends up financing domestic investment. If the saving schedule shifts to the right, the capital market no longer clears at the initial rate of return. Given the excess supply of funds, the rate of return will fall, which will induce additional investment but deter some saving. Once equilibrium is restored, we can ask what proportion of the net increase in saving translates into increased investment within the nation. In other words, we can calculate the SRC.

The manipulations are as follows. First, the SRC is defined as:

$$SRC = (dI/dB)\,/[(dS/dB)-1] \qquad (4)$$

Combining (3) and (4), we have:

$$dF/dB = (1-1/SRC)\,dI/dB \qquad (5)$$

---

[3]National saving equals total private saving minus government dis-saving (as represented by the fiscal deficit). The amount of private saving that finances public spending, including public investment, is therefore subtracted from private saving in determining national saving.

David F. Burgess

Next, define the responsiveness of saving and investment to the rate of return in derivative form, so $dS/dr = e\,S/r$, and $dI/dr = \eta\,I/r$.

But $dS/dB = (dS/dr)(dr/dB)$, and $dI/dB = (dI/dr)\,(dr/dB)$, so

$$dS/dB = (e/\eta)\,(S/I)\,dI/dB \qquad\qquad (6)$$

Now, substitute (5) and (6) into (2). The EOCK can then be written as:

$$EOCK = \{r\,(e/\eta)\,(S/I) + MCf\,(1-1/SRC) - \rho\}\,dI/dB \qquad (7)$$

And substituting (5) and (6) into (3), we can express dI/dB as:

$$dI/dB = 1/\{(e/\eta)\,(S/I)\,{-}1/SRC\} \qquad\qquad (8)$$

Combining (7) and (8), the EOCK can be written as:

$$EOCK = \{\rho - (e/\eta)\,(S/I)\,r + (1/SRC{-}1)\,MCf\}/\Delta \qquad (9)$$

where $\Delta = 1/SRC-(e/\eta)\,(S/I)$.

If $F=0$ in the initial equilibrium, then $MCf=r^{*}$, where r^{*} represents the average cost of foreign funding. The economic opportunity cost of capital can then be expressed in terms of the rates of return ρ, r, and r^{*}; the ratio S/I; the elasticities of response of S and I with respect to the rate of return, e and η; and the SRC as follows:

$$EOCK = \{\rho - (e/\eta)\,(S/I)\,r + (1/SRC{-}1)\,r^{*}\}/\Delta \qquad (10)$$

where $\Delta = 1/SRC-(e/\eta)\,(S/I)$.

Implications for the EOCK

Table 1 below provides implied estimates of the EOCK under various assumptions about key parameters. Throughout, the marginal rate of return to capital is assumed to be $\rho = 11\%$, and the marginal rate of return to incremental saving is assumed to be $r = 6.5\%$. In the first two columns, there is no accounting for systematic risk. In the third and

Table 1: The EOCK for Canada

	No deductions for systematic risk $\rho = 11\%; r=6.5\%$		2% risk premium deducted $\rho = 11\%; r=6.5\%$	
	e = .2	e = .4	e = .2	e = .4
SRC = .4	7.82	7.72	6.84	6.74
SRC = .5	8.30	8.13	7.12	6.95
SRC = .6	8.69	8.46	7.33	7.10

fourth columns, I follow Jenkins and Kuo and deduct a systematic risk premium of 2% from the pre-tax rate of return to capital and the net of tax rate of return to incremental saving.

Two values are assumed for the compensated elasticity of supply of national saving with respect to the rate of return: $e = .2, .4$. Three values are assumed for the SRC $= .4, .5$, and .6. There are two additional maintained hypotheses behind the table. First, national saving is assumed to equal investment (public plus private), so net foreign saving, F, is zero, and private investment is assumed to be 90% of total investment. Second, the interest elasticity of demand for private investment, η, is assumed to be equal to -1.0.

The evidence on SRCs for OECD countries leads me to a preferred estimate of the SRC in the range of .4 to .5. These values imply that the proportion of incremental funding obtained from abroad to finance any project is between 41% and 51% of the required funding. Taking the pre- and post-tax rates of return calculated by Jenkins and Kuo as accurate measures of the economic opportunity costs of each source of funding, the EOCK for a project of average risk is approximately 8%. However, if there is a 2% risk premium embedded in the measured rate of return to capital and the measured rate of return to saving, the appropriate EOCK for a project with zero systematic risk would be approximately 7%. Thus, my results are consistent with Jenkins and Kuo, but I believe they rest on a somewhat more solid empirical foundation because estimates of the SRC seem to be more reliable than estimates of the responsiveness of net foreign funding to the rate of return.

David F. Burgess

References

Diewert, W.E. and D.A. Lawrence. 2000. "Progress in Measuring the Price and Quantity of Capital", in L.J. Lau (ed.), *Econometrics and the Cost of Capital*. Cambridge, MA: MIT Press.

Elmendorf, D.W. 1996. "The Effect of Interest-Rate Changes on Household Saving and Consumption: A Survey", Federal Reserve Board, June. At www.federalreserve.gov/Pubs/feds/1996/199627pap.pdf.

Feldstein, M.S. and C. Horoika. 1980. "Domestic Saving and International Capital Flows", *Economic Journal* 90 (June).

Helliwell, J.F. 1998. *How Much do National Borders Matter?* Washington, DC: Brookings.

9

The Social Discount Rate for Provincial Government Investment Projects

Peter S. Spiro

Introduction

Benefit-cost analysis is a way to make rational comparisons between alternative investments to assess whether they are worth undertaking. Since these investments have benefit streams that extend over long periods of time, it is necessary to calculate their present value by taking into account the time value of money. This rate of return, conceptually similar to an interest rate, is referred to as the discount rate.

For private corporations making such calculations, the discount rate is a relatively straightforward calculation of the actual cost of funds, being a weighted average of the return on equity and interest on debt.

However, in the case of government projects, the use of the actual borrowing rate as the discount rate can lead to misleading conclusions. The government is able to borrow large sums of money at low interest rates, but this interest rate may not be a good measure of the opportunity cost of capital.

The author has benefited from the comments of Aster Barnwell, Stephen Monrad, Victor Stein, and Paul Burke on earlier versions of this paper. The opinions are his own and should not be construed as the official policy of any institution with which he has been affiliated.

Unlike a corporation, the government's credit rating does not derive from its balance sheet, and it is able to borrow money primarily due to its power to collect revenue through taxation. If the interest rate is used as the discount rate for evaluating government investment projects, it may lead to inefficient use of the government's borrowing capacity.

The social discount rate (also known as the economic opportunity cost of capital) seeks to mimic the rate of return that would be earned on private sector investments. Inefficiencies in the government's use of capital are minimized by requiring government investments to meet a rate of return hurdle similar to what is earned in the private sector.

Suppose that the government can borrow at 3% because there are some investors who need to put a portion of their funds into a very low-risk instrument. Should the government treat 3% as its discount rate and undertake a road project whose benefits equal costs at a discount rate of 3%?[1] The answer would generally be no. In order to make the citizens as well off as possible, the government should invest public resources where they have the opportunity to earn the highest rate of return.

There is no universally accepted method for choosing the discount rate, and a number of different approaches have been recommended, as discussed in a very comprehensive survey of the literature by Zhuang *et al.* (2007). The choice depends on various philosophical issues and views about the sources and alternative uses of the funds. These go beyond merely empirical questions to more fundamental issues about the choices that are (or ought to be) open to various entities. The "dissonance" that exists about this issue is ably reviewed by David Burgess in his chapter in this volume.

The approach taken in this paper is a common-sense compromise between the alternative viewpoints. The discount rate should approximate the rate of return that could be earned on a notional balanced portfolio of financial investments, even if in practice this might

---

[1]It has sometimes been argued that additional borrowing raises the interest rate. However, empirical evidence finds that from a province's viewpoint, this impact is negligible. Booth, Georgopoulos, and Hejazi (2007) estimated that an increase of government debt equal to 1 percentage point of GDP raises the interest rate on provincial debt by only 0.6 basis points (that is, less than a hundredth of a percentage point). The latest international evidence similarly suggests that for advanced countries, the supply of funds is very elastic, and interest rates would only be impacted if deficits became very large, as in Aisen and Hauner (2008).

Peter S. Spiro

not be its most likely alternative use.[2] To earn a lower rate of return than on a passive investment could be characterized as poor stewardship, which clearly fails to maximize real wealth in the economy. It will be seen that the numerical estimate derived using the approach in this paper is close to halfway between the high and low ends of the alternative approaches to social discount rates.

Should Risk Be Reflected in the Benefit-Cost Stream or the Discount Rate?

It has sometimes been argued that benefit-cost analysis should apply different discount rates in different kinds of projects to adjust for the project-specific risk of failure in its intended achievements.

However, the general consensus in cost-benefit evaluation tends toward the view that the discount rate should not be adjusted for the risk of the investment and that, instead, the dollar amounts of the future estimated benefits and costs should be adjusted to "certainty equivalents". The latest version of the Canadian Treasury Board's Benefit-Cost Analysis Guide (2007) also suggests a similar approach, in which a range of scenarios representing the uncertainty of future costs and benefits is discounted.

One recent exception is Brean *et al.* (2005), who propose a method for adjusting the discount rate for risk, focusing specifically on investments in transportation.[3]

---

[2]Public sector portfolio investments of this type already exist in the form of the Alberta Heritage Fund and the Canada Pension Plan. Recently, concerns about the inadequacy of voluntary private retirement savings have led to calls for the establishment of supplementary public pension plans above the CPP, which could be run by provincial governments. See, e.g., Ambachtsheer (2008).

[3]They undertake regressions that relate the demand for various kinds of transportation services to GDP growth. Where the demand elasticity is greater than one, they assume that this represents a greater than average risk factor. This is an innovative approach, but it is of less relevance to long-term projects. Here, the important risks relate to the long-term demand, affected by such things as major population shifts and technological changes, rather than whether it will be temporarily underused in a recession.

If a particular project has an identifiable specific type of risk (e.g., environmental damage), the correct way to take this into account is to include a notional dollar cost of this risk (an estimated "insurance premium") to the future stream of costs, so as not to create a bias in favour of alternatives whose benefit stream is weighted toward the present (Bierman and Smidt, 1980).

There is a wide range of socio-economic factors that should be taken into account in a comprehensive benefit-cost analysis.

For example, it was argued above that government borrowing does not significantly affect the interest rate on private sector borrowing. However, financial capital is not the same as physical resources. Financial capital borrowed from abroad is useful if the incremental demand for physical resources can be met by using the foreign money to buy imported goods and services. Quite often this is not possible, and this has sometimes been referred to as the "transfer problem". Government projects draw on local construction resources, where bringing in foreign workers may not be practical. In periods of full employment, the government activity may lead to the postponement of private sector construction (or higher costs for these projects).

This can be a significant issue that should be factored into government decision-making, but the discount rate is not the appropriate way to deal with it. Private sector construction spending has always been one of the most volatile components of the economy. Good macroeconomic policy would dictate that the government should be concerned about these issues and should try to stream its projects as much as possible to smooth out the fluctuations in the construction sector.

Benefit-cost analysis typically takes into account socio-economic impacts such as job creation in the economy. As a corollary, any negative impact on private sector employment (caused by labour shortages) should also be taken into account as a disbenefit to help signal that projects should proceed more slowly during periods of excess demand. Similarly, the positive impact that public infrastructure has on private sector productivity should be taken into account in the benefit stream.[4]

No doubt, all these factors are hard to forecast. However, the only way to evaluate the reasonableness of the forecasts for different factors is if they are laid out individually. This creates greater transparency, and

---

[4]Harchaoui, Tarkhani, and Warren (2004) provide a methodology for estimating these benefits.

Peter S. Spiro

better decision making, than if they are all lumped together as a miscellaneous "risk factor" in the discount rate.

Estimate of the Private Sector
Return on Equity Capital

The view taken in this paper is that government borrowing does not have a material crowding-out impact on private sector investment. The opportunity cost of public funds comes from the fact that the money could instead be invested in financial markets, either directly by the government or by the citizens it represents if they received this money in the form of lower taxes. In that case, it is an after-tax rate of return on financial capital that is relevant.

This contrasts with the view often taken in previous Canadian studies, which sought to use the pre-tax rate of return. These studies were all conducted from the viewpoint of the national government. Even if one were to accept that crowding-out occurs, from the viewpoint of a provincial government, the tax share would be quite small, reflecting that provincial government's share of the total corporate tax revenue received in Canada (about 15% of the total in 2005 for Ontario and much less for other provinces).[5]

One potential approach to estimating the opportunity cost would be to look directly at rates of return on equity investments in the stock market. However, this has such extreme volatility, even over time horizons as long as a decade, that it is hard to make any reasonable inference from it for long-run trends. A still imperfect, but somewhat more stable source of information about underlying fundamentals comes from looking directly at data on rates of return on business capital.

Statistics Canada publishes data on the average rate of return on equity for corporations going back to 1988. To smooth out the volatility of profits that occurs over the course of the business cycle, average data over the latest ten years (1998 to 2007) is used, and returns for the oil

---

[5]At first glance, this might be considered a "selfish" approach. However, in the absence of an explicit decision by all provinces to do differently, it is the rational approach. There are numerous examples in intergovernmental fiscal relations (both within Canada and internationally) where greater coordination would be optimal, but unfortunately has not happened.

and gas sector are excluded. The average return on equity over this period was 9.7%. (The average is 8.8% over the whole data sample back to 1988.) As this is calculated on the book value of equity, it is a nominal rate that needs to be adjusted to reflect inflation. Subtracting 2% as the long-run average expected inflation rate leaves 7.7%.

The real rate of return derived this way, at 7.7%, is considerably higher than the historical real return from the viewpoint of a private investor. The real return on the Toronto Stock Exchange (including dividends) has averaged about 6%.[6] Therefore, it can be considered a reasonably conservative estimate of the opportunity cost of equity capital.

Interest Rate Component

In long-term financial evaluations, it is important to remember that dollars in the distant future will not have the same value as they have today, due to inflation. In recent decades, the Bank of Canada has pursued a target of maintaining inflation near 2%, but there is no certainty that this policy regime will remain unchanged in the future.

The yields on ordinary (not indexed for inflation) bonds implicitly take into account a future average inflation rate to compensate lenders for the expected decline in the real purchasing power of the money they will get back in the future.

Financial evaluations that use future streams of costs and benefits in nominal dollars should use a nominal discount rate. They need to be reasonably sure that the discount rate and the inflation rates used in the project come from consistent sources. The preferred approach is probably to use constant dollar amounts and a real discount rate so that inflation has been factored out of both the numerator and denominator.

In the past, it was necessary to make a forecast of the long-term future inflation rate in order to estimate the real interest rate. This is always a problem for borrowers and lenders in the nominal bond market

---

[6]Some would argue that this overstates the effective rate of return, as stock market investors are being compensated for risk. Conversely, it could be argued that what is risky from the viewpoint of the individual is much less risky from the viewpoint of society as a whole (as discussed below), and therefore the whole observed return to equity is part of the opportunity cost.

as well, and the bond market only imperfectly predicts the future inflation rate. Historically, the bond market has tended to base its expectations of future inflation on the average inflation over the previous ten years or so and has made substantial forecasting errors when the trend rate of inflation had a major change (Figure 1).[7] Investors who bought bonds in the 1960s earned negative real returns, as inflation continued to rise beyond what they had expected. Conversely, borrowers who issued long-term bonds in the late 1970s and during the 1980s, before the large downward trend in inflation, ended up paying extraordinarily high real yields.[8]

Figure 1: Canadian Government Bond Yield vs. Ten-Year Moving Average of CPI Inflation

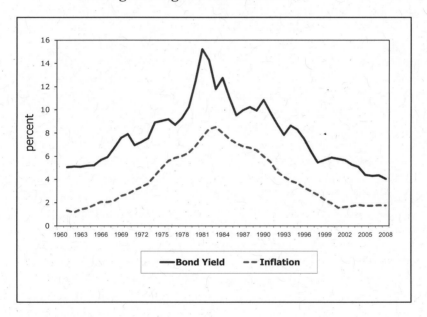

---

[7]A discussion of the problem of measuring real interest rates can be found in Spiro (1989).

[8]This was the source of a large part of Ontario Hydro's "stranded debt", which continues to impose a cost on Ontario's electricity ratepayers long after Hydro's dissolution. If real return bonds had been issued at that time, as urged by numerous economists (including the present author), Hydro's losses and debt would have been much lower.

Fortunately, an alternative source of information now exists. This is the market yield on a real return bond. These are bonds in which the value of the principal rises each year with the rate of inflation, and the yield the investor earns is applied to this rising base. The yield on this bond reflects the bond market's current forecasts of the long-term real interest rate. Along with other interest rates, this yield has been declining over the past few years and has recently been in the area of 2%.

The approach below will base the discount rate on the yield for a specific provincial government real return bond. One might ask why this synthetic discount rate combines the provincial government's borrowing rate (rather than the private sector's borrowing rate) with the private sector return on equity capital? The reasoning behind this is that the higher bond yields paid on corporate debt merely compensate lenders for the higher default risk perceived to apply to that debt. If the government, with its lower default risk, is using the capital, the social opportunity cost is to that extent lower than when the capital is used by the private sector.[9]

This view follows the analysis of Arrow and Lind (1970), which continues to offer useful guidance for benefit-cost analysis in the public sector. Arrow and Lind argued that governments represent a kind of pooling of risk that reduces financing risk to negligible levels. This has been criticized in recent years by "perfect capital markets" theorists, who argue that the private sector effectively has access to the same kind of risk pooling through diversification in the capital markets. However, as discussed by Spackman (2001), significant legal and institutional factors exist that create a greater risk in lending to the private sector than the public sector. This view received further confirmation in the private sector defaults triggered by the sub-prime mortgage collapse in 2008, which further undermined the position of efficient market theorists. In practical terms, Arrow and Lind's hypothesis still seems to hold.

This issue is particularly relevant when considering the discount rate for government-owned enterprises such as electric utilities. These companies have their own capital structures, including equity owned by the government, and may borrow without an explicit guarantee on their debt. As private sector entities, they would face considerable enterprise-specific risks, not least of which would be the effects of government regulation. Shareholders would require a higher rate of return on equity

---

[9]Montmarquette and Scott (2007), in proposing a social discount rate for Quebec, similarly make use of the yield spread between Quebec and Canadian government bonds. They recommended a real discount rate of 6% for Quebec.

to compensate for this risk. However, if the Arrow and Lind view holds, it could be argued that when these enterprises are in the public sector, their opportunity cost of capital is the general government discount rate.

Combining the Factors to Calculate the Social Discount Rate

The table below provides an example of how the reasoning described above can be used to calculate a discount rate. This example uses data for from the first half of 2008, with the province-specific values that apply to the province of Ontario. The resulting estimate of the social discount rate is 5%. This is a real rate of return since it is based on the real return on equity and the real interest rate.

A	Rate of return on equity, corporations excluding oil and gas extraction (Statistics Canada, Cansim Table 180-0002 – Financial and taxation statistics for enterprises), 1998 to 2007 average, less 2% to convert to a real rate.	7.7%
B	Ratio of debt to equity, non-financial industrial corporations	1.0
C	Yield on Government of Ontario real return bond, maturing in 2036[10]	2.2%
D	Social discount rate = [A + B*C]/(1+B)	5.0%

As I emphasize below, the estimate of the discount rate should not be viewed as a fixed value, but rather should be recalculated periodically as market conditions change. There is also a margin of error in such estimates, and sensitivity testing should be used to gauge the significance of potential errors.

---

[10]Yield as of March 6, 2008. Manitoba and Quebec have also issued real return bonds in the last several years, and the federal government began issuing them in 1991. For a province that does not have such bonds, one can estimate the yield based on their provincial spreads relative to federal government bonds.

Real versus Nominal Rates

As the 5% discount rate is a real return, it should be applied to constant dollar values of future revenues and expenses, which do not include the effects of price inflation on the cost of activities.

If a stream of future project expenses and benefits has been expressed in nominal dollars, based on a 2% inflation rate, then this should be added onto the real discount rate to arrive at a nominal discount rate of 7%.

Sensitivity Testing

The most significant risk that needs to be taken into account directly in the use of the discount rate is the uncertainty in the estimation of the cost of capital itself. There are two aspects to this.

The first is due to the fact that in practice, there are usually long time lags, stretching to several years, between when a project is analyzed and when the construction for it takes place. Major infrastructure projects such as transit lines or power plants often take five or even ten years from initial planning to the completion of financing. Even if one can know with precision what the discount rate should be today, its appropriate value might turn out to be different at the time the bulk of the investment is made.

The risk of higher future interest rates may be particularly relevant in periods, such as the present, when the real interest rate is far below its long-term historical average.

The second factor is the inherent uncertainty in any methodology for estimating the social discount rate. For example, some economists have argued that increased government borrowing makes it harder for the private sector to gain access to funds, referring to this phenomenon as "crowding-out". This was based on the view of a fixed pool of capital in a small closed economy. This may have had more relevance in the 1960s and 1970s, but international financial market integration has increased dramatically over the past few decades.

Two recent empirical studies focusing specifically on provincial borrowing illustrate that markets can absorb quite large changes in borrowing with little impact. It has sometimes been argued that additional borrowing raises the interest rate. Booth, Georgopoulos, and

Hejazi (2007) estimated that a quite substantial increase of government debt, equal to 1 percentage point of GDP, raises the interest rate on provincial debt by less than one-hundredth of a percent, while Landon and Smith (2006) found no statistically significant impact at all.[11]

This paper assumes, based on recent econometric research, that the financial crowding-out is not a material factor in the current environment. However, the econometric analysis that supports such a view can never have 100% certainty, and changing fiscal and financial market conditions could alter the situation.

On the downward side, there are some economists who argue on theoretical grounds for a social rate of time preference approach to the discount rate. This would be considerably lower, with a value of about 3% (Treasury Board of Canada Secretariat, 2007, p. 42). The UK government, which previously specified a social discount rate of 6%, has switched to a 3.5% rate based on the social rate of time preference (HM Treasury, 2003).

Based on these uncertainties, it is suggested that a range of plus or minus 2 percentage points around the central estimate of the discount rate is appropriate for sensitivity testing for long-term investment projects (20 years or more), while for short-term investments a proportionately narrower range of uncertainty would be appropriate.

The conceptual reason for this uncertainty is that the government takes on the debt and locks itself into a long-term obligation for a long-term project. Whether it is actually paid for through taxes or borrowing does not make a difference from the opportunity cost viewpoint. The longer the locked-in obligation to own and/or pay for the project, the greater the risk of "regret" that it was chosen, given changing investment opportunities in the economy. This is analogous to an investor buying a 20-year bond today with a 4% yield and suffering a loss of capital value if market yields subsequently rise.

Other things equal, a project that has a positive net present value at 7% is better than one that is only viable at 5%. However, there are obviously a great many uncertainties through all phases of an investment analysis, and a considerable amount of judgment needs to be applied. A project that appears to have a positive present value only with a low

---

[11]Even if it was believed that there is some impact, it could be argued that the relevant opportunity cost for provincial government borrowing would be the impact on private sector borrowing within its own province, which would be smaller than the Canada-wide impact that is appropriate for federal government project evaluations.

discount rate such as 5% is in a grey area, but it might be possible to justify it if there is a potential for large benefits of a type that are hard to quantify. The discount rate is just one factor in a project evaluation, and it is important to estimate the cost and benefit streams as rigorously as possible.

The Social Discount Rate Should Be Reviewed Annually

There has been a tendency for some government agencies to issue a discount rate and then never review it, as if the discount rate was a constant, like the value of *pi*. The Treasury Board of Canada was, until very recently, prescribing a 10% real social discount rate for federal government projects that had not been revised for 30 years.[12] This estimate was based on data for the return on capital for the very distant past period from 1965 to 1974.[13]

These estimates took into account factors such as the actual historical interest rates and return on capital. All of these factors can change considerably as world financial market conditions change. The high real interest rates of past decades have given way to very low real interest rates currently. In 2005-06, the Ontario government issued $1 billion of real return bonds with a maturity of 30 years at a coupon rate of 2%.

The low real interest rates prevailing since 2000 are partly due to high savings rates in countries such as China, which have undergone dramatic growth in income, as shown by Warnock and Warnock (2006).

---

[12]However, it appears that this was not universally used even in the federal government. For example, in a regulation under the *Environmental Protection Act*, a 5% social discount rate was prescribed. P.C. 2003-262, 27 February, 2003, in *Canada Gazette* Vol. 137, No. 6, March 12, 2003.

[13]This estimate, originally found in Jenkins (1977), was recently updated in Jenkins and Kuo (2007). The latter reduced the rate to 8%, but the methodology continues to assume that there is considerable crowding-out of private investment. The crowding-out is based on the assumption of a low elasticity of foreign capital inflows, but they do not provide any empirical evidence to support this, and other recent studies suggest quite high elasticities (see note 1 above). As well, they assume that increased government debt in Canada is offset partly by equity capital inflows, with a higher capital cost than debt.

The financial crisis starting in 2008 has driven interest rates even lower, to record low levels in some major countries. At the same time, government deficits and borrowing have soared due to the recession and stimulus efforts. This inverse correlation, where higher government deficits are associated with lower interest rates, is actually the common historical pattern, as noted by Spiro (1994). While higher government demand for loans might be expected to increase interest rates, this is more than offset by lower demand from the private sector during recessions.

In the future, real rates may rise again, if demand and supply conditions change, but for investment projects undertaken in the near term, it is appropriate to use a correspondingly low discount rate.

Conclusions

There is a widely held view that the opportunity cost of capital is higher than the borrowing rate on government bonds. This paper has suggested a conceptual framework for establishing that opportunity cost.

However, it is argued that the appropriate discount rate is not fixed and varies with financial market conditions. The calculations used in this paper, based on values for the first half of 2008, imply that a real discount rate of about 5% would have been appropriate for provincial government benefit-cost analysis of investment projects. In periods of significant excess capacity in the economy, the opportunity cost of capital can drop considerably. This happened in 2009, following the global financial crisis, and the implied discount rate in such a period would be even lower.

The supply and demand conditions in the economy that determine the social discount rate can change substantially over time. It is appropriate to regularly review the value of the social discount rate by examining changes in financial market indicators of the return on capital. For a variety of reasons, there is also a degree of uncertainty in choosing the appropriate values of financial market variables that go into the construction of discount rates. It is appropriate, therefore, to experiment with sensitivity analysis that looks at a range of possible values.

References

Aisen, A. and D. Hauner. 2008. "Budget Deficits and Interest Rates: A Fresh Perspective", IMF Working Paper 08/42.

Ambachtsheer, K. 2008. "The Canada Supplementary Pension Plan", Toronto, C.D. Howe Institute, Commentary No. 265.

Arrow, K. and R. Lind. 1970. "Uncertainty and the Evaluation of Public Investment Decisions", *American Economic Review* (June).

Bierman, H. and S. Smidt. 1980. *The Capital Budgeting Decision.* New York: Macmillan.

Booth, L., G. Georgopoulos, and W. Hejazi. 2007. "What Drives Provincial – Canada Yield Spreads?" *Canadian Journal of Economics* 40(3), 1008-1032.

Brean, D., D. Burgess, R. Hirshhorn, and J. Schulman. 2005. *Treatment of Private and Public Charges for Capital in a "Full-Cost Accounting" of Transportation: Report to Transport Canada.*

Harchaoui, T.M., F. Tarkhani, and P. Warren. 2004. "Public Infrastructure in Canada, 1961-2002", *Canadian Public Policy* 30(3), 303-318.

HM Treasury. 2003. *THE GREEN BOOK: Appraisal and Evaluation in Central Government.*

Jenkins, G.P. 1977. "Capital in Canada: Its Social and Private Performance, 1965-74", Economic Council of Canada Discussion Paper No. 98.

Jenkins, G. and C.-Y. Kuo. 2007. "The Economic Opportunity Cost of Capital for Canada: An Empirical Update", QED Working Paper Number 1133, Economics, Queen's University, Kingston. At http://www.econ.queensu.ca/working_papers/papers/qed_wp_1133.pdf.

Landon, S. and C.E. Smith. 2006. "Government Debt Spillovers in a Federation", Working Paper, Department of Economics, University of Alberta. At http://economics.ca/2006/papers/0316.pdf.

Montmarquette, C. and I. Scott. 2007. "Taux d'actualisation pour l'évaluation des investissements publics au Québec", CIRANO paper 2007RP-02. At http://www.cirano.qc.ca/pdf/publication/2007RP-02.pdf.

Spackman, M. 2001. "Risk and the Cost of Risk in the Comparison of Public and Private Financing of Public Services", NERA Topics No. 23. At http://www.nera.com/Publication.asp?p_ID=964.

Spiro, P. 1989. *Real Interest Rates and Investment and Borrowing Strategy.* New York: Quorum Books.

_____. 1994. "The Differential Between Canadian and U.S. Long-Term Bond Yields", *Canadian Business Economics* 2 (Winter), 16-26. At http://www.cabe.ca/cbe/vol2_2/22-spiro.pdf.

Treasury Board of Canada Secretariat. 2007. *Canadian Cost-Benefit Analysis Guide.* Catalogue No. BT58-5/2007. At http://www.regulation.gc.ca/documents/gl-ld/analys/analys-eng.pdf.

Warnock, F. and V. Warnock. 2006. "International Capital Flows and U.S. Interest Rates", NBER Working Paper No. 12560.

Zhuang, J., Z. Liang, T. Lin, and F. De Guzman. 2007. "Theory and Practice in the Choice of Social Discount Rate for Cost-benefit Analysis: A Survey", ERD Working Paper No. 94, Asian Development Bank.

Comment on "The Social Discount Rate for Provincial Government Investment Projects" by Peter S. Spiro

David F. Burgess

In recommending an appropriate discount rate for Ontario government investment projects, Spiro rejects both the social opportunity cost of capital discount rate proposed by Harberger (and supported in this conference by Jenkins/Kuo) and the social rate of time preference discount rate proposed by Marglin (and supported in this conference by Spackman).

He argues that there is no evidence of any material crowding out of private investment in Ontario when the provincial government increases its borrowing (by as much as 1% of provincial GDP). Therefore, the 7% economic opportunity cost of capital estimated by Jenkins/Kuo (which incorporates an 11% rate of return on displaced private investment) is irrelevant in determining the appropriate economic opportunity cost of capital for Ontario government investment projects.

At the same time, he argues that it would not be appropriate to use the real long-term provincial borrowing rate as the economic opportunity cost of capital, not because non-diversifiable project risk would be shifted to Ontario taxpayers but because market conditions could change and real interest rates could rise during the life of the project, leaving Ontarians worse off pursuing projects that are marginal at the government's borrowing rate.

Instead, Spiro proposes a discount rate that reflects a "compromise" between these two positions. The discount rate should equal the rate of return that an Ontarian could expect to earn on a balanced portfolio that is passively invested in Canadian stocks and bonds. The government, acting on behalf of Ontarians, should insist on a minimum rate of return on its investments equal to the rate of return that Ontarians can expect to earn on a balanced portfolio.

Spiro observes that the real rate of return on equity held in Canadian corporations over the period 1998–2007, as reported by Statistics Canada, was 7.7%, and the real rate of return on Ontario long-term government bonds was 2.2% as of March 2008. The rate of return on a balanced portfolio split equally between Canadian equities and provincial real return bonds is therefore approximately 5%.

Spiro acknowledges that a balanced portfolio invested in Canada may not necessarily represent the alternative use of the funds for public projects financed by the Ontario government. In fact, if the capital market is the marginal source of funds and there is no crowding out of private investment or consumption in Canada, and if the Arrow-Lind theorem holds (i.e., all project risk can be eliminated by spreading it over Ontario taxpayers), all of the funding for Ontario government projects would come from abroad, and the economic cost to Ontarians would be the cost of borrowing. However, if additional systematic risk were borne by Ontario taxpayers, the economic cost of funds would exceed the borrowing rate by the risk premium. The result might be a discount rate of 5%, but it would not represent the rate of return that Ontarians can earn on a balanced portfolio of stocks and bonds.

There are two further points that Spiro makes. First, he maintains that a single discount rate is appropriate for all projects financed by the Ontario government independent of their (systematic) risk because all project risk can either be covered by insurance or eliminated by pooling and spreading. Second, he maintains that the appropriate discount rate should be reviewed annually because it is likely to change with the state of the economy.

With respect to the first point, some risks can be insured but others cannot, and the conditions for the government to be able to pool and spread project risk so as to eliminate it are stringent. There are certainly practical problems in measuring a project's systematic risk, but as a matter of principle, it would seem appropriate to make some adjustment for perceived differences in risk across projects, though it might be better to adjust the project's cost or benefit estimates rather than the discount rate.

David F. Burgess

With respect to the second point, one reason why it is inappropriate to base the social discount rate on prevailing market rates, or even long-run averages of market rates, is that the rate will likely have to be changed quite frequently. But the intent of the social discount rate is to provide coherence and consistency – including time consistency – to project evaluation. Grounding the rate in terms of average real rates of return on investment and saving measured over long periods of time means that the conditions under which a change in the rate is warranted will be rare. For example, a primary reason why it is being proposed that the social discount rate for Canada be revised downward from 10% to 7% or 8% is evidence that the tax distortions that drive a wedge between the marginal productivity of capital and the consumption rate of interest have come down in recent years, plus evidence that countries like Canada are more closely integrated into global capital markets than ever before. These trends are real and important for project evaluation, but they are not likely to change materially on an annual basis or even over a decade.

To return to the issue of crowding out, it is certainly true that the Ontario economy is closer to a small open economy than Canada as a whole, and this is true about all the other provinces and territories. But if every sub-national jurisdiction took the position that its borrowing has no material impact on private investment or consumption within its boundaries, projects would be judged to be worth undertaking if their net benefits were positive at the jurisdiction's borrowing rate. Yet, for every project undertaken, a significant proportion of the funding would displace investment and consumption in the rest of Canada. The estimates that underlie Jenkins and Kuo's 7% social discount rate are that approximately half of the funding for any project comes at the expense of investment and consumption within Canada. The Canadian government's long-term borrowing rate may also be minimally affected by a substantial increase in its borrowing, but this does not mean that the economic opportunity cost of the borrowing is just the government's borrowing rate. Financial capital is indeed highly mobile between countries, but real capital appears to be much less so. The reason has to do with a "home bias" exhibited by savers with respect to their wealth holding. Thus, a province (or nation) may be able to increase its borrowing substantially with no measurable impact on its borrowing rate, but this does not mean that there is a corresponding net transfer of real capital into the country and no crowding out of private investment or consumption. A significant proportion of gross capital inflows are hedged to avoid currency risk. It is only the un-hedged component that represents a transfer of real capital.

Canadians as a whole, meaning Canadians in every province and territory, would be poorly served if projects yielding net benefits at 5% were pursued at the expense of projects yielding net benefits at 7-8%.

Part IV

The Path to Best Practice

10

Roundtable Discussion

Michael Spackman: It's been extremely interesting to see what is going on in other countries. Certainly the strengths of the arguments behind the appropriate discount rate and how to incorporate risk are a good deal clearer here than anywhere else I've been for some while.

As I said in my own paper at the beginning, in terms of the actual numbers it's not clear whether there ends up being much of a difference whether you base the discount rate on the STP rate or on the rate of return to capital after deducting an appropriate risk premium. Maybe you do, maybe you don't. I'm not entirely convinced of this notion that even if one does have a 10% rate of return churning away in the economy year after year that does really determine the appropriate discount rate. I'll think further on that, but it does seem to me to be the case.

On the PPPs, the institutional realities of the economy are important, and taking the risks into account properly is absolutely fundamental, a lot more important, probably, than the question of the discount rate. Looking at institutional capabilities, especially in less developed countries, how capable are the structures there to negotiate competently with private-sector suppliers? These are the really fundamental things, and techies like me can spend too much time theorizing about the discount rate.

Nonetheless, I'm clearly unshaken in my basic framework. I think it's fundamentally right that the social discount rate should reflect the social rate of time preference. In comparing public and private financing, it is a matter of laying out the financing streams and discounting back at the government's borrowing rate, as recommended in the United States.

Christopher Shugart: I'm going to sidestep the controversies over the economic discount rate except for the one issue of risk and get back to *my* particular concern here, which is comparing the PPP with the public-sector comparator. If I were proposing to the Ministry of a developing country, here's what I propose. I would say: Do not develop a PSC in every case. Look at types of projects; look at major types of projects that have the same kinds of technologies, or the same kinds of cash flows and so on. And if you're going to do it, do it very well for these types of projects. After you do that, come up with various criteria, rules of thumb and so on that then can guide decisions on each individual project that falls under a certain category.

I know, after having talked to the people from Ontario today, that this politically may not be feasible, where people say: For every single PPP, give me a number; give me a number comparing the PSC and the PPP. Then this won't work. But let's say this is what I would advise.

Now, how do you do the case? How do you do the analysis? You're missing so much when you compare only costs. And in many developing countries that I work in, you cannot assume that a full economic appraisal has been carried out for the project. So let's go back and, for these representative types of projects, do a full appraisal, costs and benefits, before private sector financing. You need to take into account here the costs associated with financing, the costs of intermediation. You do this on a cash flow line of some sort.

What you then do, you're doing economic analysis using an economic discount rate. What this does, I think, is extremely useful because, Number 1, it helps show up problems that might occur and comparisons on the benefits sides. And we've seen in developing countries that the benefits are not likely to be the same for both alternatives. So if you do the full appraisal, you'll see this. You won't have to fiddle around with adjustments.

Secondly, and this was inspired by Graham's presentation, it permits distributional analysis of the two projects' alternatives, the PPP and the PSC. You'll be able to see, in a very interesting way, on which parties the benefits and costs fall in both of these projects. This may help you decide things.

The final point is: What on earth do you do about systematic risk? And here, I'm going to infuriate people who think they know either there is or there isn't. I'm going to take a completely sceptical position. When I say "is or isn't", let me make that more precise: "whether or not". The systematic risk has a kind of cost that we associate with the equity market. Does it have that same kind of cost in terms of public sector financing? Not the less than 0.5% that all economists determine should be there, but the 4 or 5 or 6%, the equity premium puzzle. Is it there in public financing, or isn't it? I would say: We don't know. That's the advice given to the developing countries.

Let's say we do two scenarios. First of all, we do one in which we use an economic discount rate, adjusted to include a risk premium, for both the PSC and the PPP. How much? What do we add? You may not agree with CAPM; the theoreticians may tell you that it has lots of weaknesses. But it *is* widely used. It's widely used by regulators; it's something a lot of people can agree on. If you look at the asset beta of many PPP projects, it's going to be somewhat less than the asset beta of the normal project in the market, probably. Let's say it's 0.5. Let's say you're talking about a risk premium of 4% or 5%.

So you're talking, let's say, about 2 or 2.5 percentage points that you would add on to have the risk-adjusted economic discount rate, which you'd then use for both the PSC and the PPP. That's the worst case for the PSC. The worst case for the PSC is where there's a cost of risk on the PSC. Then do the same thing, on a second scenario, but you use a risk-free rate for the PSC. You don't add those 2.5%. And you use the risk-adjusted rate with that risk premium for the PPP only. That's the worst case for the PPP.

Clearly, if the PPP wins in the last scenario, you're fine. It's won on its worst case; you know that it's passed the test. If the PSC wins on the first scenario, that's okay; don't do the PPP. That may eliminate many, many projects and decide them without your having to take a position on whether or not there really is risk in the public sector.

Then the difficult question is: What happens if the PPP wins on the best case of the PPP, but not on the worst case of the PPP? Then risk might matter. We don't know. Unless you know for sure, unless you can say whether or not there is the cost of systematic risk in the public sector. What do we do then? Then, I think, you have to move to disaggregate the cash flows more, take a look more carefully at some of the things that Graham was talking about today, like look at the different lines. And then, frankly, probably, turn to other grounds for deciding on whether to do the PPP or not.

More fundamental grounds of structure in the project: Is it likely that you can actually write a complete contract? That would count for the PPP. Counting against the PPP, is it likely that the government's policy is fairly stable? If in fact the government's policy about this particular project, and their objectives, is going to change over 20 years, do you really want a PPP?

That sums up the approach that I would take after thinking about it today, listening to everyone and having thought about it over the last two months.

Glenn Jenkins: I think the first thing is that one of the important lessons we've learned from Chris's paper is that in deciding whether to do this public sector comparator, we really have to look at the economics in terms of the underlying resource costs rather than the particular financial flows. And that is a major change from current practice.

The other issue is that EOCK is important. And it's really important in the choice of technology. I'll give you an example that we're looking at right now in Ghana, where you've got the worst of all worlds. You've got a private sector investor whose cost of capital is very high, and the government is providing free fuel because it wants to get the equipment in there to ultimately be used more as a reserve than as a high utilization rate. But given the utilization rate, the incorrect choice of technology is resulting in an excess cost of $250 million if they get gas on an investment of $140 million. If it's oil, the excess cost is over $500 million simply because you're burning twice as much fuel. So prices matter.

Let me give you another example. In north Cyprus, they get very heavily subsidized capital, and they end up with the most sophisticated technology for water desalination – it's 2.5 times the cost of anything else – in order to reduce the running costs. Now it turns out, at $100 a barrel for oil, it's probably a good decision, but at the time it was crazy.

The point is that we're doing an analysis of what is the economic cost of capital as a way to determine whether the prices people face are leading them astray. That's why I think it's important to get a number – we're not talking about the third decimal point – but to get something that reflects what is the economic cost of capital in the economy.

On the issue of risk, it seems to me that we need to try to get the risk out of the discount rate. We shouldn't be trying to determine what is the extra cost that this private individual versus that private individual is going to demand because of their particular risk premium? We shouldn't get into the business of discounting the consumer surplus that some peasant's going to get by a risk premium demanded by some New York utility company.

That also leads to another interesting thing. There is an important issue between foreign versus domestic with respect to risk. If a foreigner requires a risk premium of 5% but a local investor will do it at 3%, that additional cost is an economic cost. We're paying for it. Or at the same time, because of the non-competitive arrangements, we're paying the foreigner 25% versus the president's cousin, who's a resident; that's a tough one. But for sure we know the foreigner's a cost. The money flows out of the country if it's a non-competitive deal. I think in some sense, trying to put these things into certain equivalents or costs may be a way to also – Graham's going down that road in terms of looking at the stakeholders, and where the money is going. That may be quite useful in terms of the methodology on PPPs.

The question whether there should be a systematic risk for public financing, I'll let Professor Harberger talk about. I think the more you look at that, it seems hard to figure out, given that – unless the project is a big part of the whole economy, and most projects are reasonably small, where are the grounds for adding a risk premium? I think a lot of times, people add a risk premium to the public sector financing just because of the optics. Anyway, I'll defer to other people who know more about that than I do.

Arnold Harberger: The first thing I want to focus on is this formula for the social rate of time preference equal to $\delta + \eta g$, which appears in the literature. I don't think a lot of people realize what is going on. So the first thing I want to do is expound what I think is going on.

We have consumption on the horizontal axis and the marginal utility of consumption on the vertical, and we have some kind of a declining curve. We have an interest rate in the market of 10%. Growth is 3%, and elasticity of marginal utility is -1. This guy starts with an income of $1,000 and ends up with income of $1,030. This thing would have grown like that, and the marginal utility would have been 1 there, to make life simple. And 3% growth is going to be 0.97 there.

Now this guy, who had that story and has an income this period of $1,000, he saves $10, and this $10 grows to $11 owing to the 10% interest. But his utility doesn't grow to 11; his utility only grows to 10.7 because of this 3% deduction coming from the combination of the growth rate of 3 and the elasticity of -1. Whoever does this kind of work would say that this person is transposing utility at the rate of 7% rather than at the rate of 10% because of this 3% deduction.

Now, if you had another guy who has a steeper curve, and has got it down to 0.94 because his elasticity is -2, again, he would save 10, the 10 would grow to 11 at the 10% interest rate, but his utility grows only to 10.4 because of the 6% deduction coming from the 3% growth rate and the elasticity of -2. That's the sort of game that is being played with this formula. Everything I've done assumes δ equals zero. I argued last night that I didn't like these deltas in the utility function. I don't mind assuming δ to be zero. But many people assume it to be a positive number; in the paper, it was assumed to be 1%. That would say that this guy, instead of using a 4% discount rate, would use a 5% discount rate. I think that's the way it works. And this guy would use an 8% discount rate.

This is just mechanics. I have no moral particularly attached yet. But I can't see how anybody could be using this. Thinking of representative consumers and all of that, without thinking of an interpersonally comparable and measurable utility function and that's what we have here are distributional weights in a disguised form. I want to tell you how this works, that here, with an elasticity of 1, we have an income of $1,000, puts utility, let's say, at 1,000, income of $500 puts marginal utility at 1. At 2, and income of $2,000 puts it at one-half.

In the literature, this elasticity of 1 is very common. And when it's not 1, it's 2. And when it's not 2, it's one-half. So it's always in this neighbourhood. Now I say, as I tried to mention last night, we take $1,000 away from this guy, and the social cost of that is only $500, and we give $1,000 to this guy, and the social benefit of that is $2,000. It's an enormous social gain to be had by extracting money from people of very modestly different incomes and giving them to people who are half or four times as poor. I point out that when you end up, the equilibrium of transfer between this guy and that guy is that we take away $1,000 from this guy, which has a cost of $500, and we give this guy $250, which times the weight of 2 has a benefit of $500.

There you carry your tax-and-transfer mechanism to its logical extreme if you're going to use this kind of reasoning. Nobody in the world would argue for that in a serious way. It means that there would be a minimum income and a maximum income in a country where the maximum could never be that size. Absurd! Unthinkable! We have Russia with much more inequality than that. Cuba has much more inequality than that. Come on! This is a logical consequence of using an exponential utility function with this kind of number. And with elasticity values of two or one half it does not change the story much at all.

How about land reform? If we take land from people who are relatively wealthy – middle income, higher income – and we give it to poorer people, but we know that the people with middle and higher income are really more fisher-farmers, and the poor people who receive this land don't have the wherewithal, don't have the knowledge, usually receive it in small enough bundles, can't manage bigger bundles. So they're much less efficient. We can carry this to the point where the degree-of-efficiency difference is 75%.

I say, take this concept and throw it out the window. And don't open doors to let it sneak in again in some sweet-sounding problem where it doesn't give you any trouble – like setting optimal marginal tax structures or something like that – without tracing the forcefulness of the assumption in areas and territories where it really is terrible.

Somewhere it was brought up about financing by taxes, and this is an interesting case. In the literature of this weighted average function, the weighted average function says, well, we pay a time-preference rate and apply that to the part where consumption is being displaced. And we pay a marginal productivity rate, and we apply that to the part where investment is being displaced. We typically use the capital market as the vehicle by which we raise our money, and we say: We're going to get these two weights, consumption and investment, from how the capital market responds.

Different people – Eckstein, Kutilla, Haveman and I'm sure others – have said: The government raises a lot of money by taxes. Why don't we use a tax framework and say: We're going to get this money by taxes, and we'll displace consumption, and we'll apply the time preference rate to that portion. And we'll displace some investment, and we'll apply the productivity rate to that. In fact, we'll follow the same procedure except the vehicle will be the tax.

Some of us objected to that because where the capital market has some sort of replicability about it, the response is – General Motors goes into the capital market, or Microsoft, or the US government, it isn't much different. You have a replicable market situation. With taxes – well, you look at the way tax laws are being generated. Sometimes you're favouring one group, sometimes another; sometimes you're favouring consumption, sometimes investment.

But some years ago, I was going to a conference at the World Bank, and they gave me the specific task of including in my paper a discussion of the shadow price of government funds. I had never used the shadow price of government funds, and I'm sure the people who asked me expected me to come down real hard against the shadow price of government funds. But when I got into it, I got driven logically to say: We have made a mistake in not incorporating the shadow price of government funds consistently and regularly into our analysis.

The logic I went through was this: Let's suppose we have an electricity project, which has this kind of a profile of costs and benefits. All the benefits are cash receipts of a new electricity company. And this project either breaks even at the correct discount rate or yields a profit. But in any case, it pays off all of its costs at the economic opportunity cost of capital.

Okay, that's fine. There's nothing wrong with our analysis. We go ahead. But now I say: This identical profile belongs to a public park or to a road that is not a toll road. The benefits definitely exist, but the government doesn't get any cash back. Our scheme is, this $10 million was raised in the capital market. So as time goes on, we have to pay interest, we forgo taxes and have to get additional funding by borrowing. All that money piles up at the, let's say, 10% social interest rate. By the time we're out here, we owe $25 million that we've never paid. And if we just let it go, we owe $50 million, $100 million, $200 million – it never stops.

I don't like that. I don't feel that we have closed the books properly on this project. What I said in that paper was, Let's set this final date and finance this project $25 million by tax. So we did that. The trouble is that it cost more than $1 to raise an incremental dollar by taxes. The simple picture is this one: We start with this tax, and now we raise the tax, and we get extra A minus B. It's the extra money we get, and the extra dead-weight loss is B. So V over A minus B can be 100%. Can be 50%. But very conservatively, can be 20 or 25 or 30%. People have tried to estimate that, and this 20, 25 or 30 is indeed in the lower end of the ranges that people can actually estimate. So we think of the government raising $25 million but having it cost 25 or 30% more. So the total cost is $33.5 million.

The way this debt is built up is not from the total costs and benefits of the project, but from the cash outlay and receipts that the government gets. In the electricity project, the government got back in cash enough to pay off with interest what it had borrowed, and everything was hunky-dory. But in this project, it does the borrowing, and nothing ever comes back. We could have this very artificial rule that says: We're going to charge $7.5 million as a final farewell to this project.

A much more elegant way is to have a shadow price of government funds equal to 1.3. That's at every single outlay. If the cost is 100, we charge 130. For every receipt of 200, we count at 260. And by the time we've done that, we have done the equivalent of this final payment, but in a much more elegant way, and in a way that fits much more into our normal thinking that shadow prices are by now second nature to us, and a shadow price of government funds is a perfectly reasonable thing.

I still prefer the capital market – I call it the canonical source of funds – because I see it as giving me the same answer when I give many, many different treatments. Whereas when we go the tax route, I don't get that same answer. But I find myself forced to go the tax route here, and I say: In the act of ignorance, let's be conservative.

Roundtable Discussion

We're introducing a new concept into this thing, a shadow price of government funds. We feel intellectually forced to do this. And when we do that and try to argue with all the people we have to argue with in the real world, better to be a little bit conservative in your estimating the premium on government funds. Don't say: The shadow price is 2.5; better to say it's 1.3. But don't say it's 1.03, which would be just caving in and paying only lip service to where the logic leads us.

Michael Spackman: With respect to the shadow price of government funds, absolutely. We almost did it in the United Kingdom. But consultation documents are the passion at the moment, and the consultation document on the new guidance as it was going to be, which was issued in 2002, we had to stick it in there. It happened to be 1.3, and I agree that it's rather at the low end. But within days of the deadline for publishing and putting it out, it was spiked by the Chancellor of the Exchequer's office. Nobody quite knows why. But one has to suspect that it's because the Chancellor was about to launch a huge expansion of public expenditure, and it was politically unacceptable to have the government at the same time producing a document that said there was a significant shadow price to be attached to it. So we tried.

After some years, the Chancellor has actually, with very grudging permission from the Treasury, with tremendous caveats, managed to get it into the public domain. It's fairly buried, and it's Department of Transport guidance. You have got this 1.3. It isn't mandatory; it's value-for-money guidance.

I would love it if that could become accepted part of government conventions. And maybe it will one day. Meanwhile, as I think I said earlier, if one has a convention of expressing benefit-cost ratios with these anomalies of being public expenditure, in a sense you do at least partly get there. The way that the guidance I mentioned, Department of Transport, it implies that that means the benefit-cost ratio of 1.3 is the absolute baseline starting point before you get anywhere. And we all know in practice that nothing could possibly get through without a benefit-cost ratio of at least 2 and quite possibly 3.

I wish Al Harberger every success in promoting that concept. But his very fierce attack on social-time preference because governments don't attach the required shadow price to public expenditure is not correct. Governments *do* behave like that! It is widely assumed, or has been widely assumed, that income tax rates are determined, fairly roughly indeed, on the basis of having an equal utility impact on everybody regardless of their income. And for that reason, one has higher marginal income tax rates, in principle, for people at higher incomes than one does for people at lower incomes – making that assumption that it's designed on an equal-utility impact.

But the other issue – and Glenn Jenkins raised this point – is the idea that, it's surely ridiculous to say that somebody on twice the income gets only half as much benefit, so you should therefore be taking money away from the rich and giving it to the poor. That would be true, actually. And yes, if you had a helicopter up in the sky, dropping a packet of dollar bills, it would be perfectly true. If the dollar bill fell in the garden of a rich person rather than a poor person, the poor person would get more utility from it than the rich person. We're talking about a modest number of dollar bills.

But that isn't life, of course. In reality, you've got two huge reasons why you don't take money from the rich, in general, and give it to the poor. First, it's simply unjust, unfair – we don't live in a totalitarian society. We've earned our money – this is Zen-type stuff, isn't it? We have a right to our money. It isn't for the government to take it away from us without a jolly good reason – income tax we broadly accept.

And the other reason, which has become more fashionable over the last 20 years, is it's inefficient. As soon as you start taking money away from the rich and giving it to the poor, you're immediately screwing up all sorts of incentives. And partly for that reason, income tax structures have tended to level out a bit over time.

David Burgess: The distinction I'd like to make here is the following. This project is an electricity-generating project. So there's income; it's a tangible project; output is measured in a market; there's a transaction once the output is sold, and the revenue stream is going to be there to pay off the bondholders.

Compare that to an investment in a park. We have a willingness to pay for the park, but we don't pay to use the park. Does the park change our mandate on other things that we were doing because we didn't have the park? We're saving our spending on other things that we were spending our money on because the park didn't exist. And it's in that way that I'm trying to differentiate; even though the thing that we're producing may not be transacted directly in a market, it may well substitute or back out other spending that we're doing.

So if this was cleaner air or water, we were spending a lot of money scrubbing our clothing and whatever because it was dirty air. Now we don't have to do that; we've saved our spending for other things. As long as the tax system is recording that income increase, it had better be recovered. In my simple model, the capital income tax is going to pick up that response that we have to the project. In that way, if that does happen, we don't have to do that shadow price of the dollars up front. I think the shadow pricing of those dollars up front is happening precisely because the project benefits are what I was calling before "fully consumed". They do not impact our behaviour in terms of reducing our spending on other things. They're not treated as income.

Christopher Shugart: What about the institutional cost of taxation?

David Burgess: The tax system is there; the assumption is that the distorted taxes are there. When we go to the capital market and borrow that money with the distortions there, if the project does generate income, we don't have to go back to raise the distorted taxes in response. If the project does *not* generate any income, what I'm suggesting is that we have to be careful. Just because it doesn't generate a marketable output for the government, it may indirectly generate tax revenue in terms of our response to the project.

If we think of it as income, it lowers our spending on other things that we were spending our money on because we now have this free public service, if you like. There is that tax – the project itself is a tax generator. I'm not saying all projects are; I'm thinking that just because the project isn't generating electricity, or doesn't produce some revenue directly. If somebody cleans the air for me, do I spend, less defensively, on the things I'm currently spending money on because of the lower air quality?

Al Harberger: I wanted to say one thing. I think that in cost-benefit analysis, the broad assumption is always that we have fully employed resources and that the resources that we do use are taken away from someplace. They're not sitting around, idle. We have that idea, which means that all income is spent either on consumption or investment. And in response to any project, people are going to reshuffle their ways of allocating, both among consumption goods, among investment goods, and between consumption and investment. All of that takes place.

Exactly what we do, when we measure externalities is we multiply each change in quantity by the tax or distortion and add them up. I think that's the structure on which our whole edifice has been constructed. I couldn't agree with you more that that kind of thing is happening, but it isn't an argument to be introduced vis-à-vis a shadow price of public funds or any other given thing. It should be there in every single step that we're doing along the way. That's part of the basic process.

Finn Poschmann: On this point, it's a familiar question in the environmental economics literature. The way they handle it is to treat the park, or a clean environment, as a complement to leisure. So it is a thing of value even though it's not transacted in a market, but it's a complementary good of leisure.

The other side of it is, of course, there's a public finance cost. The point derived from Arnold's work is that it's occurring where there are already distortionary taxes. And it's very easy to have a small tax increase in the margin that produces a very large welfare loss compared to the revenue that is generated because taxes are already distortionary.

Graham Glenday: I've always advocated the slightly modified version of this because in many of these public assets, such as when you build that park, it's probably going to last virtually forever. You're interested in, if the government actually funds the operating and maintenance, and the repayment of any – and the interest charges on that – that they charge that premium on – rather than worrying about the initial capital outlay because in fact you're probably going to keep that loan outstanding, maybe into infinity, and never actually repay it. But a minimum should target the operating and maintenance and interest repayments on it.

Al Harberger: But does it do that by further bonds?

Glenn Jenkins: I think that point is very important; it goes to the heart of the issue – the issue of PPPs. As you were saying, in India, one of the advantages of a PPP is it actually gives you the chance to get something off the tax rolls.

Andrejs Skaburskis: I come from another background in city planning. I'm certainly now feeling a little more comfortable with the higher discount rates than I did this morning after listening to your conversations. I wondered if you could make me feel even more comfortable.

Here's the kind of situation I see. I have trouble seeing that the projects that we look at are really going to shift investment out from the private sector. I have this maybe naïve impression that the government bases budgetary decisions on what the taxpayer will pay, and then you work within that kind of constraint. It's going to be a question more of how you choose between projects given that you have a fixed budget.

Then I'd be interested in how that would affect the choice of discount rate, or would it affect it? The source of discomfort that I'm still living with, with a high discount rate, say, of 10%, is that it affects the planning horizon. When I'm looking at a 10% discount rate, I'm looking at 50-cent dollars in seven years. People who I associate with don't consider 50-cent dollars as being important. That would imply that we really should be planning and looking for seven-year time horizons, push it, maybe 10 years.

With this high time-preference rate that we have, we'd be looking short-term. It almost seems to me, then, and why I'm uncomfortable with that, is that it seems that when we're in the public sector, there's some kind of a public good associated with looking into the future and looking in terms of the kinds of things that the public sector does, in that they have a longer horizon. And that maybe, again, why I like the lower rate is that I feel, let the market take care of the short run, and let there be a public sector that looks at the longer-run picture. Therefore, I favour low discount rates, provided there aren't any redistribution issues.

Michael Spackman: Interesting point. Two comments. I don't think that changing the discount rate has any material effect on actual government spending. It's much more on choice of technique than on what you actually do. I think it's one of the illusions that people in ministries of finance who are in charge of spending want a high discount rate because this will help them clamp down. My impression is that changing the discount rate – in the United Kingdom, it's been up to 10 and down to 3.5 – doesn't really make a huge difference. It makes quite a lot of difference in the choice of technique though.

But on the planning horizon, here is an anecdote to reinforce your point. The UK discount rate has been 6% for some years, which in my view is a bit on the high side. And in 2003, because the government liked public investment, it was reduced to 3.5, which strikes me as a bit too low. One consequence was that the Department of Transport, which for decades had taken 30 years as its time horizon for transport investments, decided to make it 60 years. That's another good argument against having discount rates that are really low because it does have, to my mind, an irresponsible effect on actual planning horizons. So I agree, yes.

Glenn Jenkins: I mentioned earlier that there are basically two things that are important: where is the demand, and what is the discount rate? They're somewhat related in the sense that, is it the planning horizon, or is it excess capacity? The issue is, I don't think it should affect the planning horizon, but it probably will affect the timing in which one is going to have that capacity in place. And you're going to be looking at higher utilization rates in early years. Isn't that really the issue? The issue is that with a higher discount rate, you can't afford to have excess capacity sitting there. You may have to plan more carefully in the sense that it's probably going to mean that you're going to have to meet that demand when it's there, not meet it way ahead of time and wait around until the demand comes. Isn't that really the issue?

Andrejs Skaburskis: No. We're more and more seeing it as getting a sense of how we consider the future. If we're looking at benefits and costs that occur in the future that is extending beyond 10 or 20 years, and if we regard what happens then as important, it seems to me that it requires that we use a low discount rate. And that's where I link the discount rate to the time horizon.

I can see the logic that with a higher rate you do your projects in phases and you can be more efficient in that way. But I don't think I could get much purchase with arguments based on anything happening after 10 or 20 years if I have a 10% discount rate. That's more where I'm coming from. I'm looking at the treatment of important benefits and costs that occur in the distant future.

Al Harberger: It's only a little wrong to say that the government in a place like the United States, by taking money, investing it in the broad stock market, broad capital market, reinvesting the returns, whatever tax stimulation it does, sequestering those extra taxes it collects and putting them into that capital pie, can turn $100 today into $200 ten years from now and into $400 twenty years from now. If you want to help future generations, do that. Of course, our governments do just the opposite. Instead of dumping money into the capital market, they suck it out.

David Burgess: On that note, I think it's fair to say we've had a very interesting, wide-ranging discussion. Clearly, we haven't resolved all the issues; I'm sure we'll be debating some of them for the rest of my lifetime and beyond. Nonetheless, it's useful to review the scope of the discount rate debate and how it impacts real things that are happening, including PPPs.

I appreciate very much everyone's participation. And I want to thank Sharon Sullivan, who isn't here anymore, for all her efforts to put this program together.

Glenn Jenkins: I want to say thank everyone, and especially Sharon. We will try to refine what we have produced so far, and get it into a volume worthy of publication.

Contributors

Editors

David F. Burgess   Department of Economics, University of Western Ontario

Glenn P. Jenkins   Department of Economics, Queen's University and Eastern Mediterranean University, Northern Cyprus

Authors

Donald J.S. Brean   Rotman School of Management, University of Toronto

David F. Burgess   Department of Economics, University of Western Ontario

Antal Deutsch   Department of Economics, McGill University

Graham Glenday   Duke Center for International Development, Duke University

Arnold C. Harberger   Department of Economics, University of California, Los Angeles

Glenn P. Jenkins   Department of Economics, Queen's University and Eastern Mediterranean University, Northern Cyprus

Chun-Yan Kuo   Department of Economics, Queen's University

Chris Shugart   Independent Consultant, London, England

Michael Spackman   NERA Economic Consulting and Centre for Analysis of Risk and Regulation, London School of Economics

Peter S. Spiro   Formerly Ontario Ministry of Public Infrastructure Renewal

Queen's Policy Studies
Recent Publications

The Queen's Policy Studies Series is dedicated to the exploration of major public policy issues that confront governments and society in Canada and other nations.

Manuscript submission. We are pleased to consider new book proposals and manuscripts. Preliminary enquiries are welcome. A subvention is normally required for the publication of an academic book. Please direct questions or proposals to the Publications Unit by email at spspress@queensu.ca, or visit our website at: www.queensu.ca/sps/books, or contact us by phone at (613) 533-2192.

Our books are available from good bookstores everywhere, including the Queen's University bookstore (http://www.campusbookstore.com/). McGill-Queen's University Press is the exclusive world representative and distributor of books in the series. A full catalogue and ordering information may be found on their web site (http://mqup.mcgill.ca/).

John Deutsch Institute for the Study of Economic Policy

Retirement Policy Issues in Canada, Michael G. Abbott, Charles M. Beach, Robin W. Boadway and James G. MacKinnon (eds.), 2009 Paper ISBN 978-1-55339-161-6 Cloth ISBN 978-1-55339-162-3

The 2006 Federal Budget: Rethinking Fiscal Priorities, Charles M. Beach, Michael Smart and Thomas A. Wilson (eds.), Policy Forum Series no. 41, 2007 Paper ISBN 978-1-55339-125-8 Cloth ISBN 978-1-55339-126-6

Health Services Restructuring in Canada: New Evidence and New Directions, Charles M. Beach, Richard P. Chaykowksi, Sam Shortt, France St-Hilaire and Arthur Sweetman (eds.), 2006 Paper ISBN 978-1-55339-076-3 Cloth ISBN 978-1-55339-075-6

A Challenge for Higher Education in Ontario, Charles M. Beach (ed.), 2005 Paper ISBN 1-55339-074-1 Cloth ISBN 1-55339-073-3

Higher Education in Canada, Charles M. Beach, Robin W. Boadway and R. Marvin McInnis (eds.), 2005 Paper ISBN 1-55339-070-9 Cloth ISBN 1-55339-069-5

Current Directions in Financial Regulation, Frank Milne and Edwin H. Neave (eds.), Policy Forum Series no. 40, 2005 Paper ISBN 1-55339-072-5 Cloth ISBN 1-55339- 071-7

Financial Services and Public Policy, Christopher Waddell (ed.), 2004 Paper ISBN 1-55339-068-7 Cloth ISBN 1-55339-067-9

School of Policy Studies

Taking Stock: Research on Teaching and Learning in Higher Education, Julia Christensen Hughes and Joy Mighty (eds.), 2010 Paper 978-1-55339-271-2 Cloth 978-1-55339-272-9